4 =

HOAX

H

O

A

X

Hitler's Diaries,

Lincoln's Assassins,

and Other

Famous Frauds

Edward Steers Jr.

Foreword by Joe Nickell

UNIVERSITY PRESS OF KENTUCKY

Copyright © 2013 by The University Press of Kentucky

Scholarly publisher for the Commonwealth,
serving Bellarmine University, Berea College, Centre College of Kentucky,
Eastern Kentucky University, The Filson Historical Society, Georgetown College,
Kentucky Historical Society, Kentucky State University, Morehead State
University, Murray State University, Northern Kentucky University, Transylvania
University, University of Kentucky, University of Louisville, and Western
Kentucky University.
All rights reserved.

Editorial and Sales Offices: The University Press of Kentucky
663 South Limestone Street, Lexington, Kentucky 40508-4008
www.kentuckypress.com

17 16 15 14 13   5 4 3 2 1

Library of Congress Cataloging-in-Publication Data

Steers, Edward.
  Hoax : Hitler's diaries, Lincoln's assassins, and other famous frauds / Edward
Steers, Jr. ; foreword by Joe Nickell.
    p. cm.
  Includes bibliographical references and index.
  ISBN 978-0-8131-4159-6 (hardcover : alk. paper) --
  ISBN 978-0-8131-4160-2 (epub) -- ISBN 978-0-8131-4161-9 (pdf)
  1. Fraud—History. 2. Hoaxes—History. 3. Impostors and imposture—History.
I. Title.
  HV6691.S687 2013
  001.9'5—dc23   2012047314

This book is printed on acid-free paper meeting the requirements of the
American National Standard for Permanence in Paper for Printed Library
Materials.

Manufactured in the United States of America.

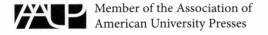
Member of the Association of
American University Presses

To Pat

You touched my heart in places I never even knew.

History is a set of lies agreed upon.

—Napoleon Bonaparte

At the heart of good history is a naughty little secret: good storytelling.

—Stephen Schiff

To steal ideas from one person is plagiarism. To steal from many is research.

—Steven Wright

Contents

Foreword

This book asks some of history's grandest questions: Did Mark Hofmann discover sensational documents—from the first example of printing in America to historical Mormon writings—that helped shape American history? Was the bombing of Pearl Harbor a consequence of treason in the Oval Office? And did madman Adolf Hitler actually pen a revealing multivolume set of diaries? Has the very burial cloth of Jesus, mysteriously imprinted with his haunting visage, survived the ages? Was the Holy Grail of paleontology, the long-sought "missing link," discovered in, of all places, a gravel pit in England? And could lost pages from John Wilkes Booth's diary provide the true, shocking account of Abraham Lincoln's assassination?

Given this book's title, one can expect that the answers are no, no, no, no, no, and—yes—no. Yet the emphatic, simple answers belie the wonderful stories that are behind each question, and then the additional, intriguing stories behind each revelation.

For these are not mere hoaxes, like the Feejee Mermaid once exhibited by P. T. Barnum. The showman later admitted it was indeed "a questionable, dead mermaid," a work of creative taxidermy. Today, no one passionately clings to the belief that the now-lost curio was authentic, despite several "originals" that occasionally remind us of the humbug.

In contrast, the cases presented in *Hoax* endure. They are not just hoaxes in history, but all would attempt, quite literally in a few instances, to rewrite history—a measure of their importance. Some continue to deceive, while others, although generally accepted as deceptions, offer lessons in how to pick our future steps through history's minefields. Moreover, these cases required teams of investigators and scientists to ferret out the facts, often employing a bewildering array of sophisticated forensic techniques or an exhaustive study of obscure but relevant documents, or both.

Just presenting the evidence in a readable fashion in such cases is a daunting task that many writers necessarily avoid, but Edward Steers Jr.

is up to the challenge. As a scientist (a molecular biochemist) turned acclaimed historian, he utilizes his enviable background and considerable talents to sort facts from pseudofacts, and he writes clearly in the process. In contrast to many other authors of books on famous hoaxes, he discusses each case fully in its historical context. His is not just a presentation of great deceptions and a treatise on credulity; it is also an engaging seminar, both on how facts and falsehoods vie for belief and on the interplay of history and science.

Along this inviting journey back in time we get ringside seats to an archaeological dig where legerdemain prevailed, to episodes of bravado and folly in the lead-up to America's war in the Pacific, and to the meticulous production of some of the world's most cunning forgeries, as well as to the further outrageous acts—including bombing murders—that were attempted to hide the trickery. Ultimately, even perhaps a bit uncomfortably, we encounter that most revealing of elements: the nearly unstoppable impulse, the frequent headlong rush to believe in fraudulent history and science when they tell us what we want to hear.

But as Steers shows us again and again, if we wish to know the truth in historical matters, we cannot begin with a desired answer and work backward to the evidence, seeking to bolster our belief. Instead, we must find the best evidence, let it lead us where it will, and then believe what it proves, like it or not.

Such an approach requires toughness of mind and spirit, but we have a guide who is both principled and fearless. So turn the page and let the adventures begin. Or as Sherlock Holmes, candle in hand early one morning, urged (in "The Adventure of the Abbey Grange"): "Come, Watson, come! The game is afoot. Not a word! Into your clothes and come!"

Joe Nickell
Senior Research Fellow
Committee for Skeptical Inquiry
Amherst, New York

Introduction

"Snap, Crackle, and Pop"

Wanting to believe is the first of the two most powerful emotions involved in the success of a hoax or forgery. The second is greed. Greed is a harsh term, but in the end it is an accurate characterization of one of the motivations behind being duped by the forger or taken in by the hoax. Believing (the desire to believe what you hear or see) turns out to be the most powerful narcotic in causing people to accept forgeries and hoaxes. This is certainly true when it comes to the Shroud of Turin. Wanting to believe can cloud a person's ability to think clearly and analytically. I have personally experienced several situations in which a forger has victimized an individual because the power of wanting to believe was stronger than all other rational thoughts. In several of the incidents where I was asked to pass judgment on a particular item, the victim sought proof only after having completed the purchase and paying out large sums of money, and with no provision to recover the money if the object proved other than authentic. Wanting to believe often dulls the mind.

My career as a scientist specializing in molecular biology and protein biochemistry exposed me to a wide variety of chemical and biological tests in the course of forty years of experimentation. Proficiency in spectroscopy, chemistry, and microscopy was essential to biomedical research. The public has come to learn that science and medicine can accomplish amazing things through the application of technology. The most common example today is that of DNA analysis, which has gained widespread attention in recent years, to the point where the average person has a reasonable understanding of what DNA is and of the power of DNA analysis in identifying individuals to nearly an absolute certainty. There are hundreds of biological and chemical tests in the scientist's arsenal that allow the identification of materials with objective certainty. For instance, blood groups can be determined with 100 percent accuracy, as opposed to handwriting analysis, which is highly subjective and frequently demonstrates a level of accuracy well below 100 percent and often below 50 percent. But even the most precise testing can prove inadequate if not applied properly.

Napoleon Bonaparte had a rather cynical view of historians and history. He is quoted as having said in one of his more lucid moments, "History is a set of lies agreed upon." That may be true in certain instances, but for the major events of history it is not lies that historians agree upon, but rather an interpretation based on minimal information. The modern historian has become a storyteller, for stories are what the general public wants to hear, or read, and historians want very much to be read. The temptation to enlarge on the basic facts and put a personal interpretation on an event often colors history in an effort to make it more interesting and, therefore, more saleable.

Not too long ago, I was asked to critically evaluate a screenplay for historical accuracy. I was instructed to pay close attention to separating fact from fiction. It seems the script was to serve as the basis for a motion picture, and the producer's primary goal was to recreate the historical event as accurately as possible rather than fictionalize it. The script was well written and interesting. Unfortunately, it bore little relation to historical truth. Having received my report, the producer assured me the author would be asked to rewrite the script, making sure to correct the errors and bringing the script into line with historical fact. The author went at it a second time and did, in fact, stay true to the actual event in most instances. It was a major improvement factually, and I was prepared to give my support as a technical adviser. The director, however, overruled the second version and rejected the revised script, choosing instead to stay with the original mythologized version of the story because, as he later said, the revised script lacked "snap, crackle, and pop." Napoleon would be pleased.

The subject matter of this book is a series of hoaxes that for a brief moment in time became part of our history. Some, not all, remain fixed in many people's minds as true history, while others have been successfully debunked. All, in my opinion, have "snap, crackle, and pop." In "Oath of a Freeman" the skill of the forger was such that he easily fooled the experts, even those who were skeptical at first. Only when the forger panicked, forcing him to resort to murder, did his scheme collapse. In "Pearl Harbor," intense dislike—bordering on hatred—of President Roosevelt was enough to sustain the fraud even to this day, despite evidence to the contrary. "The Shroud of Turin" and "Skullduggery: The Man Who Never

Was" are excellent examples of wanting to believe for ideological reasons rather than greed. In these two instances belief trumps science. In "Hah Hitler! The Hitler Diaries," we again see the seductive force of wanting to believe. The Hitler diaries represented a sea change in the history of World War II. While greed was a motivating factor, the desire to believe replaced reason. In the case of the Piltdown Man, an entire nation felt uplifted that they could now join Asia and the rest of Europe as a part of the dawn of man. After all, how could the nation that considered itself at the very top of the tree of mankind not have been among the earliest sites where modern man first lived? In "The Missing Pages from John Wilkes Booth's Diary" we see conspiracists at their extreme. Here we find most of the elements of conspiracy run amok. Treason in the highest levels of government is accompanied by claims that defy logic. It is perhaps the first example of "the big lie." Nazism and Communism taught us that the bigger the lie the more believable it becomes.

There are two kinds of myths that one finds in history: those that arise spontaneously, and those that are manufactured. The line between these two types of myths is extremely fine and can often become confused. In the end, if true history is to succeed with the public it must have "snap, crackle, and pop" or simply be ignored and soon forgotten. Of the incidents chosen for this work all have snap, crackle, and pop; the individuals behind the incidents saw to it that they did.

1

Oath of a Freeman

The King of Forgers

Mark Hofmann was unquestionably the most skilled forger this country has ever seen . . . he perpetrated by far the largest monetary frauds
through forgery that this country has ever had. He fooled me—he fooled
everybody.

—Charles Hamilton, document dealer
and handwriting expert

On October 16, 1985, a neatly dressed man in his mid-thirties clutched the
handle on the door of his blue Toyota. As he innocently opened the door a
brown paper package resting on the console slipped between the two front
seats and fell to the floor. It happened in less than a second. The inside of
the car erupted in a violent fireball, blowing the roof off of the car and lift-
ing the man several feet into the air and hurtling him backward as if he had
been suddenly pulled by a giant hand and thrown on the ground. Pieces of
the car flew through the air, landing on the parking lot's black macadam
surface as much as a hundred feet away. The air was filled with swirling
shreds of paper, fabric, and glass shards that rained down around the burning vehicle. The man lay on his back with his knees drawn up, giving the
appearance of someone resting in the warm autumn sun. His right knee
was torn apart, with blood spurting from a gaping wound. The flesh from a
finger on his right hand had been blown off, leaving the bone exposed. His
clothes were in tatters.

It was the third bomb explosion to take place in the peaceful city of

Salt Lake within the past thirty hours. The previous morning a bomb had exploded on the fourth floor of the Judge Building in downtown Salt Lake, killing Steve Christensen as he showed up for work. A few hours later, Kathy Sheets, a suburban housewife, picked up a package left by the garage door and became the second victim that morning. Now a third bomb had exploded, seriously injuring its victim. It appeared that a serial bomber was on the loose. Frightened residents became panicky, wondering who would be next. There were plenty of motives suggesting why the people were being attacked. The question bothering most people, however, was who would be next?

Steve Christensen, the first victim, had been a partner of J. Gary Sheets in an investment company. It was Sheets's wife who was the second victim. The third victim was Mark Hofmann, a thirty-one-year-old former pre-med student at Utah State University who dropped out of college and became a highly successful rare documents dealer. It wasn't long before Christensen, Sheets, and Hofmann became intimately linked, along with several other people, through Hofmann's amazing discoveries of rare church-related documents. The trail that wound its way through the heady fields of investment and rare documents, ending in murder, is one of the more fascinating stories in the area of historical fraud to occur in American history. It all began with Hofmann's fortuitous discovery of a document known to members of the Church of Jesus Christ of Latter-Day Saints (commonly known as Mormons) as the "Anthon Transcript," and ended with his discovery of America's holy grail, a diminutive document known as "The Oath of a Freeman."

The Anthon manuscript that Mark Hofmann allegedly found is a small piece of paper containing several strange looking characters. Church lore says that Joseph Smith Jr., the founder of Mormonism, created it as his key to translating the strange Egyptian hieroglyphic characters from the golden plates the angel Moroni had shown him buried in the woods near his farm in upstate New York.

At the time of his "discovery" of the Anthon Transcript, Hofmann was a twenty-six-year-old-student at Utah State University. He had been interested in history and collecting ever since he was a young boy. Hofmann's love of books and history were at the core of his personality. Like many young boys, Hofmann's interest had been in coins, but as he grew older he became fascinated with historical documents. He soon developed an uncanny knack for finding rare documents that were of great historical significance, especially to the Mormon Church. He attributed his unusual

Mark Hofmann at the time of his preliminary hearing. (Paul Fraughton, *Salt Lake Tribune*)

success to his methodology of discovery. Tracing the descendants of famous people, or people closely associated with famous people, Hofmann would contact their modern descendants in the hope of uncovering important material among family papers and keepsakes, or so he claimed.

One of his earliest discoveries came when he purchased a 1668 copy of the King James Version of the Bible that bore the signature of "Samuel Smith." Hofmann believed the signature was that of Joseph Smith's great or possibly great-great grandfather.[1] His not being sure just who Samuel Smith was in relation to Joseph Smith added a certain realistic touch to his discovery. It was the "Gosh! Gee whiz!" element used by many perpetrators of fraud—what some skeptics refer to as the "Colombo" approach to discovery. Hofmann later told church officials he purchased the Bible from an acquaintance who had bought the book from a descendant of Catherine Smith Salisbury, Joseph Smith's sister.

As significant as the signed Bible was to the Mormon Church, there was more. When Hofmann examined its pages he found a special sheet of

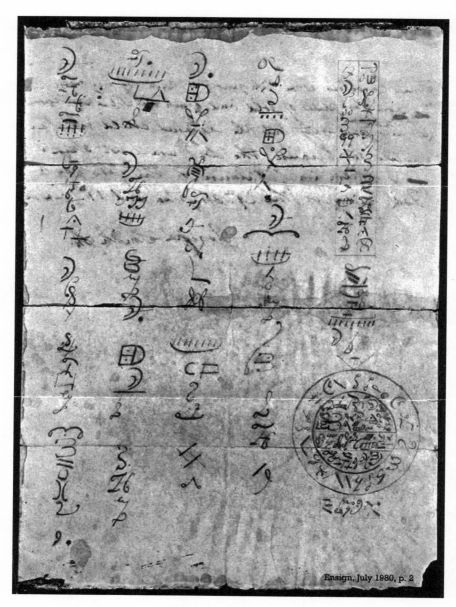

Mark Hofmann's forged copy of the Anthon Transcript containing various symbols or characters that Joseph Smith allegedly copied from the golden plates. Hofmann claimed he found the document among the pages of a Bible once believed owned by Joseph Smith's great-great grandfather. (George J. Throckmorton)

paper carefully tucked inside two pages of the Bible that had been glued together, forming a secret pocket. Freeing the paper from between the pages, he noted the faint signature of "Joseph Smith, Jr." written on the outside of the folded paper. Hofmann thought he had hit the jackpot. Only when he examined the piece of paper further did he realize just how big a jackpot he had hit. The paper was covered with strange symbols resembling Egyptian hieroglyphics. Faintly written on the back of the paper was a notation that explained their origin: "These caractors were diligently coppied by my own hand from the plates of gold and given to Martin Harris who took them to New York City but the learned could not translate it because the Lord would not open it to them in fulfillment of the prophecy of Isaih written in the 29th chapter and 11th verse. Joseph Smith Jr."[2]

The discovery was sensational. It was beyond sensational. It was akin to finding the original Ten Commandments chiseled in stone. The story alluded to in the faint inscription on the back of the document was well known to all Mormons. Joseph Smith told his followers that an angel had visited him while he was working in the fields near his home. The angel, who identified himself as "Moroni," led Smith to a spot where he told him he had buried a cache of golden plates fourteen hundred years earlier. The plates told the history of an ancient civilization that had come to America from the Middle East. The people eventually divided into two warring camps. After many battles one of the camps was wiped out and the successful camp reduced to a small number of survivors that became the ancestors of the American Indians. The angel gave Smith temporary possession of the gold plates covered in strange symbols and hieroglyphics and two magical stones he called Thummim and Urim. By placing these magical stones in his hat and placing his face against the stones and covering himself with a blanket, Smith was able to translate the strange symbols on the plates. They told the story of Nehi and his son, Laman, who left Jerusalem six hundred years before the birth of Christ, making their way across the ocean to America. It was here that the two groups, led by Nehi and Laman, went to war against each other. The Lamanites eventually destroyed the followers of Nehi. Angered by the Lamanites, God gave them brown skin as punishment for their sins. Reduced to a handful of survivors, the Lamanites eventually became the modern-day American Indians.

As Smith dictated his translation of the plates, his close friend and neighbor Martin Harris transcribed the words, which became the Book of Mormon. Harris, at the urging of Smith, took the original paper containing the symbols that Smith claimed he used to translate the Book of Mormon to Charles Anthon, a prominent Greek and Latin scholar at Columbia College in New York City, in hopes of having Anthon translate the columns of strange symbols. Anthon was unable to make sense of any of the symbols. The paper Hofmann claimed to have found glued between the pages of the 1668 Bible matched Anthon's description of the paper that Martin Harris showed him. It appeared that Hofmann had discovered the holy grail of Mormonism, missing for nearly 150 years.

Hofmann chose one of his instructors at Utah State University to be the first to see the exciting document. His name was A. J. Simmonds, the curator of the university's Special Collections Books. Interestingly, Simmonds was not a Mormon, but he knew a great deal about the religion, its history, and its current beliefs and practices. It was a clever move on Hofmann's part. He decided to make the document public by first introducing it to Simmonds, then to important members of the church who held positions dealing with church history. From Simmonds, Hofmann next took the document to Dan Bachman, a historian in church religion at Utah State University. Like Simmonds, Bachman was thrilled at the discovery. Bachman, with Hofmann in tow, took the document to Dean Jesse, the church's expert on handwriting and historical documents. Jesse was stunned by what he saw. On superficial examination it looked real. The handwriting appeared to be that of Joseph Smith, but Jesse wanted time to thoroughly examine the document before passing final judgment. This was not a trivial matter, and Jesse wanted to be certain before giving his approval. After three days of examining the writing Jesse was willing to sign a statement certifying the handwriting was that of Joseph Smith.[3] The document, he said, was real!

Hofmann was now ready for the big time. The church historians felt confident enough to take Hofmann and his document to the church leaders. It was a historic moment. Hofmann was taken into the office of Spencer W. Campbell, Prophet, Seer, and Revelator of the church. With him were his two counselors, Nathan Eldon Tanner and Marion G. Romney, and apostles Gordon B. Hinckley and Boyd K. Packer. Appearing humble and somewhat timid, Hofmann told the group of men how he came about his amazing discovery. Graciously, Hofmann agreed to leave the Anthon Transcript with the church elders so that their experts could properly test the document to verify its authenticity. Having received the experts' approval, Hofmann decided to donate the seminal document of Mormonism to the church, telling its leaders he believed it should remain within the church forever. It was a magnificent gesture considering what the document might bring financially if placed on the open market. Hofmann's generosity, however, was part of his plan to gain the confidence of the church leaders. He had cast the hook and the church elders were snagged.

It was 1980, the sesquicentennial year of the church's founding. That the Anthon Transcript should suddenly appear after a century and a half was surely a gift from God himself as a tribute to the church's great work on His behalf. A week after the initial meeting, the elders held a press conference announcing to the world the discovery of the Anthon Transcript, elevating the obscure pre-med student who found it to celebrity status. The news of the Anthon Transcript circled the globe, making headlines nearly everywhere. One prominent Mormon scholar was quoted as stating, "This offers as good a test as we'll ever get of the authenticity of the Book of Mormon."[4]

Over the next five years Mark Hofmann dazzled the historical documents world with his amazing finds. In February 1981, Hofmann again stunned the Mormon historians with an incredible find. It was known as a "blessing" by Joseph Smith. While there were numerous examples of Smith's blessings in the church archives, this one was unique. Dated January 17, 1844, it appointed Smith's son, Joseph Smith III, to succeed him as head of the church. The blessing read in part, "For he [son Joseph] shall be my successor to the Presidency of the High Priesthood: a Seer, and Revelator and a Prophet, unto the church, which appointment belongeth to him by blessing and also by right."

The blessing literally overturned the church's claim to being the true church of Joseph Smith. Following Joseph Smith's murder in 1844 in Nauvoo at the hands of religious bigots, the Mormon colony decided to pull up stakes and follow its new leader, Brigham Young, west to a new promised land. Remaining behind was a group of church members who believed that Joseph Smith's son, Joseph Smith III, was the true Prophet, Seer, and Revelator of the church, not Brigham Young. In 1860, Joseph Smith III established what became known as the Reorganized Church of Jesus Christ of Latter-Day Saints, and located his followers in Independence, Missouri. Since all of the church records were removed from Nauvoo to Salt Lake City by Brigham Young, it was believed by those who chose not to follow Young that Joseph Smith's blessing anointing his son as head of the church was ordered destroyed by Young. Now, over a century later, Mark Hofmann had uncovered the important document that, if authentic, proved the church in Salt Lake under Brigham Young was a false church, and the church in Missouri was the true church. Hofmann had once again come up with a seminal document that set church officials on their ear.

Hofmann took the blessing to Donald T. Schmidt, chief archivist of the impressive collection of early church documents held by the Mormon Church. He told Schmidt he had acquired the document along with several others from a descendant of Thomas Bullock, Joseph Smith's principal scribe. Hofmann asked Schmidt if he was interested in purchasing the important blessing. Hofmann placed a price of $5,000 on the document, a modest sum considering its significance to the church's legitimate claim as the true church of Joseph Smith. Schmidt acted indifferent to Hofmann's offer, suggesting the document was overpriced. A surprised Hofmann told Schmidt if he was not interested in purchasing the blessing, the Reorganized Church in Missouri was interested. After all, the blessing supported their claim that they represented the legitimate church of Joseph Smith.

After Hofmann began negotiating with the Missouri church, the leaders in Salt Lake met Hofmann's demands and purchased the blessing. To bolster the authenticity of the blessing, Hofmann produced a letter from the Bullock collection allegedly written by Bullock to Brigham Young. In the letter, Bullock makes reference to the blessing young Smith received from Joseph Smith. In another magnanimous gesture, Hofmann donated the letter to the Salt Lake church, telling its leader he did not want the letter to fall into the hands of those from the Reorganized Church in Missouri.

Hofmann was on a roll. He had produced the Anthon Transcript upon which the Book of Mormon was based, the Joseph Smith blessing anointing his son (and not Brigham Young) as his successor, and the Thomas Bullock letter supporting the authenticity of the blessing. It must be remembered that several experts in the field of document analysis carefully examined all three of these documents and that all three were declared authentic. Hofmann's place as the greatest discoverer of important documents in Mormon Church history was solidly established. He had gained admittance to the highest circles of church leadership. Their door was always open to him, as was the inner, restricted church archives containing a rich source of church history.

But Hofmann wasn't finished just yet, not by a long shot. Over the next two and a half years he continued to turn up interesting documents of a historical nature, including several related to other areas of American history. By now, Hofmann was a full-time dealer supporting his wife and daughter on his dealings in rare documents. In the first few months of 1981, Hofmann made $52,000 either outright or through trades.[5] One of his methods of financing his purchases involved a kind of Ponzi or Bernie Madoff scheme. Hofmann would often borrow large sums of money from friends and clients in the document-collecting field to allegedly finance his purchases. After selling the documents he would repay the loans, only to borrow again. His business grew both financially and in discoveries. Then, in December 1983, he pulled another rabbit out of his remarkable hat. It was a lengthy letter dated October 23, 1830, written by Joseph Smith's chief lieutenant, Martin Harris. It quickly became known as "The Salamander Letter." The letter talked about Joseph Smith's "magical" beliefs in forming the church, a subject taboo to the current leaders of the church.

Hofmann began to lay the groundwork for his amazing find by dropping subtle hints that his associate, Lyn Jacobs, currently doing graduate work at Harvard, had discovered a letter by Harris claiming the golden plates were guarded by a white salamander that refused to give up the plates to Smith without the presence of his dead brother, Alvin Smith. It all sounded very magical. Most importantly, it refuted the story that Smith had been visited by the angel Moroni who gave Smith the golden plates. Here was another piece of evidence that, if true, undermined the very foundation of the Mormon Church. How much more damage could the church endure and still survive? How many more potentially damaging documents would the church be forced to buy to prevent scandal? Obviously, a great deal.

Although Lyn Jacobs was a knowing partner in Hofmann's document business, he was an unknowing partner in Hofmann's forgery schemes. Hofmann had asked Jacobs to track down dealers in the East and find out what sorts of material they had for sale or trade. Jacobs, too busy with graduate work, sent Hofmann a list of dealers instead. It wasn't what Hofmann wanted, but it was enough to launch his scheme. He called Jacobs at school and told him he had acquired a sensational letter written by Martin Harris that told of Smith's discovery of the gold plates, and about the white salamander. As far as Jacobs knew, Hofmann had purchased the letter from a New York dentist, a collector of early postmarks. Hofmann told Jacobs he paid $20 for the letter, a paltry sum for such an important document. But the original owner wasn't interested in the letter for its content, only the postmark, which was worth around $20 to a postmark collector. How lucky could Hofmann get?

The letter contained Martin Harris's version of a conversation he had with Joseph Smith. According to Harris, Smith told him the true story of how he found the gold plates: "It is true I found it 4 years ago with my stone but only just got it because of the enchantment the old spirit come to me 3 times in the same dream & says dig up the gold but when I take it up the next morning the spirit transfigured himself from a white salamander in the bottom of the hole & struck me 3 times & held the treasure & would not let me have it because I lay it down to cover over the hole when the spirit says do not lay it down."

Harris goes on in his letter to state that Smith found "some giant silver spectacles with the plates he puts them in a old hat & in the darkness reads the words & in this way it is all translated & written down." Clearly, the letter, if authentic, would change the history of the founding of the church and the book of Mormon, and not in a way that would please its modern-day leaders or their followers. Hofmann had a special knack for finding documents that refuted the modern beliefs of the Mormon faithful. His success was uncanny. More importantly, it seemed his veracity was never doubted.

Hofmann magnanimously offered Jacobs a share in the letter because he had provided Hofmann with the name of the dealer where he allegedly found it. He also told Jacobs he wanted to avoid any more publicity. After all, his string of serendipitous finds was beginning to look too good to be true. Having Jacobs take credit for discovering the letter would take the focus off of Hofmann. It was a clever maneuver on Hofmann's part. He asked Jacobs if he would agree to take responsibility for finding the letter. All Jacobs had to do was tell people that he found the letter and brought it to Hofmann. Jacobs agreed. He became an unwitting accomplice. For his role, Hofmann would share the profit. Jacobs thought it was a harmless lie and that Hofmann simply wanted to stay out of the limelight.

When Jacobs arrived in Salt Lake City just before Christmas in December 1983, he began marketing the letter according to Hofmann's instructions. He first took it to President Gordon Hinckley, Prophet, Seer, and Revelator of the church. After some negotiation, Hinckley balked. He wasn't sure he should have the church buy it. Jacobs went to Hofmann and told him that Hinckley apparently had reservations about the church buying the letter. Hofmann swung into action. He contacted Brent Ashworth, a collector of Joseph Smith documents, and said the letter was available. Ashworth was reluctant because of the letter's shocking content. Ashworth told Hofmann that if the letter were authentic the church should have the letter, not a collector, and certainly not someone who wanted to hurt the church. Ashworth was repelled by its content. Hofmann then took the letter to Steve Christensen, who was intrigued, but also worried about the letter's authenticity. Christensen was aware of the rumors that had circulated over the years that Harris and Smith had had supernatural or mystical beliefs. Christensen agreed to purchase the letter for $40,000, but only after his experts examined it and certified its authenticity. His purpose was to donate the letter to the church, thereby keeping it out of the hands of the church's enemies. He hired renowned Boston rare documents dealer and handwriting expert Kenneth Rendell. Rendell sent the letter to his own experts to have the paper and ink tested. He personally examined the postmark and handwriting. When the results came back to Rendell he wrote to Christensen that there was nothing to lead him to believe the letter was anything but authentic.[6] It had passed all of the tests. Christensen purchased the letter for the agreed price of $40,000, but decided to hold on to it for one year before donating it to the church. By waiting a year Christensen created distance between Jacobs's approach to Hinckley and the final disposition of the letter. After a year of controversy surrounding the content of the letter, Christensen delivered it to President Hinckley on April 12, 1985.[7] Hofmann had struck again. It seemed he was unstoppable.

Mark Hofmann's career as a forger was not limited to documents associated with the Mormon Church. Although his most stunning discoveries had to do with the church's history, he successfully created and sold documents from across America's historical landscape. Letters attributed to such notables as Abraham Lincoln, Mark Twain, Jim Bridger, Jack London, George Washington, Paul Revere, John Brown, Daniel Boone, and George "Butch" Cassidy to name just a few. This impressive list of America's Who's Who represented the other half of Hofmann's production of forgeries. While it seemed Hofmann could successfully forge virtually anyone he wanted, there are two forgeries that attest to his real genius. The first is a poem allegedly written by the poet Emily Dickinson. It is one thing to forge a letter where creating the content is a matter of studying one's subject. But to create an unpublished poem by one of America's greatest poets and convince scholars of its authenticity takes a unique kind of talent. Not many forgers have the intellectual ability to write poetry, let alone poetry accepted as among the very best.

Emily Dickinson is often described as eccentric, which is true by normal standards, whatever they may be. But by intellectual standards she was quite normal in most ways. Dickinson was a shy, reclusive person who eventually withdrew from society, confining herself to her bedroom, where she talked to most people through her closed door. When she did emerge from her room, which was on rare occasion, she always dressed in white. Born in Amherst in 1830, she began writing poetry as a young child. By the time her poetry was collected and published in 1955, nearly seventy years after her death in 1886 at the age of fifty-six, it filled three volumes totaling an amazing 1,775 poems.[8]

Because of her voluminous output and disorganized manner of caring for her writings, she was an ideal subject for Hofmann to forge. An ideal subject, perhaps, but how does someone go about creating poetry, especially poetry of a highly recognized poet? Poetry that must pass scrutiny not just by handwriting and forensic experts, but also by literary critics who make the ultimate decision of whether a poem is worthy of publication. Such concerns were not a problem for Mark Hofmann. Years later while serving life in prison Hofmann wrote from his prison cell to Daniel Lombardo, the victim of his Dickinson forgery, that he decided to create a Dickinson poem after reading about her. "I picked Dickinson because her autograph material is among the most valuable of American poets . . . and it was a challenge." Hofmann went on to write, "I either read in a biography or concluded from her poems that she was an agnostic who provided us with a common outlook."[9]

Hofmann soon learned that Dickinson's prodigious writing produced poems of a wide range of quality—some great, some mediocre, a few poor. Surely, he thought, I can write a poem that could fit somewhere among the middling of her efforts. He was right. Hofmann created the following poem eventually attributed to Dickinson:

That God cannot
be understood
Everyone Agrees —
We do not know
His Motives nor
Comprehend his
Deeds —

Then why should I
Seek solace in
What I cannot
know?
Better to play
In winter's sun
Than to fear the
Snow

Incredibly, Dan Lombardo, the curator of Special Collections at the Jones Library in Amherst, Massachusetts, became one of Mark Hofmann's victims ten years *after* Hofmann had been sentenced to life in prison. The Jones Memorial Library consists of three libraries located in Amherst, and houses a Special Collections Department that contains works by poets Emily Dickinson and Robert Frost. It was in his role as head of the Special Collections Department that Lombardo set out to fulfill his most exciting quest, the purchase of a new, unknown poem by Dickinson for the library.

Lombardo had first become aware of the poem while reading a June 1997 Sotheby's catalogue. While the provenance of the poem was unclear, there was little doubt as to its authenticity. The poem was estimated to be worth between $10,000 and $15,000. The acquisition fund of the library totaled $5,000, not even close to what Lombardo needed to buy the rare document. Fortunately, the Emily Dickinson International Society was holding its annual meeting in Amherst at the Jones Library several weeks before the scheduled auction. Lombardo made a presentation to the Society about the poem, telling the group it was a unique opportunity to bring the poem back home where it had been written. The response was one of great enthusiasm. By the end of the meeting Lombardo had pledges from the society members totaling $8,000. This, along with the library's $5,000, gave him $13,000. Lombardo next turned to the Internet and the Friends of the Jones Library. Incredibly, he was able to raise a grand total of $24,000. Even with Sotheby's commission, Lombardo was confident he had enough to buy the poem.

Only one thing nagged at Lombardo. Was the poem truly authentic? He was sure it was. After all, Sotheby's had certified it authentic. Lombardo picked up the phone and called Ralph Franklin at Yale University's Beinecke Library. Franklin was considered by most scholars in the field to be the leading expert on Dickinson poems. To Lombardo's great relief, Franklin told him he had known about the poem for three years and was going to include it in his forthcoming volume on Dickinson's poems. All doubts had been erased, but were quickly replaced with new doubts that he would be the successful bidder. He would be up against some major heavyweights in the field of document collecting, including major institutions.

The day finally arrived and Lombardo took his seat in the famous auction house. He was not a novice to auctions, but he was also not a professional in such matters. He decided to hold back, waiting to enter his bid at the right moment. Unlike several of the bidders, he did not want to enter the bidding early and help push up the price. Bidding opened at $8,000 and soon climbed to $15,000, where it slowed. Lombardo jumped in at this point, raising the bid to $17,000. It was quickly raised to $20,000; Lombardo countered with $21,000. It was his last bid. He could go no farther. He had to reserve $3,000 for Sotheby's commission. Lombardo's anxiety changed to elation as he heard the hammer fall with the beautiful word "Sold!" Lombardo was going to return to Amherst triumphant, with the Emily Dickinson poem in hand.

Returning to Amherst, Lombardo began researching an article on the poem and preparing an exhibit where it, along with other poems and artifacts, would be on display for all to see. It was a proud moment for Lombardo. He wanted to tell as much of the story of Emily's poem as he could, so he called Sotheby's to find out its history. Where did it come from? Who consigned it? What did Sotheby's know about its history? One of Sotheby's senior experts in books and manuscripts was happy to tell Lombardo everything the auction house knew about the poem. Unfortunately, it was not much. The poem was consigned by a collector who purchased it from a dealer in the Midwest who had recently died. Lombardo was disappointed, but he still had the makings of a great exhibit. He was still feeling somewhat euphoric about his purchase on behalf of the Jones Library.

Lombardo's euphoria suddenly turned to dismay. He received a phone call from a man who identified himself as Brent Ashworth, a corporate attorney in Salt Lake City who was a collector of historical documents. Coincidentally, he was also chairman of the Emily Dickinson Society of Utah. Ashworth told Lombardo that twelve years earlier he had been offered an Emily Dickinson poem. Learning of the Sotheby sale, Ashworth obtained a copy of the catalogue with the photograph of the poem. He was reasonably sure it was the very same poem he was offered. The dealer? His name was Mark Hofmann, the man now serving a life sentence in the Utah State Prison for murder. The same Mark Hofmann who fooled the experts and sold several hundred forged historical documents. Ashworth told Lombardo that he had purchased somewhere around a half-million dollars worth of forged documents from Hofmann.

As stunning as Ashworth's call was, there was more to the story. It seems Ashworth had seen the poem a second time, approximately ten years before it showed up in Sotheby's auction room. While on business in Washington, D.C., Ashworth stepped into a shop that specialized in important American historical documents. On the wall was a beautifully framed poem by Emily Dickinson, the same poem Hofmann had offered to him two years earlier. The owner of the store and poem was a well-known dealer in historical documents, Todd Axelrod. Among Axelrod's many treasures was the famous letter written by Abraham Lincoln to Grace Bedell. Grace was the young girl from Westfield, New York, who gained national fame when she wrote to presidential candidate Lincoln in 1860 advising him to grow a beard. Grace rather audaciously wrote, "Your face is so thin. All the ladies like whiskers and they would tease their husbands to vote for you and then you would be president." Lincoln responded by writing back to Grace, "As to the whiskers, having never worn any, do you not think people would call it a piece of silly affectation if I were to begin it now?" A few days later Lincoln began growing his famous whiskers. On his inaugural journey to Washington after his election, Lincoln stopped over in Westfield, New York, and asked to see young Grace. She was introduced to him, and after kissing her on the cheek he said, "You see I have followed your advice."[10] Grace became known as "Lincoln's Little Girl," and Lincoln's reply to Grace's letter became one of the treasured documents in American presidential history. It was now one of Axelrod's prized possessions.

Wanting desperately to believe, Lombardo still had hope that the poem was authentic. Following Emily's death in 1886, her sister found a box containing over seven hundred poems. Might Lombardo's copy somehow have found its way from the box collection into private hands, eventually making its way a hundred years later into a dealer's inventory? Lombardo set out to determine the true status of his Dickinson poem. Was it authentic, or another of Mark Hofmann's masterpieces? His troubles began when he contacted Sotheby's. He was told there was "absolutely no question" that the poem was authentic—several experts had studied the poem and certified its authenticity, including the renowned documents expert Kenneth Rendell—the same Kenneth Rendell that examined the Salamander letter for Steve Christensen and concluded it was not a forgery.[11] Lombardo was reassured on hearing that Rendell felt the poem was authentic. Rendell's credentials were sterling. Lombardo, however, was not completely satisfied. He pressed on. He contacted Jennifer Larson, a rare book and document dealer whose credentials and ethics landed her in the chairmanship of the Ethics Committee of the Antiquarian Booksellers' Association of America. Larson had taken upon herself the task of researching Hofmann's non-Mormon forgeries in an effort to protect the marketplace from further damage should any of Hofmann's works show up. In her files were records of Hofmann's travels during his prolific forgery period, including records that showed Hofmann had traveled to Cambridge, Massachusetts, in 1983 and again in 1984 to visit the Houghton Library at Harvard University. She suspected it was to examine the library's large collection of Emily Dickinson poems. Larson also told Lombardo that she interviewed a television reporter who was researching Hofmann for a documentary. He had sent Hofmann a copy of an Emily Dickinson poem that appears in Todd Axelrod's book on famous documents, asking Hofmann's opinion.[12] Hofmann answered the reporter's query, "The E. Dickinson item referred to is a forgery."[13] The photograph was of the same poem that Lombardo had bought at Sotheby's. Lombardo was now all but certain that the poem was a Hofmann forgery. He next contacted one of Hofmann's couriers, Shannon Flynn. Flynn had been under intense investigation by the Salt Lake City police at the same time they were building their case against Hofmann. In the end, he was cleared and all charges against him were dropped. Flynn put the nail in the poem's coffin when he told Lombardo that he personally had delivered the poem to Todd Axelrod's Gallery of History for Mark Hofmann.

Through his own excellent research, Lombardo felt he had now established a complete provenance trail for the poem. From Hofmann's hand Shannon Flynn carried the poem to Todd Axelrod's gallery, and from Axelrod it was consigned to Sotheby's, where Lombardo purchased it. Lombardo contacted Sotheby's with his evidence and asked that they return the Jones Library's $24,000. After some hesitation, Sotheby's refunded the library's money.

Daniel Lombardo was now faced with the difficult task of letting the Jones Library and members of the Emily Dickinson International Society know that the poem was a forgery. They had been had. At least they were in good company. There was almost no one in the short history of Mark Hofmann's career as a forger that had not been fooled. He had left the landscape littered with the damaged reputations of dozens of experts who certified his work time and again as authentic. But the story does not end just yet. Hofmann had pulled off some of the greatest frauds in the history of forgery. But his greatest effort was yet to come. It would make him the unquestioned king of forgers.

As controversy swirled about the impact of the Mormon documents on the church's history, Hofmann told his closest friends his interests were moving in the direction of Americana. He was leaving the Mormon Church behind. His amazing ability to uncover documents of major importance continued, and well it should for his talent for creating documents showed no limitations of any sort. From George Washington and Ben Franklin to

Daniel Boone and Davy Crockett, Hofmann continued his uncanny success at discovery.

While Hofmann's success in document discoveries and sales helped to control the rising cost of his business and private life, his personal finances were beginning to accumulate debt at an alarming rate. He needed greater and greater discoveries to raise larger sums of money to finance his Ponzi-like schemes. He was using his stable of collectors and investors to supply him with fresh money to keep his operation afloat. At the same time he and his wife Doralee were spending money on such personal things as cars and a new house. The debts mounted, and soon Hofmann was becoming a little frantic over his financial problems.

With mounting debt Hofmann reached back to what he did best, "discovering" documents critical to Mormon Church history. While in his Mormon document mode, Hofmann claimed to have discovered the whereabouts of an infamous collection of anti-Mormon material that dated back to the founding of the church. William E. McClellin, considered by the modern church leaders to be a fallen Mormon apostle of Joseph Smith, left the church in 1838 and began a personal anti-Mormon crusade. Rumor had it that McClellin kept a journal that was highly critical of Joseph Smith and his private life. McClellin also accumulated a number of documents that were damaging to Smith and the early church. No one had seen the collection, but many believed it still existed, either lost or hidden away in some anonymous collector's files. What better source of new material for Hofmann than the mysterious McClellin collection.

Coming off of his discovery of the Salamander letter, Hofmann leaked word that he had located the McClellin collection. It was in private hands somewhere in Texas. Steve Christensen was still concerned about protecting the church's reputation. He considered it his religious duty. His purchase and donation of the Salamander letter was a generous act aimed at protecting the church. He now felt obligated to do something to prevent the McClellin collection from doing further damage. If he could arrange to buy it he could turn it over to the church leaders, who would safeguard the church from further unfavorable publicity.

In May 1985, Christensen met with Hofmann to discuss what the dealer knew and what action could be taken to buy the coveted McClellin collection. Hofmann told Christensen the owner wanted the incredible sum of $195,000. Hofmann had an option to buy the collection, but the option expired on June 30, just two days hence. Hofmann told Christensen that he didn't have the money to buy the collection, but he had a major deal pending that would give him enough money to buy the collection several times over. If he could somehow get the money to buy the collection now, he could repay the loan and donate the collection to the church. It was a good deal all around. As in the case of the Salamander letter, the church would not have to explain buying the collection since a benefactor had donated it. The two decided to go see Hugh Pinnock, an Elder and General Authority of the church who was a financial expert with numerous financial contacts, including ties to the First Interstate Bank in Salt Lake.

Pinnock was persuaded to arrange a loan to Hofmann to purchase the collection. With Pinnock's backing, Hofmann obtained a loan for $185,000 from the First Interstate Bank with a minimum of paperwork and no collateral. The bank had close ties with the church, and undoubtedly Pinnock greased the wheels, allowing the loan to go through quickly without any trouble. Hofmann now had $185,000 from Interstate Bank to close the deal. Unknown to Christensen and Pinnock, Hofmann had already marketed the alleged McClellin collection to one of his dealer-investors, Al Rust. Rust owned a coin shop in Salt Lake City and had multiple dealings with Hofmann. Hofmann told Rust he had an option to buy the McClellin collection at $185,000. He had $35,000 to put into the deal; did Rust want to invest by putting up the balance of $150,000? Hofmann told him he thought he could get $300,000 for the collection. That meant a $115,000 profit. Rust liked the idea, and the profit. He was in. Hofmann told him they had to move quickly to beat out other dealers from buying the collection.

In addition to owing Interstate Bank $185,000 and Rust $150,000, Hofmann owed a half dozen other people over $300,000 from deals he had worked previously. His travel agency was threatening a lawsuit because of a check that bounced, and he and his wife owed $200,000 as down payment on their new house. In all, Hofmann owed close to $1 million to a variety of institutions and investors. His Ponzi scheme was beginning to crumble as the amount of money Hofmann owed climbed well past the money he was bringing in. Time was running out for the talented forger.

Not all of Hofmann's dealings with his investors were bad. He was able to borrow large sums of money because he had made several legitimate transactions that generated profit—profit that he returned to his investors. In this way, he kept them on the hook and could go back to them for more money. But his juggling act was beginning to come apart. Uncanny as it seems, he was able to stall his debtors with promises that payment was just around the corner. He even went so far as to tell Christensen and Pinnock as well as Rust that he had closed the deal on the McClellin collection. He told Pinnock the collection was safely stored away in safe-deposit boxes, while he told Rust he had sold the collection to the church for $300,000, netting them a profit of $115,000. Now he not only owed Rust the $150,000 but half of the $115,000 profit. Time was about to run out for Hofmann. He needed money and he needed it in a hurry. One hundred thousand-dollar documents were not going to solve his financial problems. He needed at least five times that amount if he was going to survive. As hopeless as the situation seemed, Hofmann devised a way out. It was bold, but boldness was not new to Hofmann. It was what he needed if he was going to survive. He needed to come up with a mega-document that would bring him more money than he had ever dealt with before. That is when he decided "The Oath of a Freeman" was the answer to all his problems. It would be the greatest of all scams.

In the fall of 1638, two brothers arrived in the Massachusetts Bay Colony determined to begin a new life in a promising new world. It was a dream that millions of other immigrants would follow over the next three hundred years. Stephen and Matthew Daye left their home in England with few skills other than a determination to succeed in their new home. Stephen, a locksmith by trade, fortuitously inherited a printing press from its owner when he died during the passage across the Atlantic. It was the first printing press to arrive in the colonies, and Stephen and his brother decided the need for a printer far surpassed the need for a locksmith in the new world. Assembling the press in a small shop in Cambridge, the brothers proceeded to print the first document in the colonies. It was a small piece of paper titled "The Oath of a Freeman." The printing of the now famous "Bay Psalm Book" soon followed the Oath. Both were printed on the same press using the same set of moveable type. While several copies of the hymnbook exist, mostly in prestigious institutions, no copies of the Oath are known to have survived. Proof that it existed at one time is known because a handwritten copy survives, and a later printed version exists as part of a book printed in 1647.

The Oath was a pledge taken by male members of the colony who were freemen, who gave their pledge to defend the colony and its people and to not conspire to overthrow the government of the commonwealth. Because the Oath was the first printed document in America, it eventually became the holy grail of American printed documents. Its value, should it ever turn up, was anyone's guess. For the next several days Hofmann worked tirelessly in putting together his next scam, the biggest scam of his short career. The biggest scam, in fact, in the history of forgery—a long lost copy of the Oath.

Satisfied that he had created the perfect copy of the Oath, Hofmann took a plane to New York City, where he set his plan in motion. The day following his arrival he attended a rare book auction at Sotheby's. He sat in the audience watching as Justin Schiller, a dealer in rare children's books who had sold children's items to Hofmann and his wife over the years, acted as his representative purchasing a first edition of *Uncle Tom's Cabin* for $13,200. Before returning home to Salt Lake City, Hofmann visited the Argosy Book Store in downtown New York. Browsing through the bins of old prints, he selected several minor items and slipped his forged copy of the Oath between the pages of one. He then took the items to the unknowing clerk. Showing the clerk the Oath tucked between the pages, he asked what it was worth. The clerk, not knowing what the small printed piece of paper was worth had it been authentic, settled on $25. Hofmann paid the clerk, asking her to itemize the purchases and date the invoice. In all, the total came to $51.42, including "Oath of a Free Man," which was listed at $25. Hofmann cleverly established a believable provenance for the mysterious document. He was now ready to launch his newest scheme.

Returning to Salt Lake, Hofmann phoned Schiller back in New York. He noted that a recent Sotheby's catalogue listed a rare 1647 book that, according to the catalogue description, contained the earliest reprint of "The Freeman's Oath" printed by Stephen Daye in 1638. Was Schiller at all familiar with it? Hofmann then told Schiller he had purchased a small "broadside" while in New York at the Argosy Book Store titled "The Oath of a Freeman." Did Schiller think the Sotheby Oath might be the same Oath that he purchased at the Argosy? Schiller didn't know but said he would check around for Hofmann to see what he could find out. He asked Hofmann to mail him a photocopy of the Oath. Hofmann went Schiller one better. He told Schiller he planned on returning to New York to attend another Sotheby auction. He would bring the Oath with him.

Hofmann arrived at the Schiller-Wapner bookstore in Manhattan with his copy of "The Oath of a Freeman." Schiller took one look at it and was smitten. It certainly looked authentic, but Schiller admitted he was no expert on early printed documents. Schiller arranged to take the Oath to Francis Mattson, curator of rare books at the New York Public Library, where an original copy of Stephen Daye's Bay Psalm Book was currently on display. If Hofmann's Oath were authentic, it should match the typeface and spacing in the Psalm book.

OLD AND RARE BOOKS

ARGOSY BOOK STORE, INC.

116-EAST 59th STREET • NEW YORK, N.Y. 10022 • (212) Plaza 3-4455

Sold to:

3/13/81
INVOICE

For Mayor	5	—
For Representatives	5	—
Oath of 2 Free Men	25	—
George Washington — port	7	50
Martha Washington — port.	5	00
	47	50
tax —	3	92
	51	42

Pd.

Photocopy of the receipt Hofmann obtained supporting his claim that he found the Oath in a copy of a book he purchased from the Argosy Book Store. (James Gilreath, ed., *The Judgment of Experts*)

Comparing the two documents, Schiller and Mattson agreed they were very similar; in fact, the characters were identical. Even the spacing of the chain lines in the two papers was similar. Fortunately, Mattson also had in the library's impressive collection other early printings by Stephen Daye from the mid-1640s done on the same Cambridge Press that was used for the Oath and the Psalm book. All the characteristics of Hofmann's Oath and Daye's other printings matched beautifully. To the untrained eye, and without sophisticated forensic testing, the Oath appeared genuine. So far, Hofmann's Oath had passed its initial tests.

Schiller and Hofmann returned to the bookstore excited with what they had learned so far. Hofmann then did another smart thing in his move toward marketing the Oath: he asked Schiller if he and his partner would represent Hofmann. Schiller was delighted. Although rare documents were out of his field of expertise, dealing with upscale buyers was not. Schiller knew all of the important contacts in the field of rare books and documents. To put icing on the cake, Hofmann offered the two men an exceptionally high percentage of the final sale—so high that Schiller had to ask Hofmann to repeat his offer "several times." While the offer was much higher than standard for such dealings in the industry, Hofmann knew what he was doing. Schiller, in an article about the offer, later wrote, "That is the way to get someone committed to a project!"[14]

Once he and Hofmann reached an agreement of representation, Schiller didn't fool around. He called James Gilreath at the Library of Congress. Gilreath, an American history specialist in the Rare Book and Special Collections Division at the library, after examining a photocopy of the document, was sufficiently impressed to fly to New York. Examining the Oath, Gilreath liked what he saw. He suggested that he take the Oath back to the Library of Congress for an in-depth forensic analysis in the library's own laboratories. Such a use of the library's facilities was unusual considering that the Oath was the property of a private dealer. But Gilreath knew this was an extraordinary document. If authentic, the document belonged in the library's collection. After all, it was the very first document printed in the colonies, and before the story ended there were rumors circulating that it would be displayed along with the Constitution and Declaration of Independence. The latter two documents, of course, were not the property of the Library of Congress, nor were they on display in the library. They were in the National Archives a few blocks down the street from the library. Nonetheless, the significance of the Oath justified such rumors.

Schiller sent the Oath to William Matheson, head of the Rare Book and

THE OATH OF A FREEMAN.

I. A.B. being (by Gods providence) an Inhabitant, and Freeman, within the iurifdictiõ of this Common-wealth, doe freely acknowledge my selfe to bee subject to the governement thereof; and therefore doe heere sweare, by the great & dreadfull name of the Everliving-God, that I will be true & faithfull to the same, & will accordingly yield affiftance & support therunto, with my perfon & eftate, as in equity I am bounde and will alfo truely indeavour to maintaine and preferve all the libertyes & privilidges thereof, fubmitting my felfe to the wholefome lawes, & ordres made & ftablifhed by the fame; and further, that I will not plot, nor practice any evill againft it, nor confent to any that fhall foe do, butt will timely difcover, & reveall the fame to lawefull authoritee nowe here ftablifhed, for the fpeedie preventing thereof. Moreover, I doe folemnly binde my felfe, in the fight of God, that when I fhalbe called, to give my voyce touching any fuch matter of this ftate, (in which freemen are to deale) I will give my vote & fuffrage as I fhall judge in myne owne confcience may beft conduce & tend to the publick weale of the body, without refpect of perfonnes, or favour of any man. Soe help mee God in the Lord Iefus Chrift.

"The Oath of a Freeman," cleverly produced by Mark Hofmann and initially authenticated as a true copy of the rare document. (James Gilreath, ed., *The Judgment of Experts*)

Special Collections Division at the library under an agreement that would allow the library's laboratory to keep the Oath until their tests were completed. Should the Oath be found authentic, and the owners wished to sell it, Matheson wanted to know the selling price. Schiller thought it best not to commit to a firm price just yet. Knowing that the Bay Psalm Book printing by Daye would probably bring $1 million to $1.5 million in the current market, he told Matheson he thought the asking price would be "somewhere above one million."[15] It was not an unreasonable figure for the holy grail of printing. It would certainly solve Hofmann's financial problems, even if Hofmann had to pay Schiller and Wapner a 25 percent commission.

Hofmann's choice of "The Oath of a Freeman" as the document that would solve his financial problems was both good and bad for the con man. By choosing so rare a document Hofmann was assured of getting enough money to pay back his creditors. But such a rare document valued at such a high price would limit the buyers, and more importantly, it would subject the document to intense scrutiny and testing by the country's leading forensic experts. Was Hofmann so good that he could fool the country's best, or was he so arrogant that he had full faith in his abilities? Actually, both. Hofmann's past triumphs were good enough to fool the experts, and he knew it. He was about to move, however, onto an entirely different plateau with "The Oath of a Freeman." He was ready and anxious to get on with the testing. His one stipulation to Schiller was that he did not want his name revealed or that he had purchased the Oath from the Argosy Book Store. On reflection, this was probably another clever move by Hofmann, for it showed a certain naiveté on his part as far as the staff at the library was concerned. Hofmann, of course, was anything but naive, but it was good that his potential buyers thought he was. Eventually, he had to reveal himself and his source, but by then he had already achieved his purpose in asking for anonymity.

While the Library of Congress put the Oath through its various tests, Schiller sent photocopies to other respected analysts, including Katharine Pantzer at the Houghton Library at Harvard and Nicolas Barker of the British Library. Schiller also sent photocopies to Kenneth Rendell, and to Paul Needham of the Pierpont Morgan Library, as well as to the rare document specialists at the Folger Library in Washington. All of these people were considered experts in the field of rare documents, handwriting, and historical content. Before the negotiations surrounding the sale of the Oath were over, dozens of experts had weighed in on its authenticity. Most expressed caution, not because of any doubt but because the Oath was so rare and so valuable that it was essential to show caution before making any commitment as to its authenticity.

Since the document was printed, handwriting analysis was not a consideration except for a small notation on the back, which read, "Oathe of Freemen," in ink. All of the experts agreed that the inscription was consistent with seventeenth-century handwriting. In place of handwriting, the experts had the printer's type to analyze. Stephen Daye's type, by definition, was new to the colonies. The earliest known examples of this style of type were in Daye's printing of the Bay Psalm Book produced on the same press at approximately the same time as the Oath was printed. The type consisted of individual letters cast in lead that were arranged letter by letter in a form that held them snug row upon row. Each letter had a unique appearance and was therefore identifiable. In addition to the type used, there was the ink and the paper, both identifiable to the seventeenth century, and to Stephen Daye's Cambridge print shop. Lastly, there was the composition of the Oath. Although no known printing of the original Oath existed outside of printed books of a later date (1647 and 1648), there was a manuscript copy of the Oath in the Massachusetts Bay Colony record book. Did Hofmann's Oath comport with the known language of these later Oaths? While the wording differed slightly, it was not inconsistent with changes that might normally be expected in later forms of the Oath.

In examining the paper several features were studied. As a control for comparison, the Library of Congress used the Bay Psalm Book printed on Daye's press and dated 1647. The first feature is content. Both papers were made of flax (linen) and cotton fibers with small amounts of colored silk (red and green). No watermarks were visible, but the papers contained chain marks. These are lines that can be seen in transmitted light and come from the support form that the paper mesh is applied to during its manufacture. The five chain lines were very similar in both samples. Since the Psalm book was printed on a dozen different papers, it was not unreasonable that the Oath was not a perfect match, nor should it be. The two papers, however, were close enough in composition and structure to pass as authentic. Daye presumably printed the Oath on seventeenth-century paper similar in construction to that used in printing his hymnbook.

The second feature examined was the printer's ink used in both samples. As with tests on the paper, the ink proved to be made up of components compatible with seventeenth-century ink. Both chemical analysis and microscopic (visual) analysis of the ink showed no questionable results. With paper and ink passing analysis, the Preservation Laboratory next examined the printing features of the document. Because the method used by Daye in his seventeenth-century print shop utilized individual, moveable type, it resulted in certain "irregularities" not seen in later, more modern printing. For instance, because each character was set in place individually, some characters had a slightly higher profile than others. If one looks at the set type in cross section, then the faces of some of the letters are higher or lower than their neighbors. This gives an uneven appearance to the ink letters. Some letters appear weaker than others. If the document had been made from a photographic plate, as a forger might use, the printing would all look the same. Also, when the type was pressed into the soft paper it would leave impressions of differing depths. Close examination with a low power microscope and special lighting can reveal these differences. Once again, the Oath passed scrutiny with flying colors.

To advanced collectors and dealers, physical and chemical tests are extremely important in determining authenticity. While some tests are objective (does the ink contain synthetic dye, thereby placing it in the modern post-1860s era?), some tests are subjective (handwriting analysis, which is really based on opinion). Complementing the tests is the all-important question of provenance. What is the history of the document? Where did it come from? Can we trace it from its origin every step of the way to its present state? Provenance is key to many acquisitions. In the case of "The Oath of a Freeman," ownership and provenance were withheld from the Library of Congress until a deal had been consummated. This aspect of the negotiation was troubling to both Matheson and Gilreath, who wanted to know who owned the Oath and where it came from. Surprisingly, despite Hofmann's attempt to establish a provenance by salting his copy among items in the Argosy Book Store and then "discovering" it and purchasing it, he did not want Schiller to tell the Library of Congress before a deal was struck. This may have been a mistake. Gilreath decided to do a little detective work on his own. By recalling certain things Schiller had told him about the discovery of the Oath, Gilreath concluded the owner was a client of Schiller's who had bought children's books from him and that he probably lived in Utah. By questioning other dealers, Gilreath found out that Schiller had an active collector-dealer named Mark Hofmann who lived in the Salt Lake City vicinity. Since Hofmann's phone number was unlisted, Gilreath decided to call a book dealer he knew that had excellent contacts in Salt Lake. While Gilreath learned about Hofmann's uncanny ability in the document field (all successes to date), he also learned that he was untrustworthy and had several "suspicious" friends. He even learned that Hofmann was known to have bounced several checks and on occasion stalled clients, failing to make payments when due. All of this raised several red flags to Gilreath. He was less willing to give in to conditions set by Schiller and Wapner and was getting cold feet. As May 1985 came to an end, the Library of Congress pressed Schiller for a price and conditions for selling the Oath. Schiller told Gilreath the price was $1.5 million dollars. The library wanted a guarantee of one year, during which further tests would be carried out. If the Oath failed to pass the tests the money would be returned. Schiller accepted, but still withheld the name of the owner and provenance.

After several weeks the Preservation Laboratory of the Library of Congress issued a preliminary report of its findings. On reviewing the data from several tests, the report ended with the following statement: "Finally, the studies of the broadside entitled 'The Oath of a Freeman' conducted by the Conservation Office and the Research and Testing Office *revealed no evidence that would contravene a mid-seventeenth century date* for the broadside" (emphasis added).[16] The careful wording left the door open to either a claim for or against the authenticity of the Oath. This method of expressing the results of analyses by carefully choosing one's words has become common among experts in fields such as handwriting and chemical analyses. To state that the results of a study reveal nothing that says a document is not authentic gives the expert a way out if the document proves to be forged. After the Oath was exposed as a forgery, James Gilreath pointed out that the Library of Congress's Preservation Laboratory never authenticated the Oath despite the popular belief that it had. According to Gilreath, "it merely stated that they could find no evidence of forgery based on their examination of the material used to make the document."[17] While the wording may seem noncommittal, most people in the media received it at the time as authenticating the Oath. The reasoning went something like this: if it wasn't a forgery, then it must be authentic. A reasonable conclusion. Hofmann had basically fooled the experts once again.

Gilreath's investigation into Hofmann's reputation as well as the inability to provide a provenance for the Oath put a damper on the library's enthusiasm for acquiring the document. Time was actually on the library's side. Despite the seeming urgency of the owners of the Oath to conclude the sale, the library could always come back and reopen negotiations. It wasn't likely another party would be willing to pay $1.5 million for it. On June 5, the library informed Schiller that it had completed its studies and he could pick up the Oath. It looked to Schiller as if the library was backing off of their initial interest in purchasing the document.

On June 27, Schiller turned to the American Antiquarian Society (AAS) located in Worcester, Massachusetts. The AAS is an independent library whose collections document the period from colonial days through the Civil War and Reconstruction. Founded in 1812, the society's collection contains over 3 million items, covering all forms of printed material that deal with the history of the United States during its first two hundred and fifty years, beginning in 1639.

Three months earlier Schiller had contacted the society, informing them that an original copy of the Oath had been discovered by one of his clients, and the AAS expressed an interest in acquiring it. Schiller had offered the Library of Congress the first opportunity to buy the document, giving them until June to act. By the end of May it became obvious that negotiations were breaking down. Schiller offered the AAS the Oath with the understanding that they would be allowed sufficient time to examine the document for authenticity and to raise money should they decide to buy it. The owner would be made known along with the test results of the Library of Congress. Other minor conditions were agreed to, and Schiller delivered the copy to the society on June 28.

After subjecting the Oath to a series of tests, the society was no better off than the Library of Congress. The results neither confirmed nor refuted the claim that the document was authentic. In other words, the tests "revealed no evidence that would contravene a mid-seventeenth century date for the broadside." Once again, the ink, paper, type, and composition appeared to be authentic. Given these results, Schiller asked the AAS if they were willing to pay $1.5 million for the Oath. The answer was no. Marcus McCorison, the director and librarian of the society, argued there were too many "ifs" associated with the document. While the society was willing to accept the Oath as a seventeenth-century document, there was no proof that it was the very first document printed by Stephen Daye on the Cambridge press. McCorison pointed out that while the general understanding was that Hofmann's copy of the Oath was the first printed in the colonies (believed printed in 1638), there was no proof that an earlier version did not precede it. The renditions of the Oath that appeared in manuscript form in the 1634 records of the Massachusetts Bay Colony, and were reproduced in the 1647 book titled *New-England's Jonas Cast Up at London,* and in the printed book of Massachusetts's *General Lawes and Libertyes* (1648) show variations in wording, punctuation, and spelling. (The version that

Hofmann created differed slightly from each of these renditions.) There was always the outside possibility to the experts that Hofmann's copy was not the first printed version. This, of course, is a hypothetical argument. Without other extant copies there is no way of knowing for sure, nor would anyone ever be able to prove which copy was the first to be printed. Aside from this, McCorison did not believe this "souvenir," as he referred to it at one point, was worth that much money. The society, McCorison wrote, was prepared to pay $250,000 for Hofmann's copy. If the Oath proved authentic, the society might negotiate a price between a "half to three-quarters of a million dollars."[18]

One of the stipulations McCorison included in his list of conditions was that his governing council would have to approve the purchase, and they were not scheduled to meet until October 15. Hofmann was faced with a double dilemma: he needed at least $1 million to get out from under his debts and stave off the wolves closing in on him, and October 15 was too long to wait for the deal to be completed. Remember, Hofmann not only owed a great deal of money, somewhere around $1 million, but he owed money to two different investors (Al Rust and the Interstate Bank) for the same amount of shares in the same document. The only way he could extricate himself from his untenable position was with money—lots of money. Hofmann decided to pull another rabbit out of his amazing document hat—a second "Oath of a Freeman." If one copy fell short of earning the money he needed, he would just produce a second copy and hopefully double his money.

Hofmann went to a former college classmate who had invested heavily in one of Hofmann's earlier transactions, and made money doing so. His name was Thomas Wilding. Hofmann told Wilding his associate Lyn Jacobs had a second copy of the Oath he was willing to sell for $500,000. Hofmann said he had already sold his own copy for $1 million, but that Jacobs needed the money and was willing to sell his copy for half the price it was worth. Wilding and his friends could make a small fortune. Wilding bit on the offer and arranged to give Hofmann $206,000, his and his fellow investors' share of the asking price.

No sooner had Wilding and his associates given Hofmann cashier's checks totaling $206,000 than they began to get disturbing news. Hofmann owed Interstate Bank $185,000 on a loan that was a month overdue. They went to see Hofmann at his house and asked what he had done with their money. Hofmann showed them a receipt for a cashier's check for $142,270 made out to Lyn Jacobs as a down payment for the alleged second copy and told them the balance of their $206,000 was in a safe-deposit box. When challenged about the overdue Interstate Bank loan, Hofmann said it wasn't his fault. Several of his clients were late in paying him. Wilding had heard enough. He and his associates wanted their money back. They did not want to go ahead with the deal. Unfortunately, Hofmann had already spent the $206,000 paying off some of his other debts. What about the cashier's check for $142,270 that Hofmann had a receipt for? Shrewdly, Hofmann had purchased a cashier's check the day before but returned it that same afternoon and was able to get the money back while keeping the receipt. He was always thinking ahead.

Faced with having to produce either the McClellin collection or the $185,000 to Steve Christensen, and the $206,000 to Wilding, Hofmann decided the only solution was to kill one or both, thereby relieving him of having to produce money he didn't have and was not about to get anytime soon. The American Antiquarian Society wasn't meeting to approve the purchase of the Oath until October 15. Hofmann couldn't wait any longer. Time had run out on his scheme. He had to act. On October 5 he purchased the ingredients for making several pipe bombs. His talent did not end with formulating seventeenth-century inks or forging rare documents. On October 14 he sat in his basement carefully constructing the deadly bombs. He had decided to target Christensen as his first victim and Gary Sheets as his second. He reasoned that by killing Christensen and Sheets people would think the murders were related to Sheets's failed investment business that he and Christensen ran together. Killing the two would create a diversion, throwing suspicion on an anonymous disgruntled investor. It was desperate, but Hofmann was at the end of his rope.

On the morning of October 15, Steve Christensen arrived at his office in the Judge Building in downtown Salt Lake City, where he found a brown paper package resting against the door to his office. Bending down, Christensen picked up the package. A blinding flash of light was quickly followed by a loud explosion that sent pieces of metal and hardened nails ripping into wallboard and flesh, leaving Christensen dead. Two hours later Kathy Sheets experienced the same blinding explosion as she picked up the package that was meant for her husband. Mark Hofmann had carried out the first two murders of his plan to gain relief from his desperate financial situation. An accidental victim of his own third bomb the following day, Hofmann has never said who was next on his list. While friends and relatives were sure of his innocence, it didn't take long for the police to suspect that Hofmann, rather than being a victim, was actually the perpetrator of the bombings.

On January 23, 1987, Hofmann, now thirty-two years old, entered a guilty plea to the murders of Steve Christensen and Kathy Sheets and two counts of fraud in exchange for dropping the death penalty. As a part of the agreement, Hofmann agreed to tell all concerning the murders and all of the events that ultimately led him to take two lives. This meant he would not only tell what he had forged, but how. It was of vital importance to law enforcement authorities as well as professionals in the field of rare documents. During a series of interviews with Salt Lake County attorneys held between February 11 and May 27, 1987, Hofmann described how he went about creating his most famous forgery, "The Oath of a Freeman."[19]

When Hofmann decided to forge "The Oath of a Freeman," he knew he was going to be tested by the best forensic labs in the country, or so he thought. If he was going to fool the experts he had to make sure he left nothing to chance. One of the obvious tests that he expected to be undertaken on his forged Oath was carbon-14 dating. It is one of the most accurate and foolproof methods of dating in the forensic scientist's arsenal of tests. The element carbon exists in nature as two stable, nonradioactive isotopes, carbon-12 and carbon-13. In addition to these two stable elements there is a third, unstable form: carbon-14. The carbon-14 interacts with atmospheric oxygen to form carbon dioxide, which is taken up by plants during the normal process of photosynthesis (carbon dioxide is also absorbed into seawater, where it can be ingested and fixed into plants and animals). This process goes on continuously until the plant dies, whereupon no more carbon-14 is ingested or fixed into living tissue. Carbon-14 decays over long periods of time. It has what scientists refer to as a "half-life" of 5,730 years, which means that the amount of carbon-14 in a sample decays to half its original value every 5,730 years. The ratio of carbon-14 to carbon-12 and carbon-13 can be measured, thereby giving a fairly accurate age for certain objects. This is true even for objects only a few hundred years old.

As an example, the flax plant takes up a certain proportion of atmospheric carbon-14 and fixes it into living cells, where it becomes part of the plant's cellular fibers. Once harvested—for making paper, for example—this uptake and fixation ceases and carbon-14 disintegration, or decay, begins. By measuring the amount of carbon-14 in the paper, its age can be estimated. The technique has been greatly refined over the years to the point where test samples are relatively small and the variation in age of a sample has become smaller, and thus more accurate. It is universally accepted as an accurate measure of dating once-living objects. The fact that none of the labs bothered to check the carbon-14 levels is surprising to say the least. Such dating should have been routine in analyzing a document as rare and valuable as the Oath.

The document, if authentic, would be over three hundred years old, and while Hofmann could find paper from the mid-seventeenth century, he could not find useable ink from that period. Hofmann knew this and was prepared to meet such a challenge. To do so, he would have to make the ink himself and make it so that it passed every forensic test, including radiocarbon dating. To do this he needed to make sure he had ink that contained the right amount of carbon-14 to yield a date in the early 1600s.

Hofmann's first step was to find paper from the early 1600s. He located several books at the Brigham Young University Library that dated from the right period. Books of a religious nature from this period were not rare. He next removed several of the blank pages at the end of the books and burned them in a special apparatus with a glass chimney. As the paper burned the glass chimney collected the carbon soot from the fire. Following a seventeenth-century recipe, Hofmann mixed the carbon soot with boiled linseed oil and tannic acid that he had extracted from a leather cover from another seventeenth-century book. To this mixture he added beeswax. The result was ink that not only was made according to a seventeenth-century formula, but contained over 300-year-old carbon and ingredients that would pass any forensic test designed to determine age, including carbon-14 analysis. Hofmann obtained the correct paper in the same manner, by removing the blank end pages from books that dated from the early seventeenth century. The paper had the same chain lines and composition as the paper used by Stephen Daye in printing the Bay Psalm Book.

Now that he had the proper paper and correct ink, Hofmann needed the correct type. This was his biggest challenge. Since no type from the period existed except for a few examples recovered from excavating a privy, Hofmann had to create his own. It was a formidable task for any forger, but Hofmann was not just any forger. He created an alphabet by doing what all the experts said he hadn't done: he cut and pasted letters from a copy of the Bay Psalm Book. By cutting out the individual letters and pasting them on a matrix, Hofmann was able to make a photocopy of his created Oath, which he then took to a printer, who made a metal plate that could be used to print the Oath. However, Hofmann still had one major obstacle to overcome. The printer's plate would consist of letters that were all of the same height when viewed in profile and that would match the corresponding letters in the hymnbook if anyone thought to carefully compare the Oath to the hymnbook. To get around this problem Hofmann took the finished plate he received from the print shop and very carefully filed down certain letters at random, thereby creating an uneven plate. In addition, he used a small drill bit to subtly change the appearance of certain letters, adding small nicks and abrasions so that even on close scrutiny an examiner would conclude that while the type was similar to that used to produce the Bay hymnal, it was not identical, thereby ruling out a cut and paste forgery. Of course, that is exactly what Hofmann had created—a cut and paste forgery.

Using the correct paper and proper ink, Hofmann was able to produce a copy of the Oath that passed the careful examination of several individuals and laboratories. The conclusion reached by several of the examiners was the same as that reached by the Preservation Laboratory of the Library of Congress, which concluded, "no evidence that would contravene a mid-seventeenth century date for the broadside" was found. Hofmann had fooled the experts.

Only after Hofmann's arrest and decision to plead guilty did several of the experts change their opinions and claim they now detected certain anomalies that suggested the Oath was a forgery. None of the tests that were performed prior to Hofmann's admission of guilt were conclusive. There were signs, however, that more careful examination would have shown the Oath was a forgery. Had the Oath been authentic and printed by Stephen Daye using type from his print shop, one of the anomalies that occurred in Hofmann's Oath could not have been there: the impingement of one character of type on the space of another character located on the line above (or below) the character in question. Because each character is set in place when the type is set in its form, no two characters can occupy the same space. An example of this impinging of one character on the space of another can be readily seen in lines 26 and 27 of Hofmann's Oath, where the "p" in "perfonn" on line 26 impinges on the space of the "G" in "God" on line 27 (see page 38). There are other examples of impingement in Hofmann's Oath. However, such impingement could occur if the characters were carefully filed down so that they would fit. Because Daye was not a good printer, having been trained as a locksmith, it was concluded that he did in fact file some of his characters to make them fit tightly in his form. It should have been a red flag, however, calling for closer scrutiny of the document.

Determining the composition of ink and paper are among the first steps in analyzing a document when trying to establish authenticity. As we have seen, most successful forgers can obtain the appropriate paper,

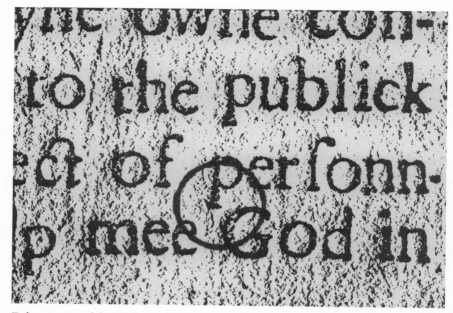

Enlargement of the Hofmann copy of "The Oath of a Freeman" showing the "p" in "perfonn" overlapping the common space with the "G" in "God." This was impossible with early typesetting procedures. (James Gilreath, ed., *The Judgment of Experts*)

and by following published formulas they can make ink that appears identical to the ink used in earlier periods. But none of the tests performed on Hofmann's Oath were able to answer the critical question of when the document was printed. That is, when was the ink actually imprinted on the paper?

There was one test that showed promise in proving the Oath was modern, and therefore a forgery. Unfortunately, it was not used until after the bombings and Hofmann's arrest had taken place. Following his arrest and prior to his plea agreement, the Salt Lake County attorney's office hired Roderick McNeil to examine the document using a relatively new and rare technique known as scanning auger microscopy (SAM). McNeil, the inventor of the method, claimed that it could determine when the ink from a document was applied to the paper. While a forger could use authentic paper, and even authentic ink, he could not alter when the ink was applied to the paper. To the best of most experts' knowledge, no forger had been able to falsify when a document was written. That is, date the relationship between ink and paper. It seemed to be the ultimate test in determining authenticity.

McNeil's technique showed enormous potential to private collectors and historical institutions at the time. Ninety percent of the material submitted to him came from private collectors and history groups, while the rest came from criminal cases.[20] Of 122 documents from the period 1760 to 1820 that McNeil examined, he determined that twenty-six were forgeries, or approximately one in five.[21] This suggests that the incidence of forgeries that passed some form of close scrutiny was high.

Scanning auger microscopy takes advantage of the fact that the migration of certain ions found in ink through a substrate (paper) is in direct proportion to time.[22] The older a document, the greater the distance traveled by the ink's ions. In essence, ink molecules attach themselves to the surface of one of the paper's fibers. Over time the individual ink molecules begin to migrate, or diffuse, along the fiber substrate. The longer the period of time, the farther the molecule migrates from its original point of application. Because these migration distances are infinitesimal, they can only be visualized by using an extremely sensitive microscope like the one developed by McNeil. By measuring the distance the ions have traveled in several test documents of known age, a standard curve can be developed from which the age of an unknown sample document can then be determined. McNeil measured the ion migration in a series of documents between 1272 and 1972, a period of seven hundred years, to establish a standard curve (see page 40). Since the ink most widely used over this period of time was iron gall ink, McNeil chose to measure the iron atom in Hofmann's Oath. The migration of the iron through the paper matrix is dependent on carboxyl groups in the fibers of the paper. Over time, the iron atoms move from one carboxyl group to another, passed along much like a bucket brigade, fanning out in all directions. When McNeil set about to test the Oath he found that the iron was in too low a concentration to accurately measure. He then chose the element lead, which was in high concentration. Because his standard curve for lead migration was based on fewer documents, the standard error was greater than that for iron.

Even with this difference in establishing standard curves for iron and lead, McNeil was still able to determine that the Oath was dated no earlier than 1940 (plus or minus fifty years). While this variation was much larger than that found in tracking iron, it clearly showed the alleged date of the Oath was within the twentieth century, a discrepancy of two hundred and fifty to three hundred years. The results of McNeil's tests placed the Oath

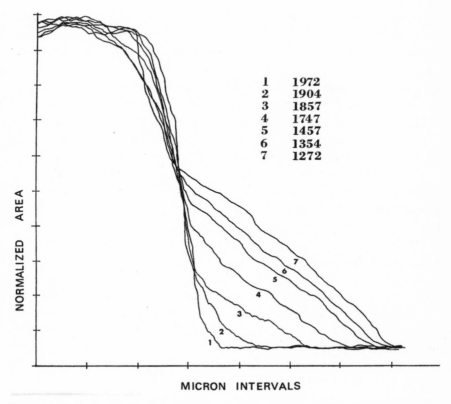

1	1972
2	1904
3	1857
4	1747
5	1457
6	1354
7	1272

MICRON INTERVALS

Roderick McNeil's standard graph showing the migration distance (micron intervals) of tested ions as a function of the document's age. The older the document the greater the migration of ions through the paper matrix. (Roderick McNeil, "Scanning Augur Microscopy Dating," in James Gilreath, ed., *The Judgment of Experts*)

well beyond the region of normal deviation, leading to the conclusion that the ink was applied in the twentieth century and not the seventeenth.

As a result of his plea bargain, Mark Hofmann was sentenced to life in prison. He is currently serving his sentence in the Utah State Prison in Draper, Utah. While a complete list of his forgeries may never be accurately known, 443 documents by Hofmann are known to have been sold, traded, or donated to various institutions. Of these, 107 (24 percent) are forged. Another 68 (15 percent) are undetermined, but suspect, which speaks to the skill of Hofmann. The remaining 268 (60 percent) are believed to be authentic.[23] But Hofmann's legacy as a forger is not based on the number of documents he was able to pass as authentic, or the historical significance of his forged documents, but rather in the number of people of expert standing he was able to fool, including many of the country's top document experts. Add to this list the hierarchy of the Mormon Church and the damage to their credibility.

There can be no argument about Mark Hofmann's title as the king of forgers. His success, however, brings to mind once again the saying, "Tell me what you want to believe and I will tell you what you will believe."

Suggested Reading

Gilreath, James, ed. *The Judgment of Experts: Essays and Documents about the Investigation of the Forging of the "Oath of a Freeman."* Worcester, Mass.: American Antiquarian Society, 1991.

Lindsey, Robert. *A Gathering of Saints: A True Story of Money, Murder, and Deceit.* New York: Simon and Schuster, 1988.

Sillitoe, Linda, and Allen Roberts. *Salamander.* Salt Lake City, Utah: Signature Books, 1988.

Tanner, Jerald. *Tracking the White Salamander: The Story of Mark Hofmann, Murder and Forged Mormon Documents.* Salt Lake City, Utah: Utah Lighthouse Ministry, 1987.

Worrall, Simon. *The Poet and the Murderer.* New York: Plume Group, 2002.

2

Pearl Harbor

Treachery in the Oval Office?

Their forces are moving across the northern Pacific and I can assure you
that their goal is the fleet in Pearl Harbor.

—Winston S. Churchill to Franklin D. Roosevelt,
November 26, 1941

This is monstrous. I think that perhaps I can find a reason to absent myself from Washington while this crisis develops. What I don't know can't
hurt me. . . .

—Franklin D. Roosevelt to Winston S. Churchill,
November 26, 1941

December 7, 1941, remains one of the definitive days of the twentieth century. Within the short span of two hours the United States was propelled
into a world war that only days before over 80 percent of its citizens had
adamantly opposed entering. The surprise attack by the Japanese on the
military bases on Oahu in the Hawaiian Islands shocked the nation to its
very core. How, people asked, could our military leaders be so utterly unprepared for such a daring undertaking? The core of America's Pacific Fleet
lay smoldering in a mass of twisted metal. The devastation was beyond
belief. The attack consisted of two aerial waves totaling 355 Japanese aircraft launched from six Japanese aircraft carriers. Eight battleships, three
cruisers, and three destroyers along with eight other ships were knocked
out of action. The four American airfields in the islands along with 288 aircraft were destroyed. Most tragic, 2,403 service men and women and sixty-

The American destroyer USS *Shaw* explodes in dry dock after being hit by a Japanese dive-bomber. She later returned to service and saw action at Guadalcanal. (National Archives)

eight civilians were killed. By contrast, Japanese losses were minimal. Only twenty-nine Japanese aircraft and five midget submarines were lost, while sixty-five servicemen were killed or wounded. It was the most lopsided battle of the war.[1]

By the time word reached the American people of the full extent of the damage inflicted by the Japanese on Pearl Harbor, accusations were being made as to just who was responsible for the disaster. How could such an attack with such a devastating effect be possible? A nation that prided itself as being among the elite nations of the world was humiliated by what many believed to be an inferior culture. Someone was to blame. Someone had to pay.

The attack transformed the American people overnight from an isolationist attitude to one of near unanimous support for entering the war, which had been raging in Europe for a little over two years, and in Asia for

The *West Virginia* and *Tennessee* under attack at Pearl Harbor. The *West Virginia* sank after receiving seven torpedo hits. (National Archives)

four. In what appeared to be a partial explanation for the success and devastation of the Japanese attack, virtually every newspaper and magazine in the country characterized it as a "sneak" attack carried out while the two nations were engaged in peaceful negotiations. While the attack was devastating, it was only successful because the United States believed the Japanese were sincere in wanting peace and thus let its guard down. Japanese envoys had been meeting with American representatives in an effort to resolve their differences peacefully, thereby avoiding war. The timing of the Japanese attack led most Americans to the conclusion that the Japanese deliberately lulled the country into lowering its guard in the belief that hostilities were not possible while negotiations were taking place.

Following on the heels of the Japanese attack were allegations that President Roosevelt was aware of the planned attack and that he knew full well that it was about to take place, and that Pearl Harbor was the target. With

Franklin Delano Roosevelt.
(Library of Congress)

the great majority of Americans opposed to entering the conflict, President Roosevelt needed a hostile act of sufficient magnitude to justify taking the country to war. The president, his critics claimed, had deliberately allowed the Pacific Fleet to be devastated, with the loss of nearly twenty-five hundred American lives, so he could plunge the country into a war that only he desperately wanted. It was an act nothing short of treason.

Pearl Harbor was chosen as the home base for the navy's Pacific Fleet, placing it dangerously close to the Japanese sphere of interest. In fact, it was deliberately chosen to put the American fleet closer to Japan and the Pacific sea lanes that would become so important in the event of a Pacific war. Its location led the majority of Americans to believe it had become an "impregnable fortress" capable of defending itself against any sort of attack from without. It was a false impression that would cost the United States dearly.

Just how unprepared the people of the United States were for such an attack is reflected in an article written at the U.S. Navy's behest in one of the nation's more popular weekly magazines. In the June 14, 1941, issue of *Collier's*, only six months before the attack on Pearl Harbor, journalist Walter

Davenport assured Americans not to worry about our military situation at Pearl Harbor. In an article titled "Impregnable Pearl Harbor," Davenport wrote with some bravado: "The Navy isn't worrying. . . . Day and night, Navy and Army planes are droning down warm skies in circles two hundred, five hundred, a thousand miles wide." The defense of Hawaii may not be one hundred percent impregnable, "but neither the Army nor the Navy believes there is any power or combination of powers existing today that can prove it in the islands (Hawaii). We have nothing to worry about," Davenport assured his readers, "to the extent that we know how many fighting ships and planes Japan has, we are kept pretty well informed where they are and what they are up to. In the continental United States there may be some doubt about our readiness to fight, but none exists in Hawaii. . . . All they wait for is the word from Washington or *an incident in the Pacific*" (emphasis added).[2]

These incredible words sum up the feeling of assurance the great majority of Americans felt. Davenport was led by the U.S. Navy to believe that "Navy and Army planes are droning down warm skies in circles two hundred, five hundred, a thousand miles wide." They were, in fact, doing nothing of the sort. Occasional reconnaissance flights did take place, but only in limited sectors well under the one thousand–mile range. Had they been flying such reconnaissance flights they would have detected the Japanese task force well in advance of its attack. The question on most people's minds was why weren't the army and navy aware of Japan's plan to attack Pearl Harbor, and why weren't both the army and navy prepared to meet the threat and blunt its effect?

The attack came with a fury unlike any experienced before that fateful day in December 1941. It was akin to the German blitzkrieg that devastated much of Europe. It was modern warfare at a new and terrifying level. But Japan's sudden attack on the United States was not as unexpected as many believed. To the contrary, the majority of Roosevelt's advisers, including the top army and navy advisers, warned that the United States's recent embargo policy would lead to war with Japan at a time when neither the army nor the navy was prepared.

Why the attack came requires some background explanation. Japan's aggressive action in China in 1937 put the United States on alert. Japan had followed an expansionist policy over the preceding decades, looking south for needed resources for its growing empire. While Nazi Germany was scoring impressive victories in Europe, Japan was giving every impression of spreading its military power throughout Asia. In 1940, Japan signed a tripartite pact with Germany and Italy that called for the partners to assist one another if any of the three parties came under attack by any power not currently engaged in war in Europe or Asia. Since the only two major powers not already engaged in war were Russia and the United States, and since Russia and Germany had signed a nonaggression treaty, that left only the United States as the obvious target of the tripartite agreement. The writing was clearly on the wall.

Roosevelt was interested in coming to Britain's aid, but an isolationist American public was adamantly opposed to going to war in Europe, or anywhere else. With an election pending in November 1940 and the public overwhelmingly against entering the war in Europe, Roosevelt was forced to walk a fine line. He remarked that he could not "bring a divided nation into war . . . if the United States publicly enters the war, it will enter united."[3] To that end, Roosevelt took calculated steps that placed the U.S. Navy in harm's way, with Germany increasing the probability of an incident that would propel the country into war, or at the very least justify Roosevelt's escalating support for Britain. Expanding the United States's territorial waters by designating sea lanes to Britain as "security zones," providing U.S. naval ships as escorts to British as well as American convoys, replacing the British garrison on Iceland with U.S. troops, authorizing navy patrol bombers and coast guard cutters to aid in the British navy's hunt for the German battleship *Bismarck* and cruiser *Prinz Eugen,* and the freezing of all German assets in the United States were only some of the provocative actions taken by Roosevelt against Germany in the spring and summer of 1941.

At the same time as the administration was provoking the Germans into an incident in the Atlantic, it also was turning the heat up diplomatically on Japan. In an effort to get Japan to stop its aggressive expansion in China, Roosevelt considered embargoing a series of goods vital to Japan's war effort. At the same time, Secretary of State Cordell Hull warned Roosevelt that cutting off vital materials to Japan would risk a war with that country, a war the United States was unprepared to fight just yet. Both the army and the navy supported Hull's conclusion, telling Roosevelt they were not prepared to fight a war in the Pacific because they did not have the necessary planes or ships, let alone men.[4] Despite these warnings, Roosevelt, in September 1940, ordered an embargo of steel, scrap iron, and petroleum products (other than crude oil and gasoline). Urged by some members of his administration to include oil in the embargo, Roosevelt responded by saying that all of his top advisers, including the military, said that doing so would surely cause the Japanese to declare war.

Not all of Roosevelt's advisers were timid about the possibility of war with Japan. Secretary of the Interior Harold Ickes told the president that if the United States waited too long to force the issue with Japan, the United States would wind up going to war with no allies left to join with them. They would have already been defeated by Japan and Germany. Roosevelt was angered by Ickes's bold position and fired back a letter telling him that foreign policy was none of his business.[5] Despite his harsh response to his secretary, Roosevelt surprised most of his staff by ordering an oil embargo against Japan just two weeks after admonishing Ickes. It appeared that Roosevelt turned his attention away from the Atlantic and Germany, and toward the Pacific and Japan.

The evidence, in hindsight, appears to support the belief that Roosevelt was looking for that one incident that would cause the belligerents to commit an overt act of war against the United States. Although Roosevelt's advisers, including the army and navy, were correct in believing an oil embargo was the one aggressive act that would compel Japan to attack, there is no evidence to suggest that the attack would occur at Pearl Harbor or that Roosevelt had any pre-knowledge of an attack. Provoking an attack and knowing precisely when and where such an attack would come are two entirely different situations.

If the United States took provocative steps that many believed would force Japan into an act of war, the question is, why was the military caught so completely off guard at Pearl Harbor? Demands for answers as to why the attack caught the military unprepared came from every sector of American life. Queries were both genuine and, at the same time, spurious. Roosevelt's political opponents in the Congress wanted to use the failure of Pearl Harbor against the president, weakening his power and eventually driving him from office. If Roosevelt knew the Japanese plans in advance and allowed the attack to take place without alerting the commanders at Pearl Harbor, he should rightfully be removed from office in disgrace. Impeachment was not out of the question. Despite the fact that the United States quickly became engaged in a two-ocean war with Japan and Germany, the president saw his party lose heavily in the 1942 off-year congressional elections. The Republican Party gained forty-seven seats in the House of Representatives, polling 50.6 percent of the popular vote. Despite this major gain by the Republican Party, however, the Democrats retained a slim three-vote majority in the House, 212 to 209.[6]

On the evening of December 7, only a few hours after the Japanese attack, Secretary of the Navy Frank Knox asked Roosevelt for permission to

Admiral Husband
E. Kimmel, commander
in chief, U.S. Pacific
Fleet, stationed at
Pearl Harbor.
(National Archives)

visit Pearl Harbor to assess the extent of the damage, and to try and find out why the military forces stationed there were caught off guard. Remember Walter Davenport's article, "Impregnable Pearl Harbor," in which he wrote, "We have nothing to worry about." How could he and others have been so wrong when the threat of a Japanese attack was uppermost in the military's mind? Secretary Knox and millions of other people wanted to know the answer to that question. The president approved Knox's request, and the secretary set out on December 9 for Hawaii. He and his party arrived in Honolulu on December 11, just four days after the attack. Rear Admiral Husband E. Kimmel, commander in chief of the Pacific Fleet at Pearl Harbor, greeted Knox. Knox set a grim tone when he told Kimmel that because of the nature of his visit "he would not be the guest of any senior officer on Oahu."[7] He did not want to be influenced by military personalities. His mission was far too important to be tainted in any way by personal relationships.

Knox interviewed several people, including the two men responsible for the army and navy units stationed at Pearl Harbor, Lieutenant General Walter C. Short and Kimmel. Both men candidly admitted to Knox

General Walter C. Short,
commander, Hawaiian
Department, U.S. Army.
(National Archives)

that they had not expected an air attack by the Japanese and were caught off guard.[8] Knox was astonished, especially since he had directed the navy to send a message to Kimmel the day before the attack warning that the Japanese representatives in Washington had received instructions to notify the Americans that negotiations were being terminated. The seriousness of this message was interpreted by most to mean that war was imminent. To Knox's astonishment, Kimmel told Knox he had received no such message. Kimmel was telling the truth. The dispatch did not arrive at his headquarters until one hour after the attack had begun.[9]

Knox gathered up the grim statistics, including casualty lists, and returned to Washington, arriving on December 14. After reporting his findings to Roosevelt, Knox held a press conference in which he notified the nation that "the armed services were to assume equal responsibility and blame for the damaged caused . . . and for the failure to be prepared for such an attack."[10] In response to questions from the press, Knox stated that the president was initiating a formal investigation. "We are all entitled to know," Knox said, "if (A) there was any error of judgment which contributed to the surprise, and (B) if there was any *dereliction of duty* prior to the attack" (emphasis added).[11] This later point sent chills through the two commands at Pearl Harbor.

Roosevelt decided to establish a special commission consisting of two army officers, two navy officers, and a civilian. On Secretary of State Cordell Hull's suggestion, Roosevelt appointed U.S. Supreme Court Associate Justice Owen J. Roberts as the civilian member, and named him head of the commission. All five members were held in high regard. The commission members were accepted by most as outstanding individuals who, in the words of the *San Francisco Chronicle,* would "learn the truth, the whole truth, and nothing but the truth," and the American people needn't fear a whitewash.[12]

But was it possible to find anyone who was truly independent and without prejudice? There was probably no one in the country who could be completely objective. That stated, someone had to undertake the onerous task of trying to find out exactly what happened and who, if anyone, was to blame for the disaster.

The committee was instructed to carry out an investigation to determine if anyone (principally Kimmel and Short) had shown poor judgment or, worse, dereliction of duty. The commission held three meetings in Washington on December 18, 19, and 20 before heading to Hawaii, where they held a series of meetings between December 22 and January 9. On January 11, upon completion of their study, the members of the commission arrived in San Francisco and then traveled by train to Washington, arriving on January 15. Still seeking information, the commission interviewed members of the military stationed in Washington. It completed its work on January 23, and Roberts handed the finished report to the president on Saturday, January 24. After being assured nothing in the report compromised national security, Roosevelt instructed his personal secretary to distribute it to the press in time for the Sunday papers of January 25.[13]

In the commission's own words, it:

> Examined 127 witnesses and received a large number of documents. All members of the Military and Naval Establishments, and civil officers and citizens, who were thought to have knowledge of facts pertinent to the inquiry, were summoned and examined under oath. All persons in the island of Oahu, who believed they had knowledge of such facts, were publicly requested to appear, and a number responded to the invitation and gave evidence.
>
> Various rumors and hearsay statements have been communi-

cated to the Commission. The Commission has sought to find and examine witnesses who might be expected to have knowledge respecting them. We believe that our findings of fact sufficiently dispose of most of them.

The evidence touches subjects which in the national interest should remain secret. We have, therefore, refrained from quotation of testimony or documentary proof. Our findings, however, have been made with the purpose fully and accurately to reflect the testimony, which as respects matters of fact, is substantially without contradiction.[14]

The conclusion of the report came down heavily on both Kimmel and Short. The report found both men guilty of "dereliction of duty," a harsh indictment that resulted in both men being disgracefully forced into retirement.

In the light of the warnings and directions to take appropriate action, transmitted to both commanders between November 27 and December 7, and the obligation under the system of cooperation then in effect for joint cooperative action on their part, it was a dereliction of duty on the part of each of them not to consult and confer with the other respecting the meaning and intent of the warnings, and the appropriate measures of defense required by the imminence of hostilities.[15]

The country had its answer to the critical question of who was to blame for the disaster. On the same day the report was released to the press, Kimmel and Short were asked to submit their resignations, and they were demoted in rank as a result of finding them guilty of dereliction.[16] The verdict of the commission placed the blame for the devastating success of the attack squarely on the shoulders of the two commanders, leaving everyone else free from blame, including Secretary of the Navy Knox, Chief of Naval Operations Admiral Harold R. Stark, Secretary of War Henry L. Stimson, Chief of Staff General George C. Marshall, Secretary of State Cordell Hull, and even President Roosevelt. Despite escaping condemnation, however, there were enough errors to taint everyone.

Rather than put the question to rest, the report only added to the firestorm that followed its release. Supporters of Kimmel and Short cried foul. Partisan opponents of Roosevelt charged treason, claiming a cover-up to protect the president, who suppressed important evidence that the administration and the top brass of the military *knew in advance of the pending attack and allowed it to take place,* impelling the United States into the war. Did not Roosevelt's advisers in both the administration and the military warn him that an oil embargo would force Japan to attack the United States?

Despite the unanswered questions surrounding the Japanese attack on Pearl Harbor, the demands of war helped to soften criticism and any further inquiry for the next two and a half years, until the election of 1944. With politics thick in the air, the claim that Roosevelt knew about the attack in advance yet allowed it to take place raised its ugly head once again. The Republicans saw a golden opportunity not only to get rid of the hated man in the White House, but also to disgrace him as a traitor to the military and the country. With blood in the water, Republican sharks began circling the president.

Kimmel's and Short's requests for retirement posed a problem for the military and for Roosevelt. Kimmel was unwilling to accept the verdict of the Roberts Commission, and requested a court-martial hearing in an effort to gain full disclosure and clear his name. He was asked, however, to wait until the war was over before pressing his case. He was told that information concerning the various Japanese messages that were intercepted and decoded prior to the attack would seriously compromise the war effort if it became known. However, an election year all but guaranteed an inquiry would go forward.

In anticipation of a hearing, Secretary of the Navy Knox appointed Admiral Thomas C. Hart to head up a board of inquiry and collect testimony that could ultimately be used during a court-martial proceeding. In July 1944, Senator Homer Ferguson (R-Mich.), acting on Kimmel's behalf, introduced legislation establishing an Army and Navy Court of Inquiry into the Pearl Harbor question. Apparently still not satisfied that all the questions concerning the attack had been asked and answered, the new secretary of the navy, James V. Forrestal,[17] asked Vice Admiral H. Kent Hewitt to head up a supplemental inquiry. This became the fifth official inquiry into the Pearl Harbor disaster. By now there should be no questions left unanswered.

It was during the Hewitt inquiry that the question of the code breaking, known as "Magic," was introduced, raising serious questions as to what was known about the Japanese war plans immediately prior to Pearl Harbor and who knew about it. The Japanese, like the Germans with their Enigma code, operated an extremely complicated code system named "Purple" by the U.S. cryptologists. The so-called "unbreakable" code was broken by the Signal Intelligence Service's William Friedman in August

1940. From then forward the Signal Intelligence Service had been reading the Japanese diplomatic messages. According to historian Gordon Prange, the Americans knew more about Japan's diplomatic positions than did its own ambassador to Washington, Kichisaburo Nomura.[18] With the subject of Magic opened up by the Hewitt inquiry, Forrestal felt the subject required further investigation. Rather than have the Hewitt inquiry reopen its hearings, he asked Major Henry C. Clausen of the U.S. Army to hold a new set of investigations, giving rise to the sixth committee to hold formal hearings. Clausen's investigation was quickly followed by an investigation into the handling of top-secret documents by the army's Colonel Carter W. Clarke. By August 1945, the hearings, inquiries, and investigations were finally over. They lasted as long as the war.

There is one thing that stood out about all of the investigations: all were conducted by the military and, therefore, subject to charges of bias. After all, the military could not reasonably be expected to indict its own. This coupled with the fact that the Roberts Commission was appointed by (and suspected of being under the thumb of) the president raised concerns among the Republican members of the Congress as to the commission's veracity. The executive branch, after all, was theoretically in charge of all seven investigations. To ensure "balance," Congress decided to create an eighth committee and hold its own investigation. Such a committee would not be beholden to the military or the president, or so the argument went. By the time the joint committee began holding hearings Roosevelt was dead and a new president, Harry S. Truman, was in charge. Still, the legacy of Roosevelt permeated every aspect of the government, and the Republican partisans in Congress were not ready to let the former president rest in peace in his grave. Should the joint committee show that the president and the top military in Washington knew of the Japanese attack ahead of time and deliberately failed to act, an outraged American people would turn to the Republican Party for leadership for the next fifty years.[19] The Republican position in the Congress was best summarized by the anti-administration *Chicago Tribune* in an editorial published on Monday, September 3, 1945: "Never before in our history did a president maneuver this country into a war for which it was unprepared, and then, thru insouciant stupidity or worse, permit the enemy to execute a surprise attack costing the lives of 3,000 Americans, *an attack which he and his cabinet members had substantial forewarning 24 hours before*" (emphasis added).[20] The belief that Roosevelt knew not only when but where the attack was coming would not die easily.

All of the once–top secret documents sent by the Japanese in the days prior to the attack on Pearl Harbor are available on a CD-ROM provided by the National Security Agency's Center for Cryptologic History. In their discussion of the deciphered messages, the authors conclude that "there simply was not one shred of actionable intelligence in any of the messages or transmissions that pointed to the attack on Pearl Harbor" (Robert J. Hanyok and David P. Mowry, *West Wind Clear: Cryptology and the West Winds Message Controversy—A Documentary History* [Washington, D.C.: Center for Cryptologic History, National Security Agency, 2008], 95). (Author's collection)

The effort by congressional Republicans shifted the emphasis of the inquiries from clearing Kimmel and Short of any blame to attacking a dead Roosevelt and thoroughly discrediting him and his administration. Surprisingly, the Democrats did not oppose a congressional investigation; they welcomed it. Senate majority leader Alben W. Barkley, Democrat of Kentucky, called for a joint committee inquiry, naively believing it would put the question to bed once and for all.

The joint committee held its first hearing on November 15, 1945. At the very beginning of the meeting the committee's chief legal adviser, William D. Mitchell, introduced an exhibit titled "Intercepted Diplomatic Messages Sent by the Japanese Government Between July 1 and December 8, 1941."[21] With this startling revelation it finally became known that the United States had broken the Japanese diplomatic code and was reading the communications between Tokyo and its diplomats during the critical period leading up to Pearl Harbor. It was an opportunity for those who were determined to show that Roosevelt and others in his administration had known beforehand that the Japanese were going to strike, and that Pearl Harbor was the target. The Republicans were sure they would find a smoking gun—or at least a cryptic message—to prove that Roosevelt knew about the planned attack and did nothing.

The hearing, however, ran into trouble from the very beginning. In addition to trying to determine the cause of the Pearl Harbor disaster, and thereby fix blame, the minority members of the committee, hoping to bring about a Republican victory in the upcoming elections, spent considerable time trying to show that Roosevelt knew of the attack in advance. Throughout the entire effort by the Republicans to tie the disaster to Roosevelt not a single document could be found indicating the president or high-ranking members of his administration had any prior knowledge of the Japanese attack.

It is not the purpose of this chapter to review all of the testimony and findings of the various inquiries, including the congressional inquiry of 1946, nor to affix blame for the disaster that befell Pearl Harbor. The Roberts Committee, the first of the investigative committees, came to the conclusion that the two commanders, Kimmel and Short, were responsible for the disaster. While subsequent hearings, especially the navy and army hearings, refuted the charge of dereliction, Kimmel and Short were found to have failed to show due diligence in defending America's most important military base. While efforts were made by various people throughout each of the eight hearings to place blame on the administration and President Roosevelt in particular, those efforts failed. Even the minority report of the joint congressional hearing failed to produce any documentation that pointed a damaging finger in Roosevelt's direction. This is not to say, however, that Roosevelt and members of his war cabinet were unaware of a Japanese plan to attack the United States.

Conditions were such in the Pacific that most advisers firmly believed war inevitable. The question that puzzled everyone was when and where the Japanese would strike. It was in America's interest to somehow control that first strike in light of the overwhelmingly isolationist views of the American people. If Japan could be maneuvered into an attack, the administration would have its necessary incident to enter the war. Secretary of War Henry Stimson wrote in his diary following a White House meeting on Japan, "The question was how we should maneuver them [the Japanese] into the position of firing the first shot without allowing too much danger to ourselves."[22] On the surface, this sounds like an indictment of the administration. There is no question that the administration had deliberately taken steps that were highly provocative in the Atlantic, where the United States increasingly invited Germany to blunder into attacking American ships escorting convoys to Great Britain. Three such incidents did occur, but for whatever reason the administration did not use the attacks to declare war on Germany, perhaps hoping that Germany would declare war on the United States first.

The failure of any of the eight official investigations into Pearl Harbor to produce concrete evidence indicting Roosevelt has not deterred critics from accusing Roosevelt of treachery in knowingly allowing the attack on Pearl Harbor to take place. In his book *The Pearl Harbor Myth,* author George Victor suggestively invites his readers to believe that Roosevelt deliberately stationed the Pacific Fleet at Pearl Harbor to lure the Japanese into an attack, thereby satisfying Roosevelt's desire for war. Victor writes: "Whether intentionally or not, Roosevelt exposed the fleet to a Japanese attack by stationing it in Hawaii. Then he intentionally used naval units as lures by ordering them on various expeditions in the Pacific. Withholding key information from Kimmel and Short increased the fleet's exposure greatly and it was most glaringly increased by not sending a warning on December 6, 1941."[23] Surely Roosevelt had a right to station the American fleet anywhere he wished without being accused of provoking an attack. Victor suggests that Roosevelt is somehow at fault for allowing U.S. naval ships to sail in international waters. His criticism is reminiscent of those pro-Confederates who blamed Lincoln for the shelling of Fort Sumter. The mere act of supplying a legitimate Federal facility somehow was considered an act of war. Exposing the fleet, however, is not the same as deliberately withholding knowledge of an impending attack, as some critics claim Roosevelt did.

In their book, *Deceit at Pearl Harbor,* Kenneth Landis and Rex Gunn take the final step and accuse Roosevelt of deliberate treachery. These authors have produced the smoking gun that shows Roosevelt knew of the pending attack two weeks before it happened and did nothing. Eight investigative hearings failed to uncover any documentation in support of such an accusation. Landis and Gunn, however, came up with evidence in the form of a transcript of a telephone conversation between Roosevelt and British prime minister Winston Churchill. In the authors' words: "The historical role played by Roosevelt as the guilty party who engineered the 'Causus Belli,' has been thoroughly uncovered by the release of the telephone warning by Churchill on November 26, 1941. This warning proves that FDR was fully aware of the impending attack and is perhaps *the most damning piece of evidence to be revealed in this greatest of American military tragedies*" (emphasis added).[24] The document is dated November 26, 1941, eleven days prior to the actual attack. It is important to understand what the document is and how it came into the hands of a few historians after the war ended, when Pearl Harbor was no longer a thorn in the side of the American public.

The consensus of most historians is that no wartime leaders shared a closer friendship and mutual trust than Roosevelt and Churchill. Beginning one week after the start of the war on September 3, 1939, until one day before Roosevelt's death on April 12, 1945, the two men exchanged more than seventeen hundred letters, telegrams, and personal messages. This extraordinary correspondence averaged nearly one message a day for five and a half years.[25] All the more amazing is the tone of openness and the sharing of information one finds in the content of these messages. The friendship endured the many petty political trials that constantly pulled at the two leaders from their own generals and political adversaries.

Their first face-to-face meeting occurred August 9–12, 1941, at Argentia Bay in Newfoundland, where the two leaders drafted the Atlantic Charter, establishing a blueprint for the postwar world as well as for the alliance between the two allies. This first meeting was followed by several more over the next four years where the two men hammered out their war strategy as well as their strategy for a postwar Europe.

In the fall of 1941 a radiotelephone link was established between the White House and Churchill's war bunker in London. This link enabled the two leaders to talk to one another directly by telephone. Although Churchill preferred the written word to the telephone, he used the device on several occasions to talk to his ally in Washington. The Germans, meanwhile, established a radiotelephone listening station on the coast of Holland and

President Franklin D. Roosevelt and Prime Minister Winston S. Churchill during their meeting in Casablanca, January 1943. (National Archives)

were able to successfully tap into the conversations. These conversations were recorded and kept in both English and German. Translated copies were supplied to Hitler and certain of his generals on a regular basis. The monitoring of this important line fell under Hitler's chief of the Gestapo, Heinrich Müller.[26]

Shortly after assuming power as chancellor in 1933, Hitler ordered the formation of a special police force to serve the Nazi Party. The new organization was called the Geheime Staatspolizei (Secret State Police), or "Gestapo" for short. It was over this organization of secret police that Heinrich Müller, a former police detective in the German state of Bavaria, was given full control. Müller was an important part of the Nazi apparatus. He participated in the infamous Wannsee Conference held in January 1942, dur-

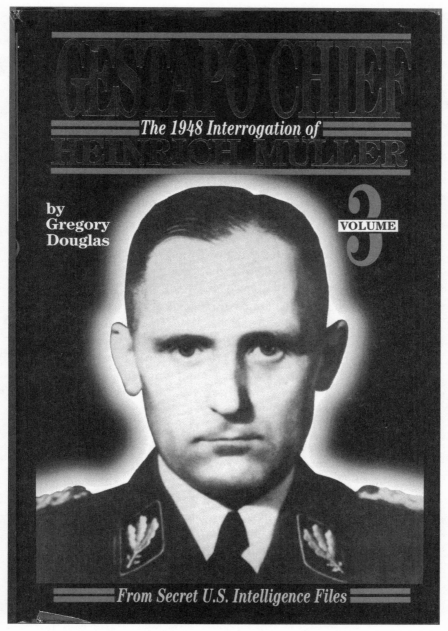

GESTAPO CHIEF

The 1948 Interrogation of

HEINRICH MÜLLER

by
Gregory
Douglas

VOLUME
3

From Secret U.S. Intelligence Files

Heinrich Müller, head of the Nazi Gestapo. (Author's collection)

ing which the "Final Solution" of what to do with the Jews of Europe was decided. As head of the Gestapo, Müller was the immediate superior of Adolf Eichmann, who was chief of the Jewish office of the Gestapo during the war.[27]

Müller's Gestapo fell within the Third Reich's security apparatus, headed by Heinrich Himmler, who is often confused as being the head of the Gestapo. Himmler was Müller's boss, but Müller was the man who ran the Gestapo. He was particularly adept at spy investigations against all enemies of Hitler and the Nazi Party, especially the communists. His knowledge of the communist espionage network may well have saved his life at the end of the war.

Müller was last seen alive on April 28, when he visited Hitler in his bunker. Müller apparently fled the bunker that day and disappeared into the fog surrounding the final days of the war in Europe. While many historians believe Müller died attempting to escape, others believe he was captured by the Russians and taken to that country, where he died. Others believe he made his way to Switzerland, where he was taken into custody by Allen Dulles, head of the Office of Strategic Services (OSS) in Switzerland.[28] The claim that Müller died in his escape and was buried in a Berlin cemetery proved unfounded when the grave marked with Müller's name and dates of birth (1900) and death (1945) was opened in 1963 under orders from the West German government and found to be empty.

One prominent World War II historian, John Lukacs, believes Müller was captured and secretly brought to the United States in 1948 by Allen Dulles, who later became head of the CIA.[29] Dulles's interest in Müller, according to Lukacs, stemmed from Müller's extensive knowledge of the Soviets' spy apparatus, which the Germans dealt with quite successfully. Müller's whereabouts and handling by the CIA were kept secret while he was housed in the United States. During his house arrest the CIA interrogated him extensively. Somehow these interrogations, along with certain documents including the November 26, 1941, telephone conversation between Roosevelt and Churchill, made their way into the hands of a historian by the name of Gregory Douglas (believed to be an alias). According to Lukacs, Douglas was a "pseudonym of an American of German origin who knew the name of at least one of Müller's interrogators and got hold of the interrogations and documents."[30] Douglas eventually published the material in a three-volume set, which included the history-revising transcript of the revealing telephone conversation of November 26 between Churchill and Roosevelt.[31]

During his questioning, Müller told his interrogator that the SS had tapped into the radiotelephone transmissions between Roosevelt and Churchill. What is more, Müller claimed to have transcripts of the telephone conversations "put away," offering to show them to his interrogator.[32] He apparently smuggled a part of his archive out of Germany, believing the documents would serve as an insurance policy guaranteeing him a safe haven with the Americans. According to Lukacs he was right.

The conversation that allegedly took place on November 26, 1941, has Churchill notifying Roosevelt that British intelligence has determined that Japan has a large task force heading for Pearl Harbor and plans a surprise air strike against the U.S. naval base. Müller's astonished interrogator warns him to "keep the matter very quiet. It would not go over too well in Washington. The subject is absolutely forbidden and we don't want to upset General [George C.] Marshall. The President [Truman] holds him in very high esteem and the General would be very upset if any of this came out."[33]

The transcript became an important part of the book by Landis and Gunn, supporting their claim of Roosevelt's treachery. Part of the conversation is reproduced here as it appears in Douglas's third volume on Heinrich Müller, and in Landis and Gunn's *Deceit at Pearl Harbor*. Churchill places the telephone call to Roosevelt at 3:15 A.M., Eastern War Time, on Wednesday, November 26, 1941:

[WSC = Winston Spencer Churchill,
FDR = Franklin Delano Roosevelt][34]

WSC: I am frightfully sorry to disturb you at this hour Franklin, but matters of a most vital import have transpired and I felt that I must convey them to you immediately.

FDR: That's perfectly all right, Winston. I'm sure you wouldn't trouble me at this hour for trivial concerns.

WSC: Let me preface my information with an explanation addressing the reason I have not alluded to these facts earlier. In the first place, until today, the information was not firm. On matters of such gravity, I do not like to indulge in idle chatter. Now, I have in my hands, reports from our agents in Japan as well as the most specific intelligence in the form of the highest level Japanese naval coded messages (conversation broken) for some time now.

FDR: I felt this is what you are about. How serious is it?

WSC: It could not be worse. A powerful Japanese task force comprising (composed of) six of their carriers, two battleships, and a number of other units to include (including) tankers and cruisers, has sailed yesterday from a secret base in the northern Japanese islands.[35]

FDR: We both knew this was coming. There are also reports in my hands about a force of some size making up in China and obviously intended to go (move) south.[36]

WSC: Yes, we have all of that (Interruption) . . . are far more advanced than you in our reading of the Jap naval operations codes, but even without that, their moves are evident. And they will indeed move South, but the force I spoke of is not headed South, Franklin, it is headed East.

FDR: Surely you must be . . . will you repeat that please?

WSC: I said to the East. This force is sailing to the East . . . towards you.

FDR: Perhaps they set an easterly course to fool any observers and then plan to swing South to support the landings in the southern areas. I have . . .

WSC: No, at this moment, their forces are moving across the northern Pacific and I can assure you that their goal is the (conversation broken) fleet in Hawaii. At Pearl Harbor.

FDR: This is monstrous. Can you tell me . . . indicate . . . the nature of your intelligence? (conversation broken) reliable? Without compromising your sources . . .

WSC: Yes, I will have to be careful. Our agents in Japan have been reporting on the gradual (conversation broken) units. And these have disappeared from Japanese home waters. We also have highly reliable sources in the Japanese foreign service and even the military . . .

FDR: How reliable?

WSC: One of the sources is the individual who supplied us the material on the diplomatic codes that (conversation broken) and a Naval officer whom our service has compromised. You must trust me, Franklin and I cannot be more specific.

FDR: I accept this.

WSC: We cannot compromise our codebreaking. You understand this. Only myself and a few (conversation broken) not even [Roosevelt aide Harry] Hopkins. It will go straight to Moscow and I am not sure we want that.

FDR: I am still attempting to . . . the obvious implication is that the Japs are going to do a Port Arthur on us at Pearl Harbor. Do you concur?

WSC: I do indeed. Unless they add an attack on the Panama Canal to this vile business. I can hardly envision the canal as a primary goal, especially with your fleet lying athwart their lines of communications with Japan. No, if they do strike the canal, they will have to first neutralize (destroy) your fleet (conversation broken).

FDR: The worst form of treachery. We can prepare our defenses on the islands and give them a warm welcome when they come. It would certainly put some iron up Congress's ass.[37]

Toward the end of the conversation Churchill tells Roosevelt his own advisers "counseled against informing" Roosevelt, allowing the strike to go forward unopposed. Churchill had been urging Roosevelt unsuccessfully to enter the war for several months. Roosevelt expresses his concern in case his own people intercept the Japanese plans. He tells Churchill, "I think that perhaps I can find a reason to absent myself from Washington while this crisis develops. What I don't know can't hurt me and I too can misunderstand messages, especially at a distance."[38]

Here is the long-sought documentary evidence Roosevelt's enemies so desperately looked for without success. Eight investigative hearings had taken place without turning up a single piece of evidence pointing to Roosevelt's treachery. The smoking gun had finally been found. Eleven days prior to the attack on December 7, 1941, Roosevelt received confirmation of the planned attack from the British prime minister. How could this critical piece of evidence elude so many historians for so long? One person it did not elude was Kenneth Landis, a naval officer who served on Rear Admiral Husband E. Kimmel's staff at the time of the Japanese attack on Pearl Harbor. Sixty years later Landis was still smarting from the attack on his commanding officer. In 2001, Landis coauthored a book with Rex Gunn, who was serving with the 7th Army Air Corps stationed at Hickam Field at the time of the attack. The book, *Deceit at Pearl Harbor,* indicts Roosevelt for treachery in knowingly allowing the attack on Pearl Harbor to take place, based almost entirely on the radiotelephone conversation between Churchill and Roosevelt on November 26, 1941. Secondarily, Landis and Gunn use their book to exonerate Kimmel and Short as "scapegoats" set up by Roosevelt to take the fall for the disaster at Pearl Harbor. The book is the first to use the evidence of the phone call to indict Roosevelt and Churchill. If true, there can be no question of Roosevelt's guilt, or of Churchill's complicity in covering up the pending attack. As the authors point out, "even Hitler knew" the attack was coming.[39]

The transcript, however, appears to be a fabrication. While a radio-telephone link did exist between Roosevelt and Churchill, and several conversations were recorded and transcribed (recorded in English and transcribed into German), there is sound evidence that certain fabrications do exist among some of these transcripts. The alleged conversation of November 26, 1941, has been judged by the eminent American historian John Lukacs to be a fabrication, believed to be manufactured by Gestapo chief Heinrich Müller or members of his staff for the purpose of gaining favor with his American captors.[40]

Lukacs's exposure of this important transcription as a fabrication has largely gone unnoticed. It appeared in the history magazine *American Heritage* in 2002 but has not made its way into subsequent writings on the subject of Pearl Harbor to date. While the transcript's publication in volume 3 of *Gestapo Chief* and in *Deceit at Pearl Harbor* may have received little notice, it is a dangerous document in one of the more dramatic and important events in American history and should be exposed as a serious hoax on history.

Lukacs has been one of the leading critics of British historian David Irving, who is described by his peers as having strong neo-Nazi sympathies. Lukacs's principal criticism of Irving is with his selective use of personal reminiscences of those who knew Hitler to cast him in a favorable light. Neo-Nazis have attempted to elevate Hitler by tearing down his adversaries, such as Roosevelt and Churchill. Lukacs believes the fabricated transcript is yet another effort to defame the two great war leaders.

A pro-Churchill historian, Lukacs believes that Churchill's greatest hour came in 1940 when he refused any accommodation with Hitler though urged to do so by members of his own war cabinet, thus laying "the groundwork for the ultimate Allied victory."[41] Lukacs's interest in the interrogation of Müller and the telephone transcripts drew his suspicion that all was not right with some of the material. As is almost always the case with fabricated documents, it is the internal inconsistencies that betray them as fabrications. In one example cited by Lukacs, Roosevelt and Churchill discuss at length whether to have Italian dictator Benito Mussolini assassinated. Yet, in the original document located in the German archives there is no mention of Mussolini. In addition, during the same week as the phone conversation Roosevelt and Churchill exchanged nineteen written messages without once mentioning Mussolini.[42] Lukacs also pointed out that Churchill never called Roosevelt "Franklin," something he did repeatedly during the alleged telephone call.[43]

His suspicions aroused, Lukacs searched the German archives for the original transcription or a summary of the November 26, 1941, telephone conversation without success. His real break came when he located one of the women that served British intelligence as a "censor" on the transatlantic phone calls. The British were sensitive to the possibility that the Germans might be monitoring the phone calls between Churchill and Roosevelt and had specially trained women listen in to the conversations and interrupt if either party began mentioning anything that was considered top secret. This woman told Lukacs that the language of the two men in the overall transcript "was far too lurid, too coarse of language, and grammatically incorrect," and, most importantly, "subjects were discussed that would never have been authorized or allowed on the transatlantic radiotelephone link." The woman also confirmed Lukacs's claim that the two men never referred to each other by their first names, Franklin or Winston.[44]

One further item should be mentioned: on the same day that the telephone conversation allegedly took place in which Churchill warned Roosevelt of the pending attack on Pearl Harbor, Churchill wrote a letter to Roosevelt in response to a message from Roosevelt dated November 24, 1941, in which Roosevelt told Churchill that the Japanese government's response to an earlier message "contains features not in harmony with the fundamental principles which underlie the proposed general settlement and to which each government has declared that it is committed."[45] There is no mention of Pearl Harbor or the British intercept of any Japanese message regarding an attack on Pearl Harbor. "In sum," Lukacs writes, "the entire transcript of the November 26, 1941, phone conversation is completely false."[46]

Revising history is the natural duty of historians. There is nothing wrong with revisionism per se if the revision results in bringing us closer to the truth. But revising history for the sake of ideology is quite another thing. Franklin Delano Roosevelt has become the target of a small group of revisionist writers intent on destroying the public's high regard for his presidency. Unable to attack his social programs with any success, these revisionist writers have accused him of "criminal negligence," and even "treasonable activity," resulting from the Japanese attack on Pearl Harbor.[47] These revisionist historians became advocates when they chose to follow the facts where they wanted them to lead them rather than wherever they may have led them. The case of the transatlantic telephone call between Churchill and Roosevelt is an example of what happens when ideology overcomes objectivity. It is an excellent example of seeking evidence to fit one's preconceived ideas in furtherance of ideology.

Lukacs sees a sinister motive behind forgeries like the radiotelephone transcript between Churchill and Roosevelt. He points out that certain historians have attempted to rehabilitate Adolf Hitler while "blackening" the images of Churchill and Roosevelt. The 1983 discovery of the Hitler "diaries" is but one example (see chapter 3). Lukacs sees the discovery of the transcript of the telephone conversation as another example of elevating Hitler by tearing down Roosevelt and Churchill. Finding the truth is a very difficult task. As Lukacs so eloquently points out, "the purpose of the historian is not the establishment of perfect truth but the pursuit of truth through the reduction of ignorance."[48]

Suggested Reading

Landis, Lieutenant Commander Kenneth, USNR (ret.), and Staff Sergeant Rex Gunn, USAR (ret.). *Deceit at Pearl Harbor*. N.p.: 1st Books Library, 2001.

Lukacs, John. "The Churchill-Roosevelt Forgeries." *American Heritage,* November–December 2002, 65–67.

Prange, Gordon W. *At Dawn We Slept: The Untold Story of Pearl Harbor*. New York: McGraw-Hill, 1981.

Victor, George. *The Pearl Harbor Myth: Rethinking the Unthinkable*. Washington, D.C.: Potomac Books, 2007.

3

Hah Hitler!

The Hitler Diaries

When I entered the back room in the Swiss bank, and turned the pages of those volumes, my doubts gradually dissolved. I am now satisfied that the documents are authentic.

—Sir Hugh Trevor-Roper, British historian
and Hitler biographer

The atmosphere in the bunker had grown increasingly tense every day since the celebration of the führer's birthday on April 20. The regular afternoon conferences in the narrow hallway outside his suite reflected the unrealistic nature of the situation. The führer's advisers became increasingly frightened of reporting the collapsing situation that was rapidly taking place all along the Russian front. As the Red Army moved closer toward Berlin, Hitler deployed his phantom armies that even if they were at full strength would be no match for the Russian assault. It was time to begin taking steps to flee the bunker and Berlin for the Alpine Redoubt in the Bavarian Alps. Only from here would a last stand be possible. Virtually all of Hitler's generals were urging him to transfer his headquarters before it became too late. When the subject was broached Hitler did not refuse; he merely put off further consideration until later, leaving his staff with some hope of getting out of Berlin before the Russian ring closed, sealing them inside with no hope of escape. The thought of capture by the Russians was unthinkable.

On April 23, Albert Speer, Reich minister for armaments and war production, made one last visit to the bunker to see his old friend. Opposed to Hitler's scorched earth policy, Speer felt he owed it to Hitler to pay his respects to the man who gave him so much. Hitler loved Speer. He held him in esteem above all his other advisers. He felt they shared a kindred love of art and architecture that none of the others could understand. Only Speer shared this precious bond with him. Now Speer was going against Hitler's orders to reduce the countryside to a blackened desert. Speer had made arrangements to save as much of the infrastructure as possible following defeat. There was still a nation of people to feed and care for. The devastated country would need rebuilding. Hitler knew of Speer's "treason," and yet he forgave him, unlike so many others he ordered shot. When Speer left on the morning of the 24th, there were no more decisions to be made. The only thing left was to secure as many of Hitler's important papers as possible for future posterity. It was important that some record remain explaining the man and his dream. If there were to be a future Reich it would need his legacy to build upon. His personal papers would form that legacy.

A short distance from the opening of the emergency exit into the Reich' s Chancellery garden a tall, handsome man dressed in a green wool uniform with several ribbons on his breast stood near a large metal drum, watching the flames dancing around the opening of the makeshift incinerator. Two Wehrmacht privates struggled to lift a heavy box containing loose papers. The officer stared into the swirling flames, his attention drawn to the changing colors of the fire as it slowly consumed the mass of material the two men were feeding into the opening at the top of the drum. They had been ordered to systematically clean out all of the papers not chosen to make the trip and burn them. The officer watched intently, making sure none of the papers escaped the fire and that every last scrap was surrendered to the flames. After the last papers from the crate were gathered up by one of the men and tossed into the funereal pyre, the officer followed the soldiers with his eyes as they walked back toward the opening in the concrete tower.

A short distance from the fire a beehive of activity was taking place around another set of papers. Bodyguards were hurriedly loading Hitler's personal papers aboard lorries to take them to an airfield near Berlin. From there they would be flown to the safety of the redoubt, where the final stand would take place. Two lower echelon soldiers that normally worked as personal valets struggled with several large, metal trunks that they loaded onto one of the lorries from the Chancellery garage. The trunks contained the personal property of Adolf Hitler and Eva Braun, Hitler's mistress, soon to be his wife. The material was destined for Schoenwalde, located ten miles north of Berlin, where several airplanes sat waiting on the runway. There, the trunks containing Hitler's papers were loaded into a Junkers 352 transport plane while another plane quickly filled up with personnel fleeing Berlin for Obersalzburg. They would accompany the sacred cargo and see to its safekeeping.

It was now only a matter of hours, thirty or forty at most, before Russian soldiers would begin breaking through the thinning German defensive lines and overrun the Chancellery and its grounds that shielded the führerbunker. The inevitable was close at hand.

While several individuals planned their escape, others planned their suicide. To their dismay, the führer finally announced his decision that he would remain in Berlin. He also made it clear that he would never be taken alive by the Bolshevik horde. He left specific instructions to his most trusted lieutenants to make sure his body and that of his new wife, Eva Braun, were cremated in the Chancellery garden so that no desecration of their corpses would occur. He still had abhorrent visions of Italian dictator Benito Mussolini and his mistress, Clara Petacci, hanging upside down from a light pole in the town square of Milan while thousands of partisans danced around the swinging corpses, spitting on them and beating them with sticks and anything else they could find that served as a club. Partisans in the small village of Mezzegra had executed Mussolini and Petacci, then taken their bodies to Milan, where they were strung on meat hooks in the center of the city. Hitler would not allow such an end to come to him. He would die a Wagnerian death consumed in flames just as his Germany was now being consumed in flames.

His papers, however, would survive to tell the story of the building of the Third Reich and provide a blueprint for reestablishing the next. Although the current Reich had failed, it was not Hitler's fault. He had not failed; those around him had failed. The German people had failed. All of the strong, loyal Germans were dead, leaving only the weak and unfaithful alive. These German people were not worthy of glory or survival. Only after complete destruction could a new Germany rise from the ashes of the betrayed Reich to finally conquer the world.

Despite his decision to remain in Berlin and die in the closing moments of the war he had created, Hitler ordered those still remaining with him to attempt a breakout. Operation Seraglio would see some eighty people and several trunks of important papers evacuated to the führer's Alpine Redoubt near the mountain village of Berchtesgaden, Hitler's favorite

Adolf Hitler at the
height of his power.
(National Archives)

retreat. Here, in the mountains of southern Germany, the Nazis would establish a new command center and carry on the fight to the bitter end.
Hans Bauer, Hitler's personal pilot, was placed in charge of providing the
fleet of ten airplanes and crews necessary for the escape. Major Friedrich
Gundlfinger, a battle-hardened veteran of the Eastern Front, would pilot
the plane carrying Hitler's personal archive. It was essential that all of the
planes take off and fly the 350 miles south under cover of darkness. The
Allies controlled the air, and if the breakout were to be successful it had to
take place at night.

Gundlfinger was charged with taking sixteen important Nazis in addition to Hitler's private papers. But something had gone wrong, causing a
delay. Gundlfinger was forced to wait until a few minutes before 5 A.M. before the last of the sixteen passengers was safely aboard. Somewhere south
of Berlin, Gundlfinger was attacked by allied fighter planes. Within minutes the Junkers 352 was on fire and falling toward the earth. It crashed
near the small German village of Boernersdorf, near the Czech border in

A German Junkers 352 like one this was used to carry Hitler's personal papers, including his alleged diaries. The plane crashed near the German village of Boern-ersdorf, killing all aboard and burning Hitler's papers. The diaries were claimed to have been rescued by villagers. (Luftwaffenphotos)

western Germany. Its destination was Ainring, the closest airfield to the Nazi retreat at Berchtesgaden. When Hitler was told of the plane's fate he was heard to howl like a wounded animal. According to Bauer, Hitler moaned, "I had sent extremely important documents and papers with him [Gundlfinger] that were to explain my actions to posterity. It is a catastrophe!"[1] It would be eight years before the story of the plane's crash and the recovery of twelve bodies would become known.[2] It would be another thirty years before the fate of the "extremely important documents and papers" would come to light as the most sensational discovery of the postwar era. The contents of the crashed plane were ideal for the conspiracy that would surface years later.

The story behind the "discovery" of the Hitler diaries actually begins on April 30, 1945, the day Hitler is reported to have committed suicide. So powerful was the image of this world nemesis that stories of his survival flooded newspapers and magazines around the globe. First-person interviews told of his flight from the bunker to France, where he was working in a casino; to a monastery in the Swiss Alps, where he became a shepherd; to a cave in Italy, where he lived as a hermit; casting nets as a fisherman in the Baltic Sea or off the coast of Ireland. He was in Albania, Spain, Argentina, France, and Italy, even England, where the British were hiding him. So powerful were these preposterous stories of his outwitting the Allies that the British decided to launch an official investigation into Hitler's final days. Code named Operation Nursery, the task was assigned to a British intelligence officer named Hugh Trevor-Roper, a young Oxford research student in history. The assignment launched Trevor-Roper on a career in history that would lead to his recognition as a World War II historian with impeccable credentials. In 1979 he was awarded a peerage and chose the title "Baron Dacre of Glanton."[3]

According to Trevor-Roper, history is an art, in which the most important attribute of any successful historian is his imagination.[4] The young historian undertook his new assignment with vigor, leaving no stone unturned in his quest for the truth behind Hitler's last days as führer. Approaching his assignment like a research project in an academic institution, Trevor-Roper first compiled a list of all the known characters who were in the bunker with Hitler during his final days, including those who were there when the announced death took place. The list included forty-two individuals in all.[5] He then set about trying to locate each of the individuals, and those he found he interviewed. At the end of his search he was able to reconstruct the events that took place during the final days and hours inside the führerbunker.

In the afternoon of April 29, Hitler had one of his cyanide capsules from his own personal stock tested on his favorite Alsatian dog, Blondi. The dog died instantly, satisfying Hitler that cyanide was both effective and quick. Later that evening he asked to say good-bye to the women working in the bunker. Having personally shaken hands with each of the ladies, Hitler retired to his private quarters. He appeared subdued and spoke only when necessary. The following morning, April 30, he lunched with two of his secretaries and his cook. Eva Braun remained in her room alone. After lunch, Hitler held his final farewell ceremony in the outer corridor to his suite. Eva Braun joined him this time. Martin Bormann, Wilhelm Burgdorf, Joseph Goebbels, Otto Guensche, Walter Hewell, Peter Hoegl, Hans Krebs, Heinz Linge, Werner Naumann, Johann Rattenhuber, and Erich Voss were present, along with Hitler's four devoted women secretaries, Gerda Christian, Gertrude "Trudl" Junge, Else Krueger, and Constanz Manzialy. Following their good-byes, Hitler and Braun retired to Hitler's small living room. A few minutes later a single pistol shot was heard.

Heinz Linge was ordered by Hitler to wait ten minutes and then enter the room.[6] Linge opened the door and entered, followed by Bormann, Guensche, Goebbels, and Artur Axmann, who had joined the group after Hitler and Eva said their good-byes. Linge, Axmann, and Guensche survived the war and years later gave separate interviews confirming the deaths of Hitler and his wife, Eva.[7] Axmann told of examining the bodies minutes after death. Linge wrapped Hitler's body in a blanket and turned it over to two SS guards, who carried the body up to the Chancellery garden area. Linge then carried Eva Braun's body up, and they both were laid in a bomb crater. Hitler's chauffeur, Hans Kempka, secured several cans of petrol from the motor garage and dowsed the bodies with gasoline. Guensche dipped a rag into petrol and, lighting it, tossed the burning rag into the crater onto the gasoline-soaked bodies. A roar of flame leapt from the hole and the funeral pyre lit the surrounding area as several of the Hitler faithful stood at attention and gave the stiff-armed Nazi salute. Over the next few hours the corpses were repeatedly dowsed with petrol to keep the fires burning until nothing was left but a few bones and ash. Surviving the fire were Hitler's dental plates, pieces of jawbone with teeth, and a skull fragment containing what appeared to be a bullet hole. The dental plates were later used by the Russians to confirm that the bodies in the crater were those of Adolf Hitler and Eva Braun Hitler. The Russians eventually released their forensic findings, even though many in Russia, including Joseph Stalin, believed that Hitler had escaped the bunker.

Trevor-Roper's study was accepted by the Western world as a masterful piece of detective work that concluded that Hitler died as originally stated, by his own hand in the bunker on the afternoon of April 30, 1945. Trevor-Roper's report eventually became a best-selling book titled *The Last Days of Hitler,* and it remains in print to this day.[8] The young history student-intelligence officer made quite a name for himself by his thorough and systematic work in proving Hitler died in the bunker. Of course, the evidence produced by Trevor-Roper was circumstantial, all of it based on individual statements gained through interviews. The forensic evidence did not emerge until later and then was based exclusively on a comparison of the dentition found in the ashes of the bomb crater to records from Hitler's dentist. There was no way at the time to prove the skull fragments recovered along with the dentition came from the same person.[9]

Despite Trevor-Roper's careful work, rumors continued for several decades that Adolf Hitler escaped and took up residence just about everywhere imaginable, positioning himself for the inevitable comeback when the British and Americans engaged the Soviet Union and its puppet states in the ultimate war for worldwide supremacy.

Following Hitler's death in the bunker, his mystique lived on, and has even grown over the decades. His malevolent personality has a magnetic power that draws many people toward it, and those who get too close become pulled into its evil center.

Hitler knew how to appeal to people's inner souls. He adorned his Third Reich with a cornucopia of pageantry and pomp that dazzled the eye and swelled the heart with nationalistic pride. The pageantry and pomp covered up the extreme acts of brutality carried out under Hitler's orders. It was not so much the individual acts of brutality that would shock the world; it was the scope of the brutality. The magnitude was unfathomable to the average person. And it was all being carried out on behalf of one man, Adolf Hitler. For Adolf Hitler was Germany, and Germany was Adolf Hitler. The Germans had a saying for it: Ein Volk, Ein Reich, Ein Fuhrer. One People, One Empire, One Leader.

Hitler's personality was so strong that it still casts a shadow more than sixty-five years after his death. There are reported to be over fifty-five thousand items in the British Library and Library of Congress relating to Hitler and the Second World War. On the one hand, there are books about nearly every aspect of his life and death, including his birth, youth, health, psyche, pleasures, hates, eating habits, personal security, art, sexual attitudes, and humor or the lack thereof. There is even a book devoted to his conversations during dinner.[10] There are personal accounts written by his valet, pilot, doctor, photographer, chauffeur, ministers, and generals.[11] And despite this plethora of writing the man remains an enigma.

Many European countries have enacted various laws prohibiting the display of Nazi symbols of any sort. The attempt to destroy Hitler's bunker where he spent the final days directing his hopeless war and ended his life on April 30, 1945, has only added to the mystique of the man. The market for Nazi memorabilia remains as strong as ever, as some people want to own a piece of the evil empire, keeping its memory alive, while others just want a piece of one the most interesting and dangerous periods of our history. Perhaps this is why the world so readily accepted the discovery of his private diaries that purported to give an insight into his innermost private thoughts.

The "discovery" of the Hitler diaries was almost an accident, as their creator never intended for them to become known outside a narrow collecting community. The story begins with the journalist Gerd Heidemann, who brought them to the attention of his publisher at *Stern* magazine. Heidemann was an unusual sort of journalist whose ability to convince his employer to keep him on the payroll is almost a story in itself. It is important to understand that Heidemann didn't discover the Hitler diaries; he merely learned of their existence and eventually persuaded their owner (creator) to sell them to *Stern* magazine. Just how Heidemann was able to accomplish this began in the mid-1950s, when he was given an assignment to dig up information about the Nazis, the Third Reich, and Nazi

HITLER'S
TABLE TALK
1941-1944

INTRODUCED AND WITH A NEW PREFACE BY
HUGH TREVOR-ROPER

Produced from an unpublished manuscript of Hitler's conversations during dinner, *Hitler's Table Talk* was not subject to the copyright law, unlike *Mein Kampf* and other Hitler assets. Hugh Trevor-Roper wrote the preface. (Author's collection) war criminals. Although the project generated little interest to his editor, it exposed Heidemann to the intriguing underworld of the Nazi Party. New assignments came and went, and each project was marked by Heidemann's obsessive nature. Once into a subject, he set about to systematically collect everything remotely connected to the project. His weakness was that he did not know when to stop or how to organize his material into a cohesive story, separating the important and relevant data from the chaff. It was not unusual for his editors to take his raw material, including his notes, and assign the final writing of the story to a more skillful writer on *Stern*'s staff.

The key that unlocked Heidemann's "discovery" of the Hitler diaries stemmed from his attempt to discover the real identity of the famous German mystery writer "B. Traven." While still obsessing over Traven long after his research had been published in an article in *Stern,* Heidemann stumbled across the *Carin II,* the ninety-foot yacht that had been presented to Nazi Luftwaffe head and Hitler confidant Hermann Goering. The badly worn yacht was sitting in her slip along the waterfront of the West German capital of Bonn. It was for sale by its present owner, who wanted to get rid of the financial liability of maintaining it. The cost had become too much. It was love at first sight for Heidemann, and his impulsiveness resulted in his purchasing the yacht. He mortgaged everything he owned and soon found that the cost of repairs and upkeep was well beyond his means as a journalist. Nonetheless, he was convinced that the derelict could be restored and later resold for a huge profit. Along the way he met Edda Goering, daughter of Hermann Goering, who helped turn the yacht into a floating museum of Goering memorabilia. With Edda's help, Heidemann began making friends with former Nazi figures, including those who had held privileged positions in Hitler's inner circle—such figures as SS General Wilhelm Mohnke, who commanded the defenses of the Reich Chancellery, and SS General Karl Wolff, Heinrich Himmler's liaison officer with Hitler and commander of SS police forces in Italy. Before long, Heidemann was hosting parties aboard the *Carin II* for major Nazi figures who sat atop the pinnacle of the Third Reich. It did not take a great deal to draw Heidemann into the lure of the Nazi mystique.

Shortly after Heidemann purchased the *Carin II* he, too, realized how costly the yacht was in needed repairs and maintenance fees and began looking for a buyer. His search led him to a prominent Nazi memorabilia collector by the name of Fritz Stiefel. Heidemann visited Stiefel at his home in the Stuttgart suburb of Waiblingen. He first tried to sell Stiefel the yacht, but Stiefel was not interested. Next, Heidemann offered Stiefel a partner-

Hermann Goering's private yacht, *Carin II,* named for his first wife. (Author's collection)

ship share in the *Carin II,* but again Stiefel turned Heidemann down. Still not ready to admit defeat, Heidemann offered Stiefel several artifacts from the *Carin II* that belonged to Goering and carried the Goering crest. Stiefel was interested and bought several artifacts for his collection. It was at this point that Heidemann brought up the diary that belonged to Hitler. Heidemann was obsessed with the idea that Hitler actually kept a diary. He pressed Stiefel to see the diary. Stiefel was still unsure of Heidemann and hesitated at first, but Heidemann's persistence finally paid off. Stiefel agreed to show him the diary.

Stiefel led Heidemann to the basement of his house, where he had a special room whose entrance was guarded by an armored door. Just beyond the door was Stiefel's personal museum of Nazi memorabilia displayed in elaborate glass cabinets and neatly arranged on shelves. It was a treasure trove unlike anything Heidemann had ever seen or even imagined. After the reporter had taken in the incredible collection, Stiefel handed Heidemann the holy of holies, a large bound book with black covers bearing what appeared to be the initials "AH" in gothic letters.[12] Heidemann immediately realized the significance of the book. It was potentially the find of the century. Where did Stiefel get it? Were there others? Stiefel told Heidemann that he purchased the diary from a man who lived in Stuttgart who had acquired it from a relative who lived in East Germany. Stiefel believed there were as many as twenty-six such diaries. Heidemann was stunned. Twenty-six diaries? Heidemann pressed Stiefel for the man's name. Stiefel refused, telling Heidemann that the man insisted on strict anonymity. Anonymity was not necessarily a red flag. It was not unusual for the owners of extremely rare and important objects to remain anonymous to the general public. It was a form of protection from the curious.

When Heidemann returned to Hamburg and *Stern* magazine, he was beside himself as he tried to explain the incredible feeling of having actually held the diary of Adolf Hitler. Incredible. Here was the publishing find of the century, perhaps of the millennium. A diary in Hitler's own hand—and there were more, lots more, as many as two dozen more. Think of the history contained in those diaries. Think of the insight into the mind of the man who conquered Europe and changed world history forever. The diary, however, came not from the mind of a madman, but rather from the mind of a minor forger.

Born in 1938 in Saxony (later East Germany), Konrad Paul Kujau was one of five children. His father was a shoemaker who became an enthusiastic supporter of Hitler and the Nazi Party. By the time Kujau was a teenager he had developed a strong interest in all things Nazi. His father had been killed in 1944, plunging the family into poverty. Separated from his siblings, Conny, as his family and friends knew him, wound up in a refugee camp. At age nineteen he was resettled near the city of Stuttgart, where he became involved in a series of petty crimes. He was arrested and convicted of forging several dozen luncheon vouchers and sentenced to five days in prison. It was the first of several scrapes with the law. Over the next twenty years Kujau tried his hand at various service-related businesses, most of which failed. It seems he could not keep from engaging in a variety of criminal activities, albeit petty in nature, which resulted in a lengthy criminal record. Throughout this period he adopted several aliases in an attempt to avert detection by the legal authorities. In 1970, Kujau and his common-law wife, Edith Lieblang, took up a new enterprise, one that reflected Kujau's lifelong interest in Nazi militaria. East Germany was a veritable treasure trove of German and Nazi artifacts that survived the war. It was not difficult to find items at modest prices and smuggle them across the border into West Germany, where a thriving black market flourished. By 1974 the selling of Nazi memorabilia had taken over Conny and Edith's lives.

While Kujau made a satisfactory living dealing in Nazi artifacts, he was not satisfied. He wanted to do something big. Something that would gain him the attention and respect he craved. The demand for Nazi memorabilia was so strong that collectors applied rather low standards in accepting provenance. Some pundits quipped that if Hitler had actually had all of the Nazi memorabilia available to him during the war that currently existed in the marketplace he wouldn't have lost. For many highly collectible artifacts of war, whether from the American Civil War or World War II, the line between authentic, reproduction, and outright fabrication becomes quite blurred. When Confederate flags and belt buckles began to escalate in price to incredible heights, skillful fakes (or reproductions) quickly followed. When the demand for Nazi memorabilia began to outstrip supply, the same phenomenon occurred.

Konrad Kujau was rather expert at exploiting such markets. By his own admission, Kujau "stumbled" into his forgery habit when he decided to use his acquired expertise about Hitler and the Third Reich to write a book.[13] In his own way of thinking, it was a small step from writing a book to forging a diary.

Heidemann was overcome with the idea that Hitler had produced as many as two dozen diaries detailing his rise to power and rule over the Third Reich. He became convinced that the editors at *Stern* were about to come into the greatest story of the magazine's existence. But, much to Heidemann's surprise, the editors at *Stern*, Henri Nannen and his deputy, Peter Koch, were not interested in Heidemann's story. They even forbid him to continue to follow his leads to the rest of the diaries, telling him to drop his crazy infatuation with Nazi history and memorabilia. They were skeptical that such a trove of material existed. Stunned at first, Heidemann was undeterred. He decided the story was too good to ignore and went to see Thomas Walde, the head of *Stern*'s history section. He told Walde about Stiefel and the diary. Walde, unlike *Stern*'s editors, became intrigued and told Heidemann to go ahead and pursue the story but to keep it secret from Nannen and Koch. Walde was taking a risk, but like Heidemann, he believed there was the potential for a blockbuster story if true.

Still unable to get Stiefel to reveal his source, Heidemann put his research talents in full gear and decided to begin at the beginning. Having read the story of the ten trunks of special papers flown from the bunker in a Junkers 352 piloted by Major Gundlfinger and its crash somewhere

Stern's reporter Gerd Heidemann posing next to the graves of two crew members of the Junkers 352 flight that crashed near Boernersdorf. (DPA)

near Boernersdorf, near the Czech border, Heidemann began tracking the possible flight path in hopes of verifying the story. He not only discovered that a plane fitting the description of the document plane did indeed crash near Boernersdorf, but actually located Gundlfinger's grave and those of the other passengers known to be on the flight. Now convinced that Heidemann was on to something big, Walde told him to go all out on the story.

Heidemann, in anticipation of convincing *Stern*'s owners, put together a dossier containing the results of his investigation. Included was a description of the missing flight with the several trunks containing Hitler's most select documents from the bunker, the crash site of the plane, the location and photographs of the graves of the pilot and other passengers on the ill-fated flight, and Heidemann's description of the diary Stiefel had allowed him to examine.

But Heidemann and Walde were not ready to go to their editors, Nannen and Koch. It was Koch who angrily told Heidemann not to spend any more time or expense money on his crazy Nazi projects. Instead, the two men took the dossier and their story to Manfred Fischer, the managing director of Bertelsmann, the media conglomerate that owned Gruner & Jahr, the publishing company that published *Stern*. Walde and Heidemann essentially went over the heads of their bosses and went straight to the man that controlled the parent company of *Stern*. Fischer was intrigued, and understood the situation between Heidemann and Koch. Fischer, who was scheduled to take over managing the parent company that owned *Stern*, did not like Koch.[14] He approved the project and authorized 200,000 marks in cash, giving Heidemann the necessary funds to begin negotiating with the owner of the alleged diaries. But Heidemann still had to physically produce the diaries, and to do so he had to track down their mysterious owner.

Stiefel, the owner of the lone diary that Heidemann had seen, refused to give him any information about the owner of the other diaries. Heidemann decided to contact Jakob Tiefenthaler, the man who first told him about Stiefel and the Hitler diary. Back when Heidemann was desperately trying to sell the *Carin II* and get out from under the growing debt the yacht was costing him, General Wilhelm Mohnke put Heidemann in touch with Tiefenthaler as someone who had significant contacts among Nazi collectors and might be able to help Heidemann sell his yacht. During the course of their efforts to sell *Carin II*, Tiefenthaler told Heidemann about Stiefel and his diary. Heidemann decided to flush out the owner of the diaries in a bold, unauthorized move. He told Tiefenthaler that he could guarantee a payment of 2 million marks (approximately $600,000) in either cash or gold to the secret dealer that had possession of the Hitler diaries.[15] If that wouldn't draw him out, then nothing would work. In addition, Heidemann said that *Stern* would protect the owner and guarantee his anonymity, using the universal right of a journalist and his paper not to divulge the source of their information.

After seven weeks, Tiefenthaler finally got back to Heidemann. The owner, a militaria dealer named Fischer from Stuttgart, was interested. Tiefenthaler gave Heidemann the man's telephone number and the address of his antique shop in Stuttgart. Heidemann, as obsessive as ever, flew to Stuttgart without contacting Fischer ahead of time and drove to the address of the antique shop, then waited. When Fischer failed to turn up, Heidemann drove to the suburban area where Fischer lived and called the number Tiefenthaler had given him. Fischer gave Heidemann his address and told him to come ahead. He had agreed to meet with Heidemann.

The cat was close to jumping out of the bag. Heidemann's dogged persistence had finally paid off and he was about to meet the owner of the infamous Hitler diaries. Now he had to convince the owner to show him the diaries and then to sell them to *Stern*. Only when he had all of the diaries in hand, or at least an agreement to buy the rest of the diaries, would he feel comfortable with going to *Stern's* editors—the very editors who had forbidden him from pursuing any more of his "crazy Nazi stories." Heidemann was confident, however, that once they learned of the cache of extraordinary diaries they would do an about-face.

Mr. Fischer, it turned out, was an alias. Fischer's real name was none other than Konrad Paul Kujau. He made his living by selling mostly bogus Nazi memorabilia to a few fanatic Nazi collectors like Fritz Stiefel. As long as he was able to sell to private collectors who wanted to remain anonymous, he was relatively safe from discovery. Selling to a magazine like *Stern* was taking on a serious risk of being exposed, especially if the money involved was in the millions of marks. Surely *Stern* would call on experts to authenticate the diaries and other Hitler items Kujau had produced, and it wasn't clear the diaries would pass expert scrutiny.

Kujau's other problem was that he had a nefarious past that included two convictions for forgery, and several petty crimes under a string of aliases, which landed him in prison. Kujau's fascination with military memorabilia eventually had resulted in his becoming a dealer in Nazi artifacts. It was a relatively easy way of making money and proved to be lucrative. Dealing in genuine articles at first, it didn't take long before Kujau's larcenous character emerged. With his artistic talent he could produce an endless supply of highly sought-after artwork that he could sell at high prices. Producing fake artwork soon led him into forging documents. By mixing forged documents in with real ones imported from East Germany, he was able to keep a steady supply flowing through his shop, to his customers' delight. He was good at his trade, and his knowledge of the Third Reich served him well.

Kujau soon mastered Hitler's handwriting and his style of painting. Hitler was a prodigious artist who turned out between two thousand and three thousand various works of art, including sketches, watercolors, and oil paintings.[16] The abundance of material made it a good deal easier for Kujau to fabricate Hitler's works and pass them off as originals. He became so well known as a dealer in Hitler and Nazi memorabilia that his clientele spread to the United States, where he regularly supplied customers with his forgeries. Fritz Stiefel soon became one of Kujau's best customers, having spent over 250,000 Deutschmarks (approximately $75,000) for memorabilia from Kujau's "collection." Among Stiefel's prized possessions was a manuscript copy of 233 pages of *Mein Kampf* written in Hitler's hand.

One of hundreds of authentic watercolor paintings by Adolf Hitler. Kujau produced several fake Hitler paintings that successfully fooled collectors. (U.S. Army)

Kujau had forged the manuscript copy of the infamous book as a way of practicing Hitler's handwriting.[17] He was so pleased with the result that he had no hesitancy in passing it off as authentic. Stiefel's passion for Hitler memorabilia blinded him to Kujau's forgeries.

Precisely when Kujau decided to forge a Hitler diary is difficult to determine. He gives various versions of how it all began. In one version he decided to put his considerable knowledge of Hitler to a more productive use by writing a legitimate biography of the führer. He soon realized that developing the biography as a diary (or diaries) was even more productive. In another version, Kujau typed out a chronology of Hitler's life for the year 1935 using a Nazi Party yearbook. When he finished, he decided to transcribe it in Hitler's handwriting to see if he could replicate it. Using one of several notebooks he had purchased to catalogue his own collection, Kujau converted the chronology into diary form. Once again he was so pleased with his effort that he showed the book to Fritz Stiefel, telling him it was a Hitler diary. Perhaps he wanted to see Stiefel's reaction as a test of how well he had made the copy. Stiefel examined the book carefully and asked Kujau if he could borrow it. Kujau suspected that Stiefel wanted to purchase the diary and needed to physically possess it for a period of time before striking a deal. Stiefel then did what any competent collector would (or should) do: he sought the opinion of an expert on Hitler's writing, August Priesack. Priesack worked as an art historian from 1935 to 1939 in the Nazi Party main archives under the direction of Hitler's second in command, Rudolf Hess. Surviving the war, Priesack made a living by representing himself as an authority on Nazi art, including that produced by Hitler.

Stiefel invited Priesack to view his collection of memorabilia. Priesack was impressed, and told Stiefel his collection was of "great historical significance."[18] After examining the diary he declared it authentic.[19] Kujau was ecstatic. Previously, his forgeries had only been inspected by amateurs, whose expertise came from owning bits and pieces of Hitler memorabilia, much of it fabricated. Impressed with Stiefel's collection, Priesack contacted Eberhard Jaeckel, a professor of modern history at Stuttgart University. Like Priesack, Jaeckel was impressed with Stiefel's collection and later gave his blessing to Kujau's diary, urging him to seek out others. Kujau must have been both confused and elated. Having plied his forgeries on collectors whose expertise was limited, he had just received the approval of his forgery by two leading experts on Hitler documents and paintings. It was too good to be true. Once again, wanting to believe apparently blinded the so-called Nazi experts.

Kujau gained increased confidence. If two of the leading experts on Hitler accepted his forgeries, surely others would, too. He was no longer afraid of his work being examined by others outside the narrow group of private collectors he normally dealt with. And, 2 million marks were beyond his wildest dreams.

But more than the money, it was Goering's uniform that caught Kujau's attention. Kujau had acquired the uniforms of several of the top Nazi leaders, including Hitler, Himmler, and Rommel, but not Goering. The uniform Heidemann had on the *Carin II* was the clincher that brought Kujau over to the journalist's side. Unknown to both Heidemann and Kujau, the uniform was bogus, a reproduction that Edda Goering had ordered and given to Heidemann to display on the yacht along with other memorabilia.

It was fitting that the master of fakery was now himself taken in by a fake uniform. Poetic justice perhaps?

Kujau was now willing to deal. There was only one problem, a small one to be sure. There were no other diaries. The diary Stiefel was holding in his special "vault room" was the only diary Kujau had forged. He was confidant, however, that he could produce more. He just needed time. Kujau told Heidemann that his brother, an East German general, was the go-between with the peasant farmer who had liberated the precious cargo from the downed plane, but that he could not afford to jeopardize his career or life by revealing his role in acquiring the diaries. The diaries would have to come out of East Germany slowly, one at a time. Kujau hoped that this ruse would buy him the time he needed. Luckily, he was prolific. He was able to work from early morning through evening nonstop, and he loved his work, which was a necessary requirement if he was to pull off the greatest hoax in Hitler memorabilia.

Kujau went to work writing new diaries. In the meantime, Heidemann returned to the *Stern* offices in Hamburg. It was time to decide where to go next in convincing the magazine to go with the story of the Hitler diaries. Heidemann began to worry that news of the diaries would soon get out and that another news organization might step in and pull the discovery out from under him. He suddenly felt the necessity of getting *Stern*'s editors to act and act quickly. Heidemann's problem was that he could not go to Nannen and Koch, who had forbidden him from involving himself in more Nazi "crap," as Nannen so brusquely put it. Heidemann would have to continue to work around the two editors and go over their heads. Meanwhile, Kujau had his first major scare concerning his other forged documents.

One of the items Kujau sold to Fritz Stiefel was a poem allegedly written by Hitler in 1916 (and so dated) that had actually appeared in the published work of German poet Herbert Menzel in 1936.[20] Eberhard Jaeckel, the history professor and expert on Hitler writings, had previously published a book on Hitler's writings and included several pieces from Stiefel's collection of Kujau forgeries, including the poem. When another professor of contemporary history called the strange anomaly to Jaeckel's attention, he concluded that the poem in Stiefel's collection was a forgery. Stiefel asked Kujau to explain. Kujau, always verbal, launched into a detailed description of the attempt to transfer Hitler's papers to his Alpine Redoubt in Berchtesgaden. He told of the plane's crash and how local peasants found several trunks in the wreckage. He ended by pointing out that he was only the go-between, receiving the material from his brother, who was purchasing it from the people who recovered the cache of documents from the crash site. What could he do? In essence, Stiefel was being told he was stuck with the forgery through no fault of Kujau's.

Jaeckel would have to publish a correction to subsequent editions of his book. Surprisingly, the discovery of a forgery did not send up any red flags or compromise the pending deal on the diaries. Heidemann, for one, was so overwhelmed by the thought of the Hitler diaries that nothing was going to deter him from moving forward as fast and as hard as he could. Heidemann had everything to lose and nothing to gain by having the deal fall through. Kujau, on the other hand, had a great deal of writing to do. His diaries had to cover thirteen years of Hitler's incredible life as he set out to conquer the world.

Returning to his home in Ditzingen, he threw himself into his project. From early morning through late evening Kujau worked on creating new diaries. He drew on every imaginable source for material, including his extensive library of Hitler books, newspapers, Nazi Party newsletters, and his Nazi friends who were close to Hitler during his reign as führer. Like so many successful forgers, Kujau possessed an extraordinary knowledge of his subject. Trying to convince the experts at the level of forgery Kujau was attempting took a very special talent. Working day and night, Kujau finally completed three of the diaries. He was ready for the next installment in this crazy episode that Heidemann insisted on carrying forward.

Over the next several months Heidemann visited Kujau and received the latest set of diaries "smuggled" out of East Germany by Kujau's fictitious brother. The story that the diaries had to be smuggled out of East Germany, a communist police state, helped Kujau pull off his scam. It gave him time, and it gave him the perfect cover for not revealing his sources.

When Manfred Fischer took over the managing directorship of Bertelsmann, the parent conglomerate that controlled Gruner & Jahr, *Stern's* publisher, he became senior to Nannen and Koch, Heidemann's nemeses. When Fischer assumed the management of Bertelsmann, Gerd Schulte-Hillen, an engineer who had been overseeing the printing operations of Gruner & Jahr, was picked to take over managing that firm. Fischer took Schulte-Hillen into his confidence and told him about the documents flown out of Berlin only to wind up in a plane crash near Boernersdorf. Fischer went on to tell Schulte-Hillen that he had already committed nearly a million and a half marks to the project and that Heidemann had obtained several of the diaries. The inner circle of those who knew about the transactions had now grown to seven: Gerd Heidemann, Thomas Walde,

Wilfried Sorge, Jan Hensmann, Manfred Fischer, Peter Kuehsel, and Reinhard Mohn, all sworn to secrecy. It was time to bring *Stern* and its editors on board with the plan to acquire and publish the diaries.

Nannen had stepped down as one of *Stern*'s editors to take over the day-to-day publishing of the magazine. Felix Schmidt and Rolf Gillhausen replaced him. On being informed about the clandestine activity of Heidemann behind his back, Koch was enraged, but there was little he could do. The owners of the parent company, Manfred Fischer and Reinhard Mohn, had decided to go ahead with the project at all costs. Having the leaders of *Stern* on board—or more accurately, in line—Fischer became concerned about an interesting question. Who owned the copyright to Hitler's diaries and other writings? It was an intriguing question. Could a monster war criminal like Adolf Hitler own the copyright to his writing? And if so, could he pass it down to next of kin? Could *Stern* legally publish the documents without approval? But approval from whom? Fischer called in Gruner & Jahr's legal adviser, Andreas Ruppert, and set him to work finding out the answers to these intriguing questions. Did the führer have any legal rights to his writings? Incredible as it sounds, he did. A lawyer had been hired by Hitler's sister Paula to represent her and other family members in dealing with Hitler's estate. Interestingly, Hitler was still owed 5 million marks in royalties from his publisher for *Mein Kampf.* In another strange quirk of law, while the state confiscated the money and certain artifacts Hitler had given to his housekeeper, it was prevented from stopping publication of another Hitler manuscript, titled *Hitler's Table Talk, 1941–1944,* compiled by Hitler and later edited by several authors, including Hitler historian Hugh Trevor-Roper, who wrote a preface to the book.[21] The law, it seems, applied only to already published manuscripts, but not to unpublished manuscripts.[22] The same ruling applied in 2006 to a newly discovered authentic Hitler manuscript written as a follow-up to *Mein Kampf.* Titled *Hitler's Second Book,* it was edited by German scholar Gerhard Weinberg.[23]

It turns out that German historian Werner Maser had negotiated a contract with family members to act as trustee for the Hitler heirs. Heidemann, taking the bull by the horns, tracked down Maser. After some negotiating, the two signed a contract giving Heidemann the sole rights to all "discovered or purchased documents or notes in the hand of Adolf Hitler." Maser received a fee of 20,000 marks, in cash.[24] All of the transactions that occurred throughout the entire episode were made in cash, suggesting distrust among all of the parties involved.

As the volumes began to accumulate, from a few at first to over sixty, Manfred Fischer decided it would be prudent to move the diaries to a special safe-deposit box in Switzerland to protect them from possible theft. In reality, it seems more likely that Fischer was fearful the West German government might step in and confiscate the diaries even though they represented unpublished material. The West German government had a strong aversion to anything Nazi and went to great lengths to suppress Nazi artifacts, including the confiscation of Nazi material.

While Kujau labored away at forging the diaries, allotting each book a six-month period in the Nazi leader's takeover as führer, Gerd Heidemann was arranging to withdraw large sums of money to pay for the diaries as they were "smuggled" piecemeal across the border from East Germany. Kujau was disciplined in his approach and was able to satisfy his victims despite the urgency they felt in wanting to acquire all of the diaries as quickly as possible. Since they needed to be created, they would have to be patient. Believing each diary was a separate negotiation, and required a separate plan for smuggling it across the East German border, the *Stern* team had no alternative but to rely on Heidemann, who had to rely on Kujau. Kujau could complete the writing of each diary in four to five hours, but the overall time it took him to create a diary was several days because of the research he had to do in creating the journal. Using his extensive library of Nazi books, newsletters, and newspapers, Kujau could focus on a particular period in Hitler's reign and complete a diary with reasonable accuracy. As pressure built to deliver more diaries faster, Kujau hurried his research, resulting in errors working their way into his writing. The errors should have been picked up by the experts, but they were missed in the early days of inspection. Only in hindsight did many of the experts acknowledge the diaries were forgeries.

As the number of diaries delivered by Kujau passed the two dozen mark, Thomas Walde, *Stern*'s editor in charge of history, decided it was time to have handwriting experts analyze the material. Like with so many frauds involving forgery, authentication was sought only after large sums of money had been paid out rather than before. Surprisingly, authentication was not made a condition of *Stern*'s payment for the diaries. The people at *Stern* had become blinded by the sensational discovery to the point where no one seriously considered that the diaries might be forgeries. Unshaken in the belief that they were authentic, *Stern* sought the analysis by handwriting experts to silence possible skeptics. The editors had no doubt as to the results of the experts' analyses, and they were right.

In seeking handwriting analyses, the people at *Stern* did a strange thing. They cut a single page from one of the diaries, submitting it or copies of it to three experts. The page contained Hitler's description of Rudolf Hess's "peace flight" to Scotland on May 10, 1941. Hess, Hitler's deputy and long-time Nazi associate, is believed to have flown to Scotland on his own initiative to offer a peace proposal to the British government. Hess, a trained pilot, flew to Scotland in a Messerschmitt 110 fighter plane and parachuted onto the estate of the Duke of Hamilton. The two men had first met during the Berlin Olympics in 1936 and had become friends. Hess's escapade is considered by historians as a futile attempt by a mentally unstable Hess to initiate unilateral negotiations with the British. When Hitler found out what his deputy had done, he was furious.

Now comes a different version of the event from the hand of Hitler himself. In the diary containing events of May 1941 there is an entry explaining Hess's flight, acknowledging that it was planned with Hitler's sanction. Should the effort fail, Hitler and his associates would deny any knowledge of Hess's act, which is, of course, what happened. The editors at *Stern* decided to test the waters by publishing an account of Hess's flight using the entry from Hitler's diary. It was a good move on *Stern*'s part. If true, the account completely contradicted accepted history and raised intriguing possibilities. If the public and press accepted the story, it augured well for going ahead with publishing the rest of the material. The time had come for the editors at *Stern* to seek authentication using the Hess page before going any further with the story.

A meeting was held between representatives of the parent publishing firm, Gruner & Jahr, and the editors from *Stern*. Presiding over the meeting was Gerd Schulte-Hillen, the managing director of Gruner & Jahr. The decision was made to go ahead and publish a major article on the Hess affair in the January 1983 issue, which coincided with the fiftieth anniversary of Hitler's coming to power. If successful, as nearly everyone at the meeting expected, the article would be followed by a book, which would be serialized in *Stern*. Wilfried Sorge, assistant to Schulte-Hillen, set out on a long tour visiting various media organizations around the world, offering the Hess story to the highest bidders. The fact that it came from one of several dozen discovered Hitler diaries was still kept a tightly held secret. Sorge's tour took him to Holland, Belgium, France, Spain, Italy, New York, and Tokyo.

The editors at *Stern*, however, were not happy with this plan. They felt Gruner & Jahr were going about the story in the wrong way. *Stern* argued that the diaries *in toto* were the scoop of the century and that an article followed by a book on Rudolf Hess's flight to Scotland was the wrong way to introduce the diaries to the public. The story, they argued, should begin with the discovery of the diaries and involve the flight of the Junkers 352 and its fatal crash near Boernersdorf. Unwilling to give up, Henri Nannen and Peter Koch pressed their case with Gruner & Jahr's managing director, Gerd Schulte-Hillen. The two editors who were once opposed to Heidemann and his "crazy Nazi" story were now on board. It seemed as if everyone had fallen under the spell of Hitler.

To nearly everyone's surprise, Schulte-Hillen gave in and agreed to quickly switch horses and go with Nannen and Koch's plan. Sorge was recalled back to Hamburg and told the strategy had changed. Thomas Walde and his assistant, Leo Pesche, saw their manuscript on Hess seriously compromised. Instead of leading the story and being serialized in *Stern,* it would simply become an accessory publication to the overall story of the discovery and serialization of the diaries.

Now it was Walde and Sorge's turn to protest. An excited Gerd Heidemann joined them. All three pointed out to Schulte-Hillen that not all of the diaries had been acquired from their alleged East German source. Exposure would surely jeopardize further acquisitions. They had not yet acquired the diaries for 1944 and the D-Day invasion, one of the more important parts of the Hitler diaries. Schulte-Hillen was unswayed by their arguments. The longer they waited the greater the possibility the whole plan would leak, exposing the diaries before *Stern* was ready to launch its publication. Schulte-Hillen told his group *Stern* would serialize the diaries beginning with their discovery. Publication was scheduled to begin with the May 8, 1983, issue of *Stern* and run for eight weeks followed by a summer break. The articles would start up again in the fall of 1984 and run for ten weeks, followed by another break until the following fall, when ten more extracts from the diaries would be published. Twenty-eight serialized articles in all over eighteen months. The word went out from Sorge to all Gruner & Jahr clients (media groups) that the syndication rights were up for sale. Interested parties were welcome to inspect the diaries in April in anticipation of the May publication date.[25]

Having settled on the plan for publishing the Hitler diaries, Walde went forward with his plan to authenticate the Hess document. If this document passed muster with a select group of experts, *Stern* would be able to silence any skeptics. Walde asked Heidemann to go with him to the Bundesarchiv, the German Federal Republic Archives, where Walde and Heidemann met with two of the archive's top officials, Josef Henke and Klaus Oldenhage. They gave Henke and Oldenhage several documents, which they said they would donate to the archive when they were finished with them. Included was a handwritten telegram by Hitler to General Franco of Spain dated January 1, 1940, a copy of a speech dated December 29, 1934, and a letter to Hermann Goering dated October 17, 1940. Two days later they submitted the page removed from the diary containing Hitler's comments on Rudolf Hess's "peace mission" to England, but did not tell the Bundesarchiv officials that the page came from one of the alleged Hitler diaries. The Bundesarchiv then forwarded the documents along with five authentic Hitler documents from its own archive for comparison to the West German police headquarters in Rhineland-Pfalz, where police experts analyzed the documents using the known Hitler examples as their standard for comparison.

A week later, on April 13, Walde and Wilfried Sorge visited Dr. Max Frei-Sulzer in Switzerland. Frei-Sulzer was the former head of the forensic laboratory of the Zurich police department. Now retired, he occasionally did consultative work as a freelance handwriting expert. Frei-Sulzer was provided with photocopies of the Hess page and a telegram from Hitler to Miklos Horthy de Nagybanya (Admiral Horthy), Regent of Hungary. For comparison, Frei-Sulzer was also given copies of the five Bundesarchiv documents and several documents from Heidemann's private collection. Incredibly, the Heidemann documents were all forgeries, meaning that Frei-Sulzer was comparing Kujau forgeries against Kujau forgeries in several instances, which invalidated his analysis.

From Switzerland, Walde and Sorge flew to North Carolina, where they hired forensic document examiner Ordway Hilton as their third handwriting expert. Hilton was retired from the New York City Police Department. He was provided with copies of the same documents given to Frei-Sulzer, compromising his analysis by contaminating the "authentic" group of documents with Kujau forgeries. Thus two of the expert examiners were using forged documents, believing them to be authentic Hitler samples. Further compromising the analysis was the fact that Frei-Sulzer's specialty was analyzing biological materials, not handwriting, while Hilton could not read German and was unable to understand the material he was examining. Most important, neither man was experienced in analyzing German documents.

Three independent experts were now in place to analyze the handwriting of the supplied documents and report back to *Stern*. Inexplicably, none of the original documents were subjected to paper or ink analysis. Had those two simple tests been performed, Kujau's forgery would have been exposed instantly. Not only was this obvious test not performed, but also Walde had contaminated the handwriting analysis by including forged documents from Heidemann's collection as authentic examples of Hitler's handwriting for use in the experts' evaluation.

Seven weeks passed before the final report reached the offices of *Stern* magazine. Not surprisingly, all three experts certified the Hess document as authentic. Hilton wrote in his report that "there is no evidence within this writing which suggests in any way that this page was prepared by another person in imitation of the writing of Adolf Hitler, and consequently I must conclude that he prepared the document."[26] Frei-Sulzer was more positive in his report, writing, "There can be no doubt that both these documents [the Horthy telegram and the Hess document] were written by Adolf Hitler."[27] The Bundesarchiv was the last to report. Not as emphatic as Frei-Sulzer, its expert nonetheless gave his approval, stating that it was "highly probable" that Hitler wrote the Hess document.[28] The fatal flaw in these analyses was in the forged documents from Heidemann's collection (purchased from Kujau) that the three experts were told were authentic examples of Hitler's handwriting.

Stern seemed unconcerned with the fact that no forensic analysis had been completed on the paper, ink, and other physical aspects of the diaries, such as the glue, wax seals, and fiber composition of the cord used with the wax seals. Tests on any one of these would have shown that the material dated from after the war. The results of the handwriting analyses were enough for officials at *Stern*.

Stern had hit a home run. They had three out of three experts certifying the Hess document authentic, satisfying *Stern* that the diaries were written by Adolf Hitler. *Stern* was now ready to go ahead with publication of the Hess manuscript. For this, Bantam Books, a subsidiary of Bertelsmann, was the obvious choice. Not only was Bantam part of the parent company, but it was experienced in the American market, something Gruner & Jahr was not. Meeting with Bantam officials, the negotiations went poorly. Louis Wolfe, president at Bantam, wanted guarantees backing up the authenticity of the material, including some form of compensation should the book come under serious challenge. Although Gruner & Jahr and *Stern* were now convinced the material was authentic, they were reluctant to give any guarantees to Bantam. Bantam was also kept in the dark throughout the talks about the Hitler diaries, which were never mentioned. Besides,

Bantam was not particularly interested in serialization of the book, which was what was really at the top of Gruner & Jahr's agenda. Over the next several months talks took place between the two groups, but in the end Bantam was never given a contract to publish the Hess manuscript. Time soon changed Gruner & Jahr's original game plan, and the publication of the book wound up on the back shelf.

Since serialization was the ultimate goal of Gruner & Jahr, the officials decided to contact an American company specializing in such rights, International Creative Management (ICM). Wilfried Sorge made sure ICM understood that "only reputable organizations" should be approached: the *New York Times, Newsweek* magazine, and *Time*. Negotiations for the American rights under way, the men from Gruner & Jahr and from *Stern* turned to the media mogul Rupert Murdoch. Murdoch, it turns out, was not only interested in the British and the Commonwealth publishing rights, but the American rights as well. Before making his offer, Murdoch wanted to have his own expert's opinion on the diaries and their authenticity. He chose one of the best, the noted English historian Hugh Trevor-Roper. Trevor-Roper also just happened to be on the board of directors of the *Sunday Times*, Murdoch's most prestigious newspaper.

Bertelsmann's executive officer, Manfred Fischer, had moved the diaries to the Handelsbank, in Zurich, Switzerland, for safekeeping. The Swiss bank was presumably beyond the reach of German authorities should they attempt to confiscate the Nazi material. Trevor-Roper was greeted by Wilfried Sorge and Jan Hensmann of Gruner & Jahr, and Peter Koch of *Stern*. Ushered into a special room at the Handelsbank, the historian was taken aback by the volume of materials that were set out for him. On a table were fifty-eight large books purported to be the diaries of Adolf Hitler. Surrounding the diaries was an archive of material, from paintings to letters to artifacts, including a steel helmet claimed to be the führer's World War I helmet.

Trevor-Roper had set out on his trip skeptical of the claims being made that Hitler had faithfully kept a historical record of his years in power from 1933 to 1945. He had been given a special report prepared by *Stern* explaining Rudolf Hess's failed peace mission in 1941 and excerpts from Hitler's diary showing that Hitler knew of Hess's plan in advance and approved of it. It was contrary to everything Trevor-Roper knew about the abortive peace initiative and Hitler's ignorance of it. It was only natural that a historian of Trevor-Roper's stature would be skeptical of such a historic find as the unknown diaries of the twentieth century's nemesis.

Although skeptical at first, Trevor-Roper began to shed his doubt. Shown the three separate reports by the handwriting experts retained by *Stern* and faced with the sheer number of diaries, the historian began to change his mind: "When I entered the back room in the Swiss bank, and turned the pages of those volumes, my doubts gradually dissolved. I am now satisfied that the documents are authentic." He then added the lines that many other historians took issue with: "the standard accounts of Hitler's writing habits, *of his personality,* and even, perhaps, some public events may, in consequence, have to be revised" (emphasis added).[29] Trevor-Roper seemed to suggest a kinder, gentler Hitler would emerge from the diaries.

The people at *Stern* and perhaps more importantly Rupert Murdoch, who hired Trevor-Roper on behalf of the *Sunday Times,* were delighted. One of the leading historians on the Nazi era and Adolf Hitler had just given his seal of approval to the diaries. It was time to complete the negotiations for syndication rights. The most expensive hoax in publishing history was about to take place. *Stern* next wanted to get Trevor-Roper's approval to quote him in announcing their discovery of the diaries. It would be the ultimate proof for the diaries' authenticity. *Stern* submitted for the historian's approval three "quotes" they had made up. Trevor-Roper did not like any of the three, but with pressure from *Stern* he finally agreed to allow the magazine to quote him as stating that the diaries were the most important historical discovery of the decade and a scoop of Watergate proportions. Given the significance of the diaries had they been authentic, the quote was modest. Watergate paled in comparison. It would later prove embarrassing to the Oxford don.

In fairness to Trevor-Roper, he maintained from the beginning that he could not make a judgment regarding the diaries' authenticity simply by examining the diaries superficially. He would need sufficient time to sit down and carefully examine typescript translations of the diaries' content. Only by examining the content of the diaries could he pass judgment on their accuracy and, thus, authenticity. The people at the *Sunday Times* understood. They told him he would have the time required to thoroughly examine the diaries' content. Unfortunately, they misled him. Murdoch wanted to move as quickly as possible to head off any competition. He understood Trevor-Roper's concern, but he needed to make his offer soon or risk losing the syndication rights. Trevor-Roper was asked to call the *Sunday Times* from Zurich with a "preliminary assessment" of the diaries' authenticity the same afternoon he began his examination.[30] After several hours of pouring through the massive archive of material and listening to

Rupert Murdoch, a media mogul with interests worldwide, upstaged the people at *Stern* and Gruner & Jahr by calling their bluff and outmaneuvering them in negotiations for serialization rights. The deal ultimately fell through when the diaries were exposed as forgeries. (Author's collection)

Wilfried Sorge tell the story of Hitler's Operation Seraglio and the crash of the Junkers 352 near Boernersdorf carrying several trunks of documents from the bunker, Trevor-Roper phoned Charles Douglas Home, the editor of the *Sunday Times,* "I think they are genuine."[31]

Back in London, Rupert Murdoch and the people at the *Sunday Times* were elated. In Zurich, however, Trevor-Roper was already having misgivings. He knew better than to make such an important judgment without carefully examining the diaries' total content. Any competent historian would have taken time to carefully read the diaries, looking for errors, inconsistencies, and false statements. Once the story broke exposing the diaries as forgeries, Trevor-Roper regained his senses and lamented what he had done. But it was too late. His prestige throughout the world as a first-rate historian meant his endorsement of the diaries' authenticity would make international headlines. He would forever regret his poor judgment.

After the hoax was exposed and criminal proceedings were moving forward against the perpetrators, Trevor-Roper stepped up and apologized for his actions: "Whether misled or not, I blame no one except myself for giving wrong advice to the *Times* and *Sunday Times,* whose editors behaved throughout with more understanding than I deserve."[32]

Stern had always looked to the Hitler diaries to significantly boost sales and subscriptions to the magazine. The plum would be the syndication rights sold to British and American media companies. At the top of the British list was Rupert Murdoch. Murdoch owned the British *Times* and *Sunday Times,* along with a television station in Australia and several other newspapers throughout the Commonwealth, while *Time* magazine and *Newsweek* magazine along with the *New York Times* represented the American interests. The potential market was huge, and *Stern* stood to make millions on selling the rights to the diaries.

Murdoch was enthusiastic over the potential sales associated with the diaries, and now with Trevor-Roper's approval he was anxious to negotiate a deal. *Newsweek,* intent on closing the circulation gap with *Time,* was also anxious to get in on the money machine, but prudent enough to seek its own expert's opinion. It hired the University of North Carolina's esteemed historian Gerhard Weinberg. Born a German Jew, Weinberg fled Nazi Germany with his family at age twelve and became an American citizen. Highly respected as a scholar of the Third Reich for his *Guide to Captured German Documents,* published in 1952, Weinberg would go on to enhance his credentials as a leading scholar of the Nazi era and Hitler with his monumental history of World War II, titled *A World at Arms,* published in 1994, and his editing of *Hitler's Second Book,* published in 2006.[33]

A fastidious historian, Weinberg's initial reaction to the Hitler diaries was skepticism, but curiosity spurred him into wanting to examine the volumes. On learning that Murdoch had already had Trevor-Roper examine the diaries, *Newsweek* was anxious for Weinberg to see them. They were falling behind and wanted to move quickly. Weinberg flew to Zurich and the Handelsbank, where the diaries were safely stored. The examination did not go well at first. The entries Weinberg examined were too sketchy for him to compare to known events. They predated the entries in the diary of Heinz Linge (Hitler's valet), and Weinberg was unable to use Linge as a test against which to examine the entries. Hitler's handwriting was difficult to read and there were no transcripts to work from. When Weinberg came to the diary containing Hitler's meeting with Britain's Neville Chamberlain, he found what he was looking for. Hitler had praise for Chamberlain as a negotiator, something Weinberg firmly believed. That coupled with the fact that Hitler signed every one of the diary pages at the bottom convinced Weinberg that the diaries were authentic. No one in their right mind would attempt to forge Hitler's signature hundreds of times, expecting to get away with fooling the experts. The sheer scale of the forgery added to its plausibility. *Newsweek* was satisfied. It was ready to negotiate.

Negotiating for *Stern* and its publisher, Gruner & Jahr, was the publisher's financial director, Jan Hensmann. Among Murdoch's entourage was his *Sunday Times* editor, Charles Douglas-Home. Murdoch did not fool around. Disappointed at not being able to secure the book rights (that was reserved for Bantam Books), Murdock offered *Stern* $750,000 for the serial rights for Britain and the Commonwealth, and $2.5 million for the American syndication rights—a total offer of $3.25 million. Hensmann was pleased. He told Murdoch he would give him an answer within forty-eight hours, no later than five o'clock Monday afternoon.

At the very moment Murdoch was negotiating for serial rights, the editors of *Newsweek* were examining the diaries. Later that night following his meeting with Murdoch, Jan Hensmann met with William Broyles, editor-in-chief, and Maynard Parker, managing editor, at *Newsweek*. After several rejected offers, Hensmann told the two men the price for serialization was $3 million.[34] Broyles and Parker said they would have to get back to Hensmann following their return to New York, where they would presumably go over the demand and decide whether or not to pay the asking price.

On Monday, April 11, the *Newsweek* team phoned Hensmann at Gruner & Jahr and agreed to the $3 million for serialization rights on the condition that the diaries were authentic. Hensmann was flying high. Having promised Murdoch he would call him by five o'clock Monday evening with his answer, Hensmann told Murdoch the deal was off. *Newsweek* had topped his offer by $500,000 for the American rights. If Murdoch wanted the American rights he would have to raise his offer by that amount to stay in the game. Murdoch exploded! He thought he had a deal when he and Hensmann shook hands on Friday afternoon on Murdoch's total package of $3.25 million.

Ever the cunning negotiator, Rupert Murdoch got hold of the people at *Newsweek* and made them an interesting offer, to say the least. Instead of allowing Gruner & Jahr to pit the two organizations against one another, why not join together and make a joint offer, splitting the costs and the diaries. The details could be hammered out later. *Newsweek* agreed, and the new consortium arrived at Gruner & Jahr's headquarters, where its chief executive officer, Schulte-Hillen, took over the meeting. Stunned to find the two former competing groups now allied, the *Stern* and Gruner & Jahr people were crestfallen. They assumed the combined $3.75 million deal was off the table and that the new offer would be substantially lower. To their surprise, the original offer was still acceptable, $3.75 million. The members seated around the table were stunned once again when Schulte-Hillen decided to try and outsmart Rupert Murdoch. "We no longer think that is enough. We want $4.25 million."[35] As if prearranged, Murdoch and his entourage, followed by the *Newsweek* team, got up from their seats and silently filed out of the room. The deal was dead. All negotiations were over. Schulte-Hillen had overplayed his hand with the master and his bluff cost him dearly. The teams from Gruner & Jahr and *Stern* were left in stunned silence. Greed had killed the goose along with her golden egg.

The people at *Stern* now had two major problems, both exceedingly bad. They had lost the two top clients for syndication rights and they had given *Newsweek* copies of several documents along with copies of the first four articles that *Stern* planned to run. *Newsweek* was under no legal obligation to maintain secrecy about the diary discovery or even the contents of the *Stern* articles. Even if *Stern* moved up its publication to the earliest possible date, *Newsweek* could break the story ahead of them by running an article in its next scheduled edition on Tuesday, April 26, 1983. *Stern* decided to break its normal publication date, scheduled for Thursday, April 28, and move it to Monday, April 25, beating *Newsweek* by one day and thereby regaining the initiative.

Negotiations had broken down on Friday, April 15, when Murdoch and *Newsweek* walked out following Schulte-Hillen's attempt to up the ante after the buyers thought they had a deal. For the next three days Schulte-Hillen had tried to reach Murdoch in an attempt to reopen negotiations. There was no one else big enough to pay the kind of money Murdoch and *Newsweek* could pay. Despite Schulte-Hillen's efforts, Murdoch refused to talk to him. On the fourth day, April 19, Murdoch agreed to meet and reopen negotiations—only this time on his terms. He dropped his offer of $750,000 for the British and Commonwealth rights to $400,000, and the American rights from $3 million to $800,000. Schulte-Hillen had no choice but to humbly accept Murdoch's offer. He had cost Gruner & Jahr and *Stern* $2.5 million by his arrogant attempt to shake down Murdoch.

Having settled with Murdoch on the mogul's terms, Gruner & Jahr would announce the discovery of the diaries on Friday, April 22, followed by publication of their first article on Monday, April 25. Murdoch would publish Trevor-Roper's article authenticating the diaries in the Saturday edition of the *Times,* followed by the first of several articles on the diaries in the *Sunday Times* of April 24. Trevor-Roper would write the lead story. He worked all day Thursday, April 21, on his article and handed it in to the *Times* on Friday, the 22nd. That evening he and his wife joined a group of Cambridge University colleagues in attending the Royal Opera at Covent Garden in London.[36] It would prove to be a disturbing night for the renowned historian. The more he thought about the diaries and the circumstances surrounding their discovery and "authentication," the more troubled he became. By the time he returned home it was too late to withdraw his article. The presses were already running.

All the while that Trevor-Roper was skillfully weaving his qualified endorsement of the diaries, Dr. Arnold Rentz, a forensic chemist, was working overtime analyzing three sheets of blank paper removed from two of the diaries and handed to him by Dr. Josef Henke of the Bundesarchiv along with a telegram allegedly sent by Hitler to the Italian dictator Mussolini. At long last someone was doing forensic analyses on the diaries other than handwriting and content analysis. Rentz determined that the pages did not contain the special whitening substance used in the manufacture of paper after World War II, but that the telegram did contain a whitening substance and was created post-1945, and was therefore a forgery. The editors at *Stern* were troubled by the results of Rentz's tests. Peter Koch, the senior editor, was afraid that any question involving the authenticity of any of the documents in Heidemann's possession equally cast doubt on the diaries' authenticity. *Stern* was hours away from holding a press conference announcing the discovery of the Hitler diaries and their publication. Koch raised his concerns with Schulte-Hillen, asking him to get Heidemann to reveal the source of the diaries and confirm their origin. Heidemann refused, standing by his original claim that revealing his source would jeopardize the lives of people in East Germany who were involved in smuggling the documents to him. In his concern, Heidemann may well have believed his position. Schulte-Hillen was satisfied that Heidemann was telling the truth and that the diaries were authentic. Besides, there was the endorsement of the genuineness of the diaries by one of the leading historians of the Nazi era, Trevor-Roper. Unfortunately, no one at *Stern* or Gruner & Jahr was aware that Trevor-Roper was having second thoughts about his endorsement.

Enter David Irving. Irving was a World War II historian of considerable controversy. Recognized by his peers as an excellent discoverer of doc-

Controversial World War II historian David Irving challenged the authenticity of the diaries from the beginning, only to reverse himself a few days before forensic analysis proved they were fake. (*Searchlight*)

uments, Irving was something of a pariah for his views of Hitler and the Holocaust. His sympathetic view of Hitler and his conclusion that the Holocaust never happened the way leading historians wrote about it in their books left Irving outside the circle of World War II scholars. While biased in his ideology, he was, nevertheless, respected by many of his colleagues as a research historian. While they recognized that he got his facts right, it was his conclusions that were wrong.[37] On learning of the diaries, Irving began a persistent search for copies, as well as for copies of other Hitler documents that appeared to have come from the same source before making their way into the collections of certain Nazi memorabilia collectors. He acquired copies of several documents from collectors along with several pages from the diary that Kujau had given to Fritz Stiefel. From the very beginning, there was no doubt in Irving's mind that the documents were forgeries. Upon learning that *Stern* was holding a press conference on Friday, April 22, announcing the diaries' discovery, and that they were publishing the first installment in a special issue of the magazine on Mon-

Stern reporter Gerd Heidemann (right) holding some of the alleged Hitler diaries at the April 22, 1983, press conference. Peter Koch, editor of *Stern* (left), watches along with the head of the magazine's history section, Thomas Walde (center). (DPA)

day, April 25, Irving began a series of interviews with several media publications stating his opinion that the diaries were forgeries. One of the West German newspapers, *Bild Zeitung,* offered to pay Irving a fee if he would attend the upcoming press conference and confront the *Stern* spokesmen with his claim that the diaries were forged. Irving gladly accepted. It was just the sort of controversy that he seemed to thrive on. Thanks to several of *Stern*'s competitors, Irving would quickly emerge as the chief critic of the magazine's claim that the diaries were authentic.

Friday morning arrived to find the basement canteen at *Stern* headquarters packed with journalists representing the media from around the world. More than two hundred journalists and twenty-seven television crews packed the room.[38] *Stern*'s pending announcement was clearly major news. No sooner had the press conference begun than it started to collapse in a shambles. Were the diaries authentic? Was it a trick to rehabilitate Hitler, or perhaps promulgated by the East German government to embarrass the West Germans and raise badly needed hard currency by selling the bogus diaries for large sums of West German marks?[39] *Stern* officials grimaced as embarrassing questions came from every section of the room.

To uphold the authenticity of the diaries, *Stern* turned to its top gun, Lord Dacre, Hugh Trevor-Roper, sitting quietly at the front of the room. Unfortunately for *Stern*, the Oxford don was having even greater second thoughts. He had been lied to by *Stern*'s editor Peter Koch, who told him that he knew the source of the diaries, and he had no doubt as to their authenticity. By the morning of the press conference Trevor-Roper had heard of up to three different sources for the diaries. Which was the correct one? The source, according to the famous historian, was linked to the diaries' authenticity.[40] When a reporter asked him his opinion on the diaries' authenticity, he said, "the link between the airplane and the documents is not absolutely established."[41] Not a very convincing answer. Immediately after the press conference he was asked again about the diaries' authenticity. He replied, "I am not saying they are not genuine. I am saying they cannot be pronounced genuine."[42] It was a subtle distinction that only scholars could understand. The subtlety escaped the reporters. Why a renowned historian should place such reliance on the source of the diaries was a mystery to them. Surely Trevor-Roper was sufficiently familiar with the methodology of historical research that it mattered little where the diaries came from. Their source, so important to Trevor-Roper, was of far less importance than their content. Gerhard Weinberg hit the nail squarely on the head: "The authority of these documents does not depend on a name of someone who tossed these things over a wall or sneaked them out [of East Berlin] on a subway . . . what matters is the documents themselves."[43] Indeed. A simple reading of any of the diaries would have uncovered any number of inconsistencies and errors that should have led any examiner to question their authenticity.

Stern officials held fast. They were unflinching in their resolve that the diaries were authentic despite their prize historian's sudden wavering. After all, they pointed out, three leading handwriting experts concluded that Hitler was the author. Peter Koch told the audience, "I am a hundred percent convinced that Hitler wrote every single word in those books," pointing to the stack of journals on the table in front of him and his colleagues.[44]

Stern's position was further eroded by historian David Irving, who had shown up on behalf of *Der Bild* to challenge the *Stern* claims. Midway through the press conference Irving grabbed the microphone and

British historian and World War II scholar Hugh Trevor-Roper (left) and *Stern* editor Peter Koch (right) during the press conference in Hamburg, Germany, on April 22, 1983, declaring the Hitler diaries to be authentic. (DPA)

unleashed an attack on the diaries. How, Irving demanded, could Hitler have written the entry on the day (and the day after) the July bomb plot to kill him when his right arm and hand were so badly injured that he had to shake hands with his left hand?[45] Irving went on to point out that the diaries were part of a larger collection of documents containing numerous forgeries.[46] Irving stole the show, including the post-press conference meeting where he was surrounded by reporters and television cameras. He had rehabilitated his damaged reputation of being pro-Nazi, and was once again viewed as a reputable historian.

Once the walls began to crumble around the Hitler diaries the house of *Stern* quickly collapsed. The number of experts commenting on the diaries was clearly shifting to the side of their being forgeries. *Stern,* undeterred although shaken, went ahead with publication. The fact remained that whether authentic or fake, publication of the diary excerpts increased *Stern* sales tremendously. The people at *Stern* must have made a deliberate decision that it didn't matter if the diaries were fake or real, sales would skyrocket. The reading public did not seem to care about authenticity. They did not let the facts get in the way of a good story. Rupert Murdoch summed it up best when he told one of his editors who questioned the decision to go ahead and publish in light of the forgery claims, "After all, we are in the entertainment business. . . . Circulation went up and it stayed up. We didn't lose money or anything like that."[47] Circulation for Murdoch's *Sunday Times* and Gruner & Jahr's *Stern* did go up, and stayed up after the dust finally settled. This is a phenomenon that one sees in most hoaxes and fabrications: they sell, and even after being exposed as fake they continue to sell, which is certainly one of the major reasons they continue to be manufactured. Truth may be stranger than fiction, but it is not nearly as titillating, nor as profitable.

The people at Gruner & Jahr and *Stern* had a new problem to worry about as a result of the challenge to the diaries' authenticity. One of *Stern*'s attorneys expressed concern that the editors faced possible prosecution for "disseminating Nazi propaganda" should the diaries prove to be forged.[48] If proved authentic, the editors could hide behind the shield of disseminating historical information. If forged, however, that protection would vanish, leaving the people at *Stern* vulnerable. This strange situation resulted from the laws passed by the West German government following World War II in an effort to distance the new government from the Nazi Party and Adolf Hitler, and to blunt a neo-Nazi reformation. Under these new laws, wearing Nazi uniforms or displaying the swastika can carry a penalty of up to three years in prison. The law prohibits the display of a swastika in any form or fashion, even if used satirically or as part of an anti-Nazi political statement. More importantly, any publication that promotes in any manner Nazi propaganda is unlawful and the author is subject to prosecution and fines and/or imprisonment if found guilty. The editors of *Stern* were subject to accusations of promoting a sympathetic view of Hitler by publishing excerpts from the diaries if they turned out to be forged and if the editors at *Stern* were aware of the fraud.

One of *Stern*'s lead lawyers, Herr Hagen, decided that *Stern* should seek a definitive analysis of the diaries to determine beyond a shadow of a doubt whether they were authentic or not. At Hagen's urging, *Stern* turned over three of the diaries, including the "Hess diary," to the Bundesarchiv for analysis. Previously, the Bundesarchiv had been given only select samples from the collection of documents acquired by Heidemann for *Stern*. The Bundesarchiv turned the three diaries over to the Federal Institute for Forensic Investigation, located in West Berlin.[49] The scientists at the insti-

Stern magazine, in which the story of the diaries first appeared. (Author's collection)

tute conducted a wide range of tests, not just handwriting analysis. Within a week *Stern* had an answer. The diaries were bogus. The institute concluded that the paper contained a whitener not available until after 1955 as well as traces of synthetic polyester produced after 1953. Still unconvinced, the people at *Stern* tried to find evidence that would explain the scientists' findings without compromising the authenticity of the diaries. Like Hitler in his bunker, the people at *Stern* continued to deny the obvious. Victory was still possible. They delivered four more diaries to the Bundesarchiv for analysis of their content while delivering eleven diaries to a Swiss lab for forensic analysis. While this was taking place, Peter Koch traveled to the United States, where he undertook a tour attempting to shore up the rapidly sinking diaries.

On May 6, Hagen visited the director at the Bundesarchiv, Hans Booms, to get a full report. Booms had bad news for the *Stern* attorney. The results of various tests were completed and confirmed earlier results. The paper was of poor quality made from wood pulp and contained a chemical whitener manufactured after 1955. The cords adorning the cover of several diaries contained synthetic polyester and viscose fibers manufactured after the war. The most damaging findings related to the ink that was used in writing the diaries. By measuring the amount of chlorine in the ink the scientists were able to determine that the ink used in the "Hess diary" was only two years old while that used in the 1945-dated diary was less than twelve months old. Significant errors were also found in the content of several of the diaries. Historians at the Bundesarchiv determined that the content closely followed the wording found in a compilation of Hitler's speeches and proclamations edited by Max Domarus.[50] Where nothing occurred on a given day as reported by Domarus, nothing appeared in the diaries. Where Domarus recorded an error, it was reproduced in the diaries. The most glaring error in one of the diaries that was copied from Domarus was a telegram from General Ritter von Epp to Hitler congratulating him on the fiftieth anniversary of his enlistment in the German army. The telegram was actually sent by Hitler to von Epp rather than the other way around.[51] Kujau had it reversed.

At the same time that the Bundesarchiv was overseeing an analysis of the diaries at Hagen's request on behalf of *Stern,* Kenneth Rendell, an American documents dealer and forensic expert, was undertaking an analysis of two of the diaries on behalf of *Newsweek* magazine.[52] The editors at *Newsweek,* along with Rupert Murdoch, were still interested in buying the rights to publish excerpts from some of the diaries under an arrangement whereby *Newsweek* and Murdoch would agree on which diaries would be divided between them. Before closing the deal, *Newsweek* wisely sought the opinion of Rendell as to the diaries' authenticity.

Rendell had bought and sold hundreds of Hitler documents. He was given two diaries to examine, the diary allegedly written in 1932 and the diary for 1945. The diaries covered the beginning and end of the Third Reich. In preparation for his examination Rendell gathered nearly a hundred authentic examples of Hitler's writing. Rendell went about his examination in a methodical way, looking at three areas for telltale signs of forgery. He examined the handwriting characteristics, reviewed the content of the documents, and performed chemical tests on the materials. The diaries failed all three in Rendell's opinion. In his examination of the handwriting Rendell first photocopied twenty-two pages from the 1932 diary. From those copies he carefully cut out all of the capital letters and pasted them on a separate sheet of paper. In all, he collected twenty-one different capital letters. He repeated the exercise using photocopies of authentic documents for his samples of capital letters. Comparing the two collections, he found several glaring differences. The three most glaring were found with the letters "E," "H," and "K." He also noted that the crossbar on the "f" of Hitler's abbreviated signature differed between the signatures in the diaries and the ones on the authentic documents. In the authentic signature the crossbar slanted down from left to right while the signature in the diaries was horizontal *in every instance.*[53]

Rendell showed his evidence to Peter Koch, who finally was realizing that the diaries were a forgery. According to Rendell, Koch was "stunned." Koch could not understand how the three experts hired by *Stern* could have concluded the diaries were authentic. Rendell pointed out to Koch that the three experts were given forged materials to use as a standard for their analysis that they were told were authentic. In several instances they were comparing the forged diary pages with forged documents, all written by Konrad Kujau. However, not all of the documents given to the experts were forged. They were given several authentic documents provided by the Bundesarchiv. Had they been careful they should have detected significant differences.

When it is all said and done, handwriting analysis remains a subjective form of examination. It is not absolute, and errors are common in examining documents. Rendell, for example, failed to identify the "Salamander Letter" and the poem by Emily Dickinson as forgeries, albeit by the king of forgers, Mark Hofmann. It is in the forensic analyses where one finds objective results. For instance, the presence of chemicals not available un-til after the war, the chemical composition of the ink, and the presence of synthetic fibers in the cords all show that the diaries were postwar or after Hitler died. These types of analyses do not require opinion or guesswork. The third conclusive piece of evidence was in the content of the diaries. Re-peated errors throughout the diaries as to people and dates were conclusive in showing the diaries to be fake.

Back at the Bundesarchiv, Hagen learned that the results of the tests were being passed along to Friedrich Zimmermann, the Minister of the In-terior, who was going to hold a press conference within the hour announc-ing that the diaries were forgeries. Zimmermann told the press gathering, "The Federal Archive [Bundesarchiv] is convinced that the documents do not come from Hitler's hand but were produced after the war."[54] The peo-ple at *Stern* now had the word from two separate authoritative sources, Kenneth Rendell and the Bundesarchiv, that the diaries were forged. They quickly held a meeting to decide their course of action in light of the di-sastrous news.

With the exposure of the diaries (and many of the documents sur-rounding them) as forgeries, the remaining questions revolved around who at *Stern* would take the fall for the fiasco. It was decided rather quickly that management was not at fault, but merely persuaded to go along with the story by the editorial staff. Manfred Fischer, the managing director of Bertelsmann, the parent company, who enthusiastically endorsed the proj-ect, overruling editors Nannen and Koch, had left Bertelsmann earlier in the year to become the head of Dornier Aircraft Corporation. He was no longer the company's problem. Gerd Schulte-Hillen, managing director of Gruner & Jahr, *Stern*'s publisher, who supported Heidemann and his ob-sessive belief in the diaries' authenticity, submitted his resignation, but it was turned down by Reinhard Mohn, the majority owner of Bertelsmann. All apparently agreed that responsibility for the fiasco resided with the edi-tors of *Stern,* Henri Nannen, Peter Koch, and Felix Schmidt. It seems ironic in hindsight since both Nannen and Koch opposed Heidemann's efforts early on and ordered him to stop fooling around with SS and Nazi stories. At first it was Heidemann and Thomas Walde, head of the history sec-tion at *Stern,* who went over Nannen and Koch. Nannen was already semi-retired and therefore buffered from management's efforts to place blame. Schmidt and Koch became the principal scapegoats, with the major part of the disaster falling on their shoulders. They finally agreed to a settlement with *Stern* for approximately $1 million each to go away and keep quiet.

Time magazine joined *Newsweek* in exposing the Hitler diaries as forgeries. (Author's collection)

Newsweek magazine declared the diaries to be forgeries in its May 16, 1983, issue. (Author's collection)

Gerd Heidemann and Konrad Kujau were a different story. Heidemann still believed Kujau had received the diaries from an East German source. He did not yet believe that Kujau was the forger. Heidemann retreated to his apartment, while Kujau fled to Austria, hoping the whole affair would blow over, missing him somehow. Both men were still living in a fantasy world. Kujau was watching television one evening when a photograph of him was shown on the screen identifying him as the forger of the diaries supplied to Heidemann. The announcer then shocked Kujau by stating that *Stern* had paid a grand total of over 9 million marks for the sixty-two diaries. Kujau was outraged. Heidemann had paid him less than a third of that amount, apparently pocketing over 6 million marks. It was ironic that Kujau, the master deceiver, was outraged at being deceived. There was truly no honor among thieves. Kujau contacted his lawyer in Stuttgart, who told him it was best if he came home and turned himself in to the authorities who were looking for him.

On May 13, the police visited Kujau's home and began searching through his belongings when the phone rang. It was Kujau calling home. When Kujau learned the man on the other end was the Hamburg prosecutor, he agreed to turn himself in voluntarily. During his interrogation Kujau continued to lie about his role in the diary fiasco. He was just the middleman, he said. It was preposterous to think he had forged sixty-two diaries, let alone hundreds of documents and paintings. Even Heidemann believed Kujau lacked the talent and skill to forge so much and get away with it for so long. But such views frequently help forgers deceive their victims. Kujau was a pathological liar and good at it. When Heidemann learned that the police believed Kujau was the forger, he still refused to believe it. Heidemann believed that if Kujau did produce the diaries, then he must have done nothing more than copy them from the original diaries, which were still out there somewhere. In the end, both men would go to jail, convicted of creating and carrying out one of the greatest—and most expensive—hoaxes in history.

But not everyone believed Kujau was the originator of the diaries. A variety of theories sprang up, reminiscent of the UFO and 9/11 conspiracies that still exist today. The Russians claimed it was all an American CIA plot to glorify the Third Reich. Kujau was nothing more than an American stooge.[55] Henri Nannen came to the conclusion that the diaries were created by East German intelligence agents and "smuggled" into West Germany in an effort to destabilize the democratic government. Others claimed the East Germans created the diaries as a way of supporting the neo-Nazi groups in the West to further damage the Federal Republic. And the *Sunday Times* ventured a guess that the diaries were actually an effort to raise hard capital for the HIAG, an organization supporting former Nazi SS men who lost their pensions.[56] All of these conspiracy theories had believable aspects to them. For most conspiracy-minded advocates, these theories will continue to thrive no matter how much evidence is produced to the contrary. In the end, the diary fiasco proves that Hitler sells, a fact of which every publisher is very well aware.

In his defense, Heidemann lashed out at the editors of *Stern*: "It was the job of the magazine to check the authenticity [of the diaries]. I am no Hitler researcher. I never said, 'Don't examine the notebooks.' I limited myself to supplying them." Heidemann had a point. How could *Stern*, or Gruner & Jahr, go ahead and publish without undertaking a thorough examination of the diaries to ensure their authenticity? They had only themselves to blame. It did little good.

Both Heidemann and Kujau were charged with fraud and placed on trial. The two defendants could not have been more different on the witness stand if they had rehearsed their roles. Kujau was an instant hit. Jocular, witty, seemingly indifferent to his situation, he readily acknowledged his culpability in forging the diaries and the rest of the large archive of paintings and documents that found their way into major collections. He even drafted a document giving the prosecutor a promotion for doing an excellent job and signed it, "A. Hitler." Kujau became the darling of the public for having fooled the major publishing corporations and experts. The people loved him. Heidemann was just the opposite. Withdrawn and morose, he suffered from depression. He tried to defend himself from Kujau's accusations that he knew all along that the diaries were forgeries. The longer Heidemann testified, the crazier he sounded—claiming that Martin Bormann was still alive, that he had purchased an unknown diary by Hitler containing an account by the führer that Jesus Christ did not die on the cross but was later resuscitated by his disciples only to die years later of natural causes. When asked about this strange account Heidemann testified, "Until that moment I was a faithful Catholic. Now I am utterly confused."[57]

The trial lasted ten months and heard thirty-seven witnesses. Heidemann's defense was simple: he believed the diaries were authentic. As to what happened to the difference between the money *Stern* gave to Heidemann and the actual amount Heidemann paid Kujau, nothing was ever proven. Over six million marks (approximately $1,800,000) went unaccounted for. Heidemann maintained he gave all of the money to Kujau. No

Konrad Kujau (right) surrounded by photographers and journalists in July 1985. His lawyer, Eric Groenewoldt, is to the left. (DPA)

one in the courtroom believed him, and if he would lie about his skimming millions of marks for himself he would also lie about his part in the whole fiasco. Found guilty, Heidemann was sentenced to four years and eight months in prison; Kujau received four years and six months. Not charged, and therefore not judged, were the executives of *Stern* and Gruner & Jahr. The judge unleashed a scathing rebuke of both companies, accusing them of caring nothing about the diaries' authenticity, caring only about boosting their circulation. *Stern,* he said, "was virtually an accomplice in the fraud."[58]

On his release from prison, Konrad Kujau picked up where he left off, forging paintings and documents of famous artists and persons, only this time telling his clients that what they were buying was an "authentic forgery" by the famous Kujau. His forgeries became highly desirable collectibles, so much so that forgers began making forgeries of Kujau's forgeries and selling them as authentic Kujau forgeries.[59] In 1996 he ran for the office of mayor of Stuttgart and received just over nine hundred votes. He died four years later, at the age of sixty-two, from stomach cancer.

Heidemann fared better than Kujau, thanks to something the forger later said. While serving his sentence, Kujau told a reporter it was Heidemann who had affixed the wax seal emblem of the Third Reich and the modern cord to several of the diaries. Kujau claimed Heidemann did it after he had purchased the diaries and before he turned them over to *Stern*. Kujau maintained he would never have been so stupid as to use a modern cord and the symbol of an infantry corps as that of the Third Reich. Kujau's mistake here was in the fact that one of his major clients, Fritz Stiefel, owned several documents that bore the exact same symbol as that found on the diaries. Heidemann never had any of these Stiefel documents in his hands, had never seen them, had never even been aware of them. The judge, on reading Kujau's account, realized the forger was lying and, in reviewing the evidence against Heidemann given by Kujau, decided to commute Heidemann's sentence and ordered his release from prison on September 21, 1983, four months into his four-year sentence. Heidemann, age seventy-eight in 2011, lives in a small apartment, a pensioner on a social security payment of approximately $500 a month.[60] He is divorced; his son died of AIDS and his daughter moved to Australia to begin a new life away from any memory of the Hitler diaries scandal.

Everything about this sordid episode was wrong. As in the case of most frauds, success was dependent on the willingness and desire of the victims to want to believe. The experts' opinions were shaded by that old maxim, "Tell me what you want to believe and I will tell you what you will believe." The editors put their journalistic ethics aside for the sake of making money, lots of money. Even when the diaries' authenticity was crumbling, circulation was increasing dramatically. Red flags appeared all over the landscape of these diaries even before the forensic tests were completed. The cheap quality of the books themselves, the phony wax seal, the red cord affixed to some of the diaries, and the gross errors in content were dead giveaways that the diaries were fakes. But the lure of fame and money overpowered the participants. Rupert Murdoch hit the nail squarely on the head when he said, "After all, we are in the entertainment business. . . . Circulation went up and it stayed up. We didn't lose money or anything like that."[61]

Suggested Reading

Hamilton, Charles. *The Hitler Diaries: Fakes That Fooled the World.* Lexington: Univ. Press of Kentucky, 1991.

Harris, Robert. *Selling Hitler: The Story of the Hitler Diaries.* London: Faber and Faber, 1986.

Hitler, Adolf. *Hitler's Table Talk, 1941–1944: His Private Conversations.* 1953. Reprint, New York: Enigma Books, 2008.

Rendell, Kenneth. "Cracking the Case." *Newsweek,* May 16, 1983, 58–59.

———. "The Hitler Diaries: Bad Forgeries but a Great Hoax." In *Forging History: The Detection of Fake Letters and Documents,* 106–123. Norman: Univ. of Oklahoma Press, 1994.

4

The Shroud of Turin

Tell Me What You Want to Believe and I Will Tell What You Will Believe

Then took they the body of Jesus, and wound it in linen clothes with the spices, as the manner of the Jews is to bury.

—John 19:40

To believers, the Shroud of Turin is the authentic burial cloth that covered the body of Jesus Christ following his crucifixion prior to his resurrection. To skeptics the shroud is a man-made object created in the fourteenth century by a medieval painter as a religious icon to attract pilgrims and their money. The shroud first came to light in 1357 and passed through several hands and places before ending up in the royal chapel of the Cathedral of Saint John the Baptist in Turin, Italy, where it is preserved today. Once privately owned, it is now the property of the Roman Catholic Church, which oversees its care, and its public display on rare occasions.

Controversy has followed the shroud since it first appeared in the mid-fourteenth century and continues to the present. One would think that modern science with all of its sophisticated technology could settle the controversy beyond a reasonable doubt. Unfortunately, as in the case of evolution, the controversy continues in spite of the science. In fact, as with evolution, it is science that comes under attack, not the shroud, whenever the authenticity of the relic is questioned. At times one wonders if it is worthwhile to devote so much effort to determine the true nature of the

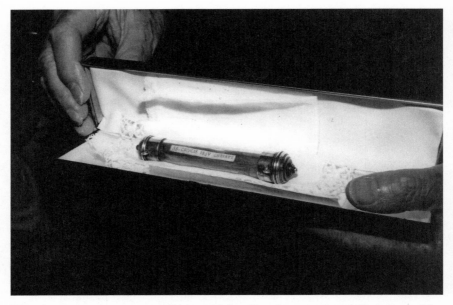

This glass tube protects a small piece of the alleged true cross of Christ's crucifixion, carried to the Maryland colony by Father Andrew White aboard the *Ark and Dove* in 1634. The relic resides in St. Ignatius Church in Port Tobacco, Charles County, Maryland. (Photograph by the author)

shroud since no amount of evidence has changed opinions on either side of the controversy.

It is not surprising that of all the revered relics from time immemorial the most treasured are those of a religious nature. Religious relics of the most extraordinary kind abound throughout Christendom, ranging from Christ's foreskin (carefully preserved following his circumcision), to his mother's breast milk, to pieces of the cross on which he was crucified, to the nails that held him to the cross, to a thorn removed from the mock crown placed on his head by Roman soldiers, to the spear that pierced his side, to blood collected from the wound caused by the spear, to the *Titulus Crucis* or plaque placed on the cross bearing the inscription "King of the Jews." Joe Nickell, Senior Research Fellow of the Committee for Skeptical Inquiry, expertly describes these relics, and many others, in his book *Relics of the Christ*.[1]

Of all of the religious relics that exist today, none are more sacred or more revered than the Shroud of Turin. While most of the relics mentioned above are treated with considerable skepticism by even devout Christians, the Shroud of Turin is embraced as genuine. Considered the holy of holies, the shroud is a piece of linen cloth approximately fourteen feet in length by four feet in width. Its most important feature is the image of a man, believed to be that of Christ. The image depicts a man carefully posed with his hands folded in front of him covering his genital area. The image depicts both the front and the back of the man along with traces of what appears to be blood emanating from wounds on the head (presumably from a crown of thorns), the right side (caused by a Roman spear), wrists and ankles (from nails), and on the upper back (presumably caused by scourging). The cause of the image is unknown, but many of those who believe the shroud to be authentic explain it as being the result of a sudden burst of energy released at the moment of resurrection. Other believers reject this theory, simply stating that various tests have failed to reveal the source of the image. To nonbelievers the image is a clever painting, the product of a medieval artist.

What is the history of this interesting piece of cloth? When did it first appear, and where did it come from? As mentioned above, the first recorded description of the cloth occurred in 1357, when a man by the name of Geoffroy de Charney presented the cloth to the dean of the church in Lirey, France. De Charney claimed the cloth was the burial shroud of Christ, but left no information as to its history between Christ's death around 30 A.D. and its first appearance in 1357. If authentic, the shroud escaped recognition for over thirteen hundred years. This in itself is troublesome for an object so important to Christianity.

The shroud was put on public display for the first time in 1357. It immediately began to draw large crowds of people, including pilgrims who journeyed from all over Europe to witness the relic. Certain members of the church hierarchy at the time, however, were skeptical of the shroud's authenticity. Their skepticism resulted from the fact that no mention of the exceptional shroud appears anywhere in the Bible, nor can its existence be accounted for prior to its appearance in 1357. In response to the clergy's skepticism an investigation was ordered by the bishop of Troyes, Henri de Poitiers. In 1389, the bishop's successor, Pierre d'Arcis prepared a report of the findings of the investigation, which he forwarded to Pope Clement VII. In the report d'Arcis claimed the shroud was not the shroud of Christ, and that the image on the shroud was a clever painting. D'Arcis further reported that the dean of the church in Lirey knew the shroud was not authentic yet used it to raise funds from the many pilgrims who visited his

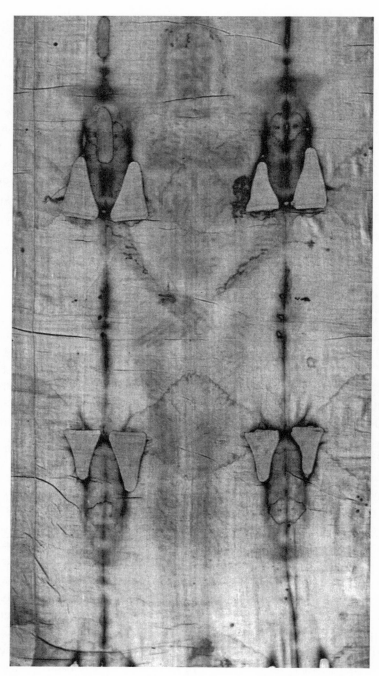

The Shroud of Turin showing a full frontal view. (Joe Nickell)

church. In further support of his findings, d'Arcis cited a predecessor who had located the artist, who confessed to painting the image. D'Arcis wrote: "the said cloth had been cunningly painted, the truth being attested by the artist who painted it." D'Arcis accused the dean of "avarice" and of "falsely declaring and pretending that this was the actual shroud in which our Saviour Jesus Christ was enfolded in the tomb."[2] One would think that the story of the shroud would have ended with Bishop d'Arcis's report and that the cloth would have faded away, being only an icon rather than a relic. But the story was only just beginning, as was the controversy.

In spite of d'Arcis's findings, Geoffroy de Charney and the dean of the Lirey church continued to display the shroud as a moneymaking device. Determined to put an end to what he considered a fraud on the people and the Church, d'Arcis went to King Charles VI with his evidence. Convinced by d'Arcis's evidence, Charles ordered the shroud seized. De Charney and the dean, however, ignored the order and continued to display the shroud. Undeterred, d'Arcis went to Pope Clement VII and pleaded his case. Hearing d'Arcis's evidence, the pope, like Charles, was convinced the shroud was not authentic. Rather than order the shroud removed from display, however, Clement allowed de Charney and the dean to continue to display it with the proviso they announce to all that the shroud was not the burial cloth of Christ, but merely a painting—that is, a religious icon. Its use was solely as an object to aid pilgrims and the pious in their meditations on the passion of Christ. The year was 1390. Despite the official order that the shroud was not the burial shroud of Christ, the public chose to believe it was authentic. It was far better to worship a false relic than a true icon. Here the matter ended, a stalemate between de Charney and d'Arcis.

Twenty-eight years later, in 1418, the Hundred Years' War raged in the region around Lirey, threatening the safety of the shroud. The granddaughter of Geoffroy de Charney, Margaret de Charney, sought permission from the church authorities to remove the shroud to her family's castle for safekeeping. Permission was granted by the canons of the church with the proviso that it would be returned on the war's end. Not surprisingly, Margaret refused to return the shroud to the church canons at war's end as promised, thereby becoming the owner of the shroud by little more than theft. Secure in her possession, Margaret took the shroud on tour, claiming it to be the authentic burial shroud of Christ. In 1453, apparently tiring of the shroud, and perhaps believing that it was a fabrication, Margaret de Charney sold it to Duke Louis I of the Italian House of Savoy.[3]

Angered by Margaret's actions, the canons of the Lirey church in

Cathedral of St. John the Baptist, located in Turin, Italy. The Shroud of Turin is housed in this church. (Photograph by Joe Nickell)

France continued their fight to recover the shroud, claiming to be the rightful owners. After several attempts, including appeals to Duke Louis to return the shroud, Louis agreed to pay the canons of Lirey fifty gold francs a year as compensation for the annual revenue lost to them by the shroud's absence. These payments continued until Louis's death in 1465. Following his death the shroud passed to his son, Amadeus IX, who requested permission from Pope Sixtus IV for construction of a special sanctuary to house the shroud. Sixtus granted Amadeus's request, and in 1502 the Sainte Chapelle of the Holy Shroud accepted the relic, where it remained until its transfer to Turin, Italy, on September 14, 1578. Today the shroud resides in the royal chapel of the Cathedral of Saint John the Baptist in Turin. The shroud, now known throughout the world as the Shroud of Turin, remained in the royal chapel from 1578 until the present except for six years during the Second World War (1939–1945), when it was removed to the Abbey of Montevergine in southern Italy for safekeeping.

While housed in the Sainte Chapelle, the shroud was nearly lost to fire in 1532 when the chapel burned. Kept locked in a silver reliquary, the fire melted part of the box's silver lining, which fell onto the folded shroud, burning holes through a part of the cloth and leaving burn marks. The shroud was rescued from the reliquary and doused with water, causing additional stains, which are still obvious today.

During the periods in which the shroud was housed in Sainte Chapelle and Turin it was placed on public display at irregular intervals, drawing large crowds of worshipers. Throughout this period the Church was always careful not to endorse the shroud as authentic, although it continued to be accepted by most of the public as Christ's burial cloth. In 1670, when the shroud was placed on display in Rome, a committee overseeing the event on behalf of the Church stated that the display was "not for venerating the cloth as the true Shroud of Christ, but rather for meditating on his Passion, especially his death and burial."[4] The Church considered the shroud a man-made object whose purpose was to help those who viewed it in their pious meditation on Christ's crucifixion.

The on-again, off-again history of the shroud's authenticity has accompanied it for all of its nearly seven hundred years of known existence. What makes the shroud different from the dozens of relics of Jesus Christ is the number of seemingly qualified experts who have examined it and judged it to be authentic. The list consists of a broad class of society, from religious leaders of mainstream theocracy to scientists to those who believe in the supernatural. All areas of society are among those who publicly profess a belief in the authenticity of this unusual relic.

The Shroud of Turin is not the only such cloth claimed to be the true burial shroud of Christ. There are as many as forty-three burial cloths claiming to be the true shroud, the earliest dating to 1098 A.D.[5] What distinguishes the Shroud of Turin from all of the other pretenders to Christ's burial shroud is the presence of an image of a man on the cloth. The image fits all of the accepted characteristics of a crucified individual and includes the facial image of what many people believe is the face of Jesus Christ. The image is accompanied by samples of blood appropriately located at positions on the image that correspond to the crucifixion wounds described in the Bible. This image, with its alleged bloodstains, is the principal evidence of those who maintain the authenticity of the shroud.

The cloth itself consists of a single piece of linen made from the flax plant. Unusual in its large size, the shroud measures fourteen feet, four inches by three feet, eight inches. Also unusual—if not unique—for the period of Christ's death is the weave pattern of the yarn in a special three-to-one herringbone twill pattern, giving the surface of the cloth a stylized appearance of diagonal lines running through the fabric. Both the twill pattern and the large size make the cloth unique for the period and region where Christ lived and died.

If the cloth is indeed the burial shroud of Christ, it should conform to the standard practices of first-century Jews in treating their dead. After all, Jesus was a devout Jew, as were the people who prepared his body following his death. The earliest writing on the subject of Christ's death and burial preparation comes from the Gospel According to St. John. This particular Gospel is believed to have been written sometime between seventy-five and ninety years after the death of Christ.[6] The writer of the Gospel is anonymous, and while most scholars are in disagreement as to the actual author, the majority agree it was not John.[7] Regardless of who wrote the account of Christ's burial preparation or when it was written, it is accepted by religious scholars today as an accurate account based on knowledge of the events and practices among Jews at the time. Certainly it is accepted as an accurate account by most of the individuals who proclaim the shroud authentic, and therefore it serves as evidence in discussing the shroud that covered the body of Christ.

The following statement appears in John 19:38–42 and 20:1–7.

Chapter 19:

38 And after this Joseph of Arimathea, being a disciple of Jesus, but secretly for fear of the Jews, besot Pilate that he might take away the body of Jesus: and Pilate gave him leave, He came therefore, and took the body of Jesus.

39 And there came also Nicodemus, which at the first came to Jesus by night, and brought a mixture of myrrh and aloes, about an hundred pound weight.

40 Then took they the body of Jesus, and wound it in linen clothes with the spices, as the manner of the Jews is to bury.

41 Now in the place where he was crucified there was a garden; and in the garden a new sepulcher, wherein was never man yet laid.

42 There laid they Jesus therefore because of the Jews' preparation day; for the sepulcher was nigh at hand.

Chapter 20:

1 The first day of the week cometh Mary Magdalene early, when it was yet dark, unto the sepulcher, and seeth the stone taken away from the sepulcher.

2 Then she runneth, and cometh to Simon Peter, and to the other disciple, whom Jesus loved, and saith unto them, They have taken away the Lord out of the sepulcher, and we know not where they have laid him.

3 Peter therefore went forth, and that other disciple, and came to the sepulcher.

4 So they ran both together; and the other disciple did outrun Peter, and came first to the sepulcher.

5 And he stooping down and looking in, *saw the linen clothes* [emphasis added] lying; yet went he not in.

6 Then cometh Simon Peter following him, and went into the sepulcher, and seeth *the linen clothes* [emphasis added] lie.

7 And the napkin, that was about his head, not lying with the linen clothes, but wrapped together in a place by itself.[8]

This description contains a great deal of information relevant to the question of the shroud's authenticity. The Gospel confirms the cloth was linen, but refers to it in the plural, "clothes." It also refers to the "napkin," a cloth Jews traditionally placed over the face of the deceased (known as a "sudarium"). The Gospel also refers to "*as the manner of the Jews is to bury.*" Is the Gospel accurate? Or are we to take liberties in interpreting what the Gospel tells us? Did the Shroud consist of more than one cloth wrapping (clothes), as the Gospel of John states, or was it a single length of linen like the Shroud of Turin? Was there a "napkin" placed over Christ's face in addition to the shroud or is the Gospel mistaken? These questions all figure into the argument over the Shroud's authenticity. If we are to believe the Gospel, Christ's body was wrapped in linen clothes with a separate napkin placed over his face. While this was the standard practice of the Jews, it is not what the Shroud of Turin appears to depict. Christ's body was covered in several places with blood, suggesting that the body was not washed as tradition requires, and there was no separate napkin placed over his face, since a complete image of his face is clearly a part of the intact shroud. If a separate napkin or sudarium had been placed over Christ's face, as the Gospel states, it would have prevented the facial image from becoming a part of the shroud.

The most basic approach to an examination of the shroud must begin with the cloth itself. Everything else, from the "image" to other substances, such as blood, pigment, sweat, DNA, pollen, "dirt," etc., is problematic because its origin cannot be determined with any assurance. Any one of the substances, or all of the substances, associated with the shroud could have come at any time in the shroud's history. After all, the Shroud of Turin has been handled by hundreds of people over several centuries, and has even been used ceremonially at times in its early history. It is not unreasonable to believe that people held, kissed, even cried over the shroud. Sweat, tears, and saliva, even in trace amounts, surely touched the cloth at various times throughout its venerated history. That the shroud came in contact with biological material over the centuries seems a given fact. Therefore, the presence of material on the cloth is not definitive proof of its authenticity as the burial shroud of Jesus Christ. The most basic piece of evidence in the shroud's identity is the linen cloth itself. Any attempt to authenticate the shroud must begin with the linen fabric, its composition, and most importantly, its age.

The cloth is made from the fibers of the flax plant. Of the four natural fibers (cotton, flax, wool, and silk), flax is the oldest known fiber used by man, dating back some twelve thousand years, to around 10,000 B.C.[9] Flax is a straw-like plant (*Linum usitatissimum*) that is distributed widely throughout the world, including the Middle East and Europe. Archeological evidence has shown that the Neolithic lake dwellers (around 10,000 to 9,000 B.C.) of the late Stone Age constructed their fishnets from fibers of the flax plant. By 5,000 B.C. linen was widely in use by the Egyptians to wrap the mummified bodies of their nobility, giving rise to the earliest known burial shrouds made of linen.

The flax fiber, made up of cellulose polymers, is located in bundles or "basts" inside the woody stem of the flax plant. The fibers are collected by physically breaking the woody stems, thereby separating the fibers, which are then collected and combed before spinning into yarn. The process requires soaking the woody stems in water to facilitate the bacterial breakdown of the woody tissue, freeing the internal fibers in a process known as "retting." The woody stems normally contain between twenty and forty fiber bundles, arranged in a ring-like pattern, each yielding between two hundred and sixteen hundred primary fibers. The microscopic appearance of the primary fiber is characterized by transverse striations at regular intervals along the length of the fiber known as "nodes." The striations give the appearance of breaks in the fiber along its length, and are part of the normal growth of the fiber. The striated appearance makes for easy microscopic identification of the fiber since the other three naturally occurring fibers do not have this distinct feature.

Cotton represents the second oldest fabric associated with man, dat-

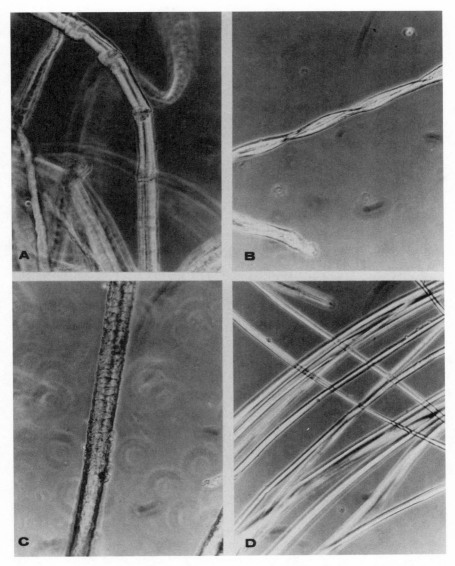

Photomicrographs of the four naturally occurring fibers: (A) flax, (B) cotton (note the helical twist), (C) wool, and (D) silk. (Photomicrographs by the author)

ing back six thousand years. Indigenous to warm climates, the cotton plant grows between two and six feet in height, with a growing season of eight to ten months. The plant consists of numerous pods that contain spidery fibers. Each fiber, which ranges in length from one to three inches, is the

Photomicrographs showing examples of basket weave of a fabric made from cotton yarn. (Photomicrographs by the author)

An example of twill weave pattern similar to that found in the Shroud of Turin. The example is from the strap to a Union soldier's canteen from 1861. (Photograph by the author)

growth of a single epithelial cell of the cottonseed. Like the flax fiber, the cotton fiber is made up of polymers of cellulose. Following elongation of the cotton fiber, additional layers of cellulose are laid down inside the hollow cell until the fiber is several layers thick. This thickening of the cotton fiber results in both the flattening of the fiber (oval shape in cross-section) and its growth producing twists or convolutions along its length, resulting in a spiral appearance. It is this spiral appearance that gives the cotton fiber its unique pattern when viewed microscopically, allowing for easy identification. Modern processing (beginning in the late 1800s), known as mercerization, includes heating the cotton fibers in strong alkali. This process results in removing the spiral twist of the fiber, resulting in a long, straight fiber, and gives the final product added strength and the resulting fabric a sheen. Removal of the spiral pattern by mercerization dates the fabric to the late nineteenth century and after.

Once fibers have been obtained and processed into thread or yarn they are made into cloth by weaving. There are three weaves that are basic to early cloth production because they may be carried out on a simple loom without the need for specialized equipment or elaborate manipulations of the loom. These three weaves are known as: plain (or basket), twill, and satin. Plain, or basket weave, is the simplest and most economical weave that can be produced on a loom. The fabric is produced by simply alternating the warp and weft yarns over and under one another, yielding a simple pattern of durable construction. It was the earliest weave developed by man and remained the dominant weave found throughout the first millennium.

In the case of twill weave, the weft or filling yarn interlaces two or more warp yarns. The obvious feature of this pattern is its overall diagonal ap-

Close-up view of the twill weave pattern of the shroud. The pattern would be unusual if not unique among fabric weaves found at the time of Jesus. (Joe Nickell)

pearance. The Shroud of Turin is woven in a twill pattern referred to as 3/1. It is an unusual pattern for linen cloth dating from the time of Christ—unusual because the pattern one finds from the period of Christ is the plain or basket weave. According to the theologian David Sox, former secretary of the British Society for the Turin Shroud, there are no known examples of the kind of weave we find in the shroud from the period in question. The weaves of all of the ancient Egyptian linens to survive differ from that of the shroud. "All of the extant Palestinian linens, including the wrappings from the Dead Sea Scrolls, are of a basket weave—decidedly different from the shroud."[10] Hence, the weave found in the Shroud of Turin is unique in that it differs from all known weaves from the time of Christ.

The unusual length of the Shroud also places it in a special class of surviving cloth from the period of Christ, if authentic. In discussing the unusual size of the shroud Sox wrote, "you just don't find anything the size of the Shroud except for Egyptian mummy wrappings—certainly nothing that measures fourteen feet, the size of the Shroud."[11]

Close-up view of a fragment of shroud cloth recovered from a Jewish grave in Jerusalem dating from the time of Jesus. Note the basket weave pattern. (Shimon Gibson)

Aside from the physical composition (flax), size (fourteen feet by four feet), and weave of the cloth (herringbone), there is the image that appears on the shroud. There is no doubt that it is the image of a man, both front and back, that has all the marks of crucifixion. The image shows the hands folded over the genital region. The feet, right side, and scalp bear wounds, as does the back, all showing traces of what appears to be blood. The physical aspects of the image comport neatly with the biblical accounts of Christ's crucifixion.

How such an image came to be fixed upon the shroud is an important question, and one that divides students of the shroud. One explanation given by those who believe the shroud authentic is that the image represents a stain created by the oils and spices used to prepare the body for burial.[12] A second explanation is that the image is the result of some sort of unknown radiation given off by Christ's body at the moment of resurrection (a miracle). A third explanation is that the image is a clever painting created during the fourteenth century as claimed in the report of Bishop d'Arcis. While the first two explanations challenge credulity, they have substantial advocates. The red stains are considered to be caused by Christ's blood seeping from his wounds, and therefore natural, a relatively easy explanation to test scientifically.

Aside from the cloth itself, the composition of the image, the alleged blood stains, and other foreign matter that might be attached to the cloth, such as pollen, sweat, epithelial tissue (from a severely scourged individual), and of course DNA, lend themselves to forensic analysis. All of these specimens have been examined with varying results. But all of these items, if present, may not be original to the shroud. Any one of them could have been added at any time over the past centuries, either by accident or deliberately.

If the shroud was created by someone as an icon or as a hoax, one would assume the person was capable of satisfying every detail of the Gospel account, even using real blood (either human or animal) to simulate the blood of Christ. Fortunately, chemical testing is capable of answering such questions, if done properly, and herein resides the problem.

Following d'Arcis's inquiry the shroud survived unexamined for the next six hundred years. Then, in 1969, the Archbishop of Turin appointed a commission and granted it approval to examine the shroud. Interestingly, the appointment of the commission and its work was carried out in secret, but word of its existence eventually became known, to a flurry of criticism.[13] The examination was essentially visual and the report of the commission was a series of recommendations for future examinations. Since the commission's examination was of little use in dating the shroud and determining its authenticity, requests for a more thorough forensic examination of the shroud and its image persisted.

In 1973, an Italian commission appointed by Archbishop Cardinal Michele Pellegrino carried out additional studies. The archbishop asked the commission to focus its attention on the red stains and determine if they were in fact blood. The results of Pellegrino's commission were reported in 1976. Among the select list of tests performed on the shroud were several that examined the red-stained areas portraying blood. Among these tests were light microscopy, ultraviolet irradiation testing for fluorescence, attempts at solubilization of the stain using chemicals in which blood is normally soluble, thin-layer chromatography to separate certain components of blood for identification, a reaction with benzidene HCl (a chemical known to specifically react with trace amounts of hemoglobin in blood), and serological typing with antibodies in an attempt to detect blood group antigens. Significantly, *all* of these tests proved negative for blood. Light microscopy revealed particulate matter (red granules) that did not dissolve in the standard solvents that dissolve blood, and the reaction to benzidene HCl was negative. UV spectral analysis did not give a spectrum associated with blood, nor did the samples fluoresce when treated as they should have if they contained blood. Thin-layer chromatography proved negative, as did the serological tests for ABO antigens specific for human blood.[14] It is important to understand that any stain or pigment visible to the naked eye should give positive results to most if not all of the tests applied by the commission if the stains contain human blood. Unfortunately, the individuals carrying out the tests fell short in their analyses. While concluding the granular material was not blood, they made no effort to determine what the red stains were made of.[15] If not blood, what? Even more baffling is the fact that the report received marginal attention at the time and has been completely ignored in nearly every modern discussion of the shroud's authenticity. It has simply been discarded by the proponents of the shroud's authenticity. This in itself casts doubt on the objectivity of those claiming the shroud is the authentic burial cloth of Christ. If the stains do not contain blood, that clearly points to their being man-made and not a product resulting from crucifixion.

There are four dates subsequent to the 1976 report of the Italian commission that are important to the study of the shroud: 1978, 1980, 1981, and 1988. We will consider all four.

In 1978, a major step forward was taken with the establishment of the Shroud of Turin Research Project, known as STURP for short. STURP consisted of religious and scientific people from various disciplines who were granted access to the shroud for investigative purposes. Whatever the motivations behind the appointment of this group or of its individual members, it should have been able to answer the question of the shroud's authenticity once and for all. STURP included both prominent religious individuals as well as individuals with varying scientific skills, including an internationally renowned expert in forensic chemistry and analytical microscopy, Dr. Walter C. McCrone. McCrone was an important member of STURP because of his training and his commercial laboratory, where he carried out the very sorts of analyses on historic documents and questionable objects that were needed for the shroud.[16] McCrone was the only professionally trained forensic chemist and microscopist on the STURP team. In all, two dozen individuals were permitted to examine the shroud over a period of five days. The examination took place continuously for 120 hours. While some members of the group worked, others slept, taking turns examining the relic.

The shroud was studied using a wide variety of optical and microscopic methods as well as through several "sticky-tape" samples that were taken from select areas of the cloth. The tape was deemed the safest way to remove particulate matter from the cloth while causing as little damage as possible. Among the tests performed were low-power X-ray irradiation and ultraviolet light scanning. Because the shroud had received a cloth backing sewn to it by Belgian nuns during medieval times as a support, a side edge of the shroud was unstitched and the exposed back or reverse of the shroud was examined visually.

In 1981, the STURP group issued a report of its findings with one important omission. During the interval between 1978 and the release of the STURP report in 1981, Walter McCrone, the forensic chemist and microscopist, left the group following a dispute over his research findings. McCrone claimed he was "drummed out of STURP" as a result of his conclusion that the shroud was fabricated.[17] He had spent the interval examining one of two duplicate sets of thirty-two sticky tapes taken from various areas of the shroud. The set of thirty-two tapes consisted of fourteen tapes from nonimage areas and eighteen from body-image areas, including six from "blood"-image areas. Each tape measured approximately 3 inches by 3/8 of an inch. McCrone estimated that there were at least a thousand individual fibers on each tape, along with "orange-red particles" associated

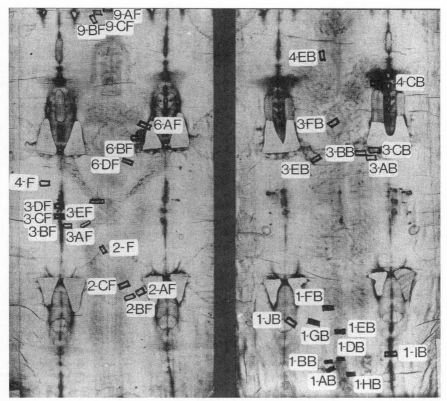

Front and back images of the Shroud of Turin showing the "sticky tape" sample locations (with identifying symbols) used by Walter McCrone for his forensic analysis. (Walter McCrone)

with many of the fibers.[18] McCrone wrote that the thirty-two tapes yielded "at least 40,000 'Shroud' linen fibers with hundreds of extraneous loose particles of all kinds: pollen, pigment particles, fibers, hair, and dust are on those tapes to tell anyone able to identify them what the 'Shroud' image is and how it got there."[19] The linen fibers existed in two forms: clear or colorless, and yellow to faint yellow. The yellow-appearing fibers were predominantly in the image area, while the nonimage area consisted mainly of clear or colorless fibers. Most significant, McCrone found that the yellow fibers in the image area were covered by a collagen tempera medium (collagen is an animal protein), which was colored by red ochre and vermilion pigments. The vermilion was prominent in the areas of the alleged blood stains found on the image.[20]

Collagen tempera was a common medium used by medieval artists, as were red ochre and vermilion. (It should be noted that vermilion is a pigment that was not invented until circa 800 A.D.) If vermilion did exist on certain of the fibers, it could only have been put there some eight hundred years after the death of Christ. In addition to using microscopic analysis to visually identify the presence of pigments (in granular form), McCrone also used standard chemical tests to support his visual observations. The red particulate matter that McCrone identified as vermilion paint pigment was found associated with the alleged blood fibers that were described by two of the STURP examiners as "blood sherds" and "blood flakes."[21] Mc-Crone disproved their conclusion by showing that the refractive index of the red particles was nearly double that of human blood (3.00 versus 1.60, respectively), and none of the red particles dissolved in the chemical hydrazine, which readily dissolves blood but not paint pigments.[22] McCrone concluded that since the image contained significant amounts of paint pigments common to the medieval period, it was the work of a medieval artist (as determined by Bishop Pierre d'Arcis) using collagen tempera medium along with the pigments red ochre for the image and vermilion for the blood.

In December 1979, McCrone submitted his first scientific paper containing the results of his study to the STURP committee for approval (all members had signed a secrecy agreement in 1979 that required STURP approval before publication of data). The committee rejected McCrone's findings in a letter to him that stated in part: "your data is [*sic*] misrepresented, your observations are highly questionable, and your conclusions are pontifications rather than scientific logic; I [the author of the letter was Eric Jumper] cannot permit this paper to carry the Shroud of Turin Research Project's seal of approval."[23] McCrone was also reminded that he had signed a secrecy agreement requiring STURP approval,[24] and that before any journal would publish his work members of STURP would be asked to review the paper, which would result in their recommendation that the paper be rejected.[25] McCrone, dismissed without even being asked to defend his findings, submitted his resignation to STURP in June 1980. Once the secrecy agreement expired in late 1980, McCrone went ahead and published his findings in a journal for which he served as an editor, thereby bypassing any chance of STURP members blocking publication. He followed this initial publication with two more papers providing additional evidence for the presence of pigments in the shroud image.[26]

Completely ignoring McCrone's findings, STURP issued its own report

Walter McCrone, head of McCrone Associates, was one of the original members of STURP. After releasing his findings, McCrone was denied further access to shroud materials. (Joe Nickell)

in 1981 emphatically denying that any pigment (paint, dyes, or stains) were found on the shroud. In the interim between McCrone's publications and STURP's release of its report, efforts were made to discredit McCrone as a scientist and his results as false. In justifying its position, STURP reported that "thousands of photographs, photomicrographs, X-rays, and spectra" were performed.[27] The techniques used in the examination impressed the lay public, who waited anxiously for the group's conclusions as to the authenticity of the shroud. The final report was summarized by STURP as follows:

No pigments, paints, dyes or stains have been found on the fibrils. X-ray, fluorescence and microchemistry on the fibrils preclude the possibility of paint being used as a method for creating the image. Ultraviolet and infrared [light] evaluation confirm these studies. Computer image enhancement and analysis by a device known as VP-8 image analyzer show that the image has unique three-dimensional information encoded in it. Microchemical evaluation has indicated no evidence of any spices, oils, or any biochemicals known to be produced by the body in life or in death. It is clear that there has been a direct contact of the shroud with a body, which explains certain features such as scourge marks, as well as blood. However, while this type of contact may explain some of the features of the torso, it is totally incapable of explaining the image of the face with the high resolution that has been amply demonstrated by photography. The basic problem from a scientific point of view is that some explanations which might be tenable from a chemical point of view, are precluded by physics. Contrariwise, certain physical explanations which may be attractive are completely precluded by the chemistry. For an adequate explanation for the image of the shroud, one must have an explanation which is scientifically sound, from a physical, chemical, biological, and medical viewpoint. At the present, this type of solution does not appear to be attainable by the best efforts of the members of the Shroud team. Furthermore, experiments in physics and chemistry with old linen have failed to reproduce adequately the phenomenon presented by the Shroud of Turin. The scientific consensus is that the image was produced by something which resulted in oxidation, dehydration and conjugation of the polysaccharide structure of the microfibrils of the linen itself. Such changes can be duplicated in the laboratory by certain chemical and physical processes. A similar type of change in linen can be obtained by sulfuric acid or heat. However, there are no chemical or physical methods known which can account for the totality of the image, nor can any combination of physical, chemical, biological or medical circumstances explain the image adequately.

Thus, the answer to the question of how the image was produced or what produced the image remains, as it has in the past, a mystery.

We can conclude for now that the Shroud image is that of a real human form of a scourged, crucified man. It is not the product of an artist. The blood stains are composed of hemoglobin and also give a positive test for serum albumin. The image is an ongoing mystery and until further chemical studies are made, perhaps by this group of scientists in the future, the problem remains unsolved.[28]

This summary report is troubling in that it tells us very little. It reports the absence of "pigments, paints, dyes or stains," and then proceeds to tell us that the image cannot be explained by chemistry or physics. Unfortunately, the report does not tell us why physics and chemistry cannot explain the image. It should be able to explain it. Is STURP suggesting that the image is made up of substances unknown to man or science? By acknowledging that attempts to explain the presence of the image by known physics and chemistry failed, the STURP committee set the stage for a "divine" or "supernatural" basis for producing the image. Absent from this summary report is the conclusion reported by certain members of the STURP team that explains the origin of the image as a result of "flash photolysis" or a sudden "burst of radiation" during resurrection, and as such, the result of a miracle.[29] Even so, the composition of the image surely contains known elements, particularly carbon. Or is STURP suggesting the image consists of heretofore unknown substances not found in the near universe? While STURP leaves its readers wondering if some supernatural force created the image, it omits such claims by certain of its own members from the report. Is STURP avoiding the "miracle" explanation for fear it might discredit the report? By concluding no explanation the committee leaves it to the general public to supply the answer. This is not how the scientific method works.

So far we have overlooked the most obvious and most definitive test of all, radiocarbon dating of the linen cloth. While it was proposed—even urged—by several people, including some members of STURP, the owners of the shroud refused on the grounds that the testing was still not accurate enough (having a range of plus or minus two hundred years) and that such testing would require a large sample of the shroud, which they were not prepared to give up. Both criticisms are invalid. The difference between the first century and fourteenth century (thirteen hundred years) is well beyond the two hundred–year range cited by certain STURP members and by the owners of the shroud. Modern methodology requires a quite small sample for radiocarbon testing. Critics of STURP felt the organization was not prepared to accept the results from radiocarbon dating, just as they were not prepared to accept the results of Walter McCrone's forensic testing. But the definitive test was soon to come.

Following the 1983 death of the exiled Italian king, Umberto II (the custodian of the shroud at the time), the Vatican inherited the shroud. In 1988, after considerable negotiations between STURP and several laboratories, STURP agreed to allow small samples to be radiocarbon tested under a special protocol.[30] The man chosen to independently oversee the protocol was Michael Tite, scientific director of the British Museum in London. Originally seven laboratories were selected to take part in the testing. In the end, however, only three were chosen: the University of Arizona in Tucson, Arizona; the University of Oxford in Oxford, England; and the Eidgenössische Technische Hochschule in Zurich, Switzerland. A sample measuring 90 mm by 10 mm (approximately 3 inches by 3/8 inch) weighing 150 mg was cut from the shroud and divided into three equal segments. Along with the shroud sample given to each laboratory were three control samples: an Egyptian burial fragment previously carbon-dated to 110 A.D., a mummy wrapping previously carbon-dated to 200 A.D., and a sample from the cloak of Louis IX of France woven between 1240 and 1270 A.D.[31] Interestingly, the entire process of removing and dividing the sample of the shroud for testing and delivery to the laboratories was videotaped, ensuring that each of the labs received a sample of the shroud and not a sample that had been switched.[32]

The element carbon exists principally as two stable nonradioactive isotopes, carbon-12 and carbon-13. In addition to these two stable elements there is a third, unstable form, carbon-14. Carbon-14 is created by cosmic rays interacting with atmospheric nitrogen, converting it into carbon-14. The carbon-14 interacts with atmospheric oxygen to form carbon dioxide, which is taken up by plants during the normal process of photosynthesis. (Carbon dioxide is also absorbed into seawater, where it can be ingested and fixed into plants and animals.) The plant material containing carbon-14 is ingested by animals, where the carbon-14 becomes incorporated into the animal tissue. This process goes on continuously until the plant or animal dies, whereupon no more carbon-14 is ingested or fixed into living tissue. Because carbon-14 decays over time at a steady rate, the amount of carbon-14 in the plant or animal is slowly reduced at a fixed rate. Carbon-14 decays over long periods of time. It has what scientists refer to as a "half-life" of 5,730 years, which means that the amount of carbon-14 in a sample decays to half its original value every 5,730 years. The ratio of carbon-14 to carbon-12 and carbon-13 can be accurately measured, thereby giving a fairly accurate age for certain objects.

As an example, the flax plant takes up a certain proportion of atmospheric carbon-14 and fixes it into living cells, where it becomes part of the plant's cellular fibers. Once harvested, this uptake and fixation ceases and carbon-14 disintegration, or decay, begins. By measuring the amount of carbon-14 in the linen, the age of the cloth can be determined. The technique has been greatly refined to where samples are relatively small and the variation in age has become more precise. It is universally accepted as an accurate measure of dating once-living objects. It should be remembered that the shroud is composed of linen made from flax plants that once were living. Radiocarbon dating was performed by the three independent laboratories on their respective swatches of shroud material, which had been removed from "one end of the main portion of the shroud."[33]

On October 13, 1988, all three laboratories released the results of their radiocarbon dating. The dates for the samples ranged from 1260 A.D. to 1390 A.D. These dates are consistent with the finding of Bishop d'Arcis's report that a medieval artist produced the shroud with its image around the middle of the fourteenth century. The authors of the paper concluded, "These results therefore provide conclusive evidence that the linen of the Shroud of Turin is mediaeval [medieval]."[34] The results also supported the findings of Walter McCrone, who determined that the image on the shroud consisted of pigment and tempera traditionally used during the medieval period, consistent with Bishop d'Arcis's findings. McCrone and his colleagues felt vindicated.[35]

The radiocarbon dating results from the three different labs were devastating to believers in the shroud's authenticity. To those convinced the shroud was the true burial cloth of Christ, there had to be an explanation that would explain or discredit the radiocarbon dating. It is important to note that advocates of the shroud's authenticity did not challenge the laboratories' integrity in carrying out the tests. Instead, they attacked the results of the tests. The laboratories were quite excellent. It was the data that had to be wrong. Something must have happened to give a false reading of the date. Initially, authenticity advocates suggested that heat from the fire in 1532 somehow affected the carbon-14 ratio, thus giving a false reading for the shroud's age. Experts in the field quickly dismissed this criticism. No such effect of heat is known to alter the decay rate of carbon-14. In fact, carbon-14 dating of burnt material thousands of years old is not uncommon in archeological studies. Still, proponents insisted something else must have happened to alter the carbon-14 rate of decay.

In 2005, in a publication in the journal *Thermochimica Acta,* chemist Raymond N. Rogers claimed the radiocarbon-14 dating was erroneous because it had been performed on a swatch of fabric that was from a medieval repair to the shroud, and not part of the original shroud. The material tested, Rogers claimed, was from a much later addition.[36] Rogers's criticism would be valid if the claim of a medieval repair were true, and if the test material were taken from the repair area. It would explain the medieval date. The advocates of the shroud had found their answer.

In April 1534, four nuns from the Poor Clare Convent in Chambery, France, repaired the damage caused by the fire in 1532 by sewing over the seriously burned areas using two dozen linen patches taken from an altar cloth. In addition, they sewed a backing cloth onto the entire shroud to give it stability. Here then, could be a possible source of linen not original to the shroud that might account for the fourteenth-century date.

There are several problems with this explanation. First, the scientists who tested the samples were not stupid. They maintain the swatches of cloth did not come from obvious "repair" areas of the shroud. Second, the swatches were destroyed in the process of testing, so how could the critics know what the swatches that were tested looked like? Rogers based his claim on two surviving small threads that allegedly came from one of the test swatches. And third, the repairs were done in 1534, not 1260 to 1390, 144 years to 274 years after the carbon-14 dating. This time frame was outside the margin of error for modern carbon-14 testing. If the test had been performed on a repair patch, the dates would have run in the 1500s, not the 1300s.

Subsequent critics of the radiocarbon dating claimed that one of the surviving two "threads" from one of the swatches contained a dye found in the madder root, a natural plant, along with a "binding medium" believed to be gum arabic, thus "proving" the swatch tested "was not part of the original cloth." The theory developed by Rogers was that the nuns used madder dye and gum arabic to "color" the repair area so it would "blend" in with the rest of the shroud. This might be evidence to challenge the dating if it were not for the fact that forensic chemists (in particular, Walter McCrone) found both red madder and gum arabic on shroud fibers taken from the several *image areas* (not the repair area), leading them to conclude the image on the shroud was, in fact, created by a medieval artist.[37] Hence, the advocates' argument actually supported McCrone's original finding. Despite the response to Rogers's claim, shroud advocates continued to dismiss the radiocarbon data as erroneous, clinging to their claim of authenticity.

Unfortunately, skeptics of the shroud's authenticity have been unable to convince the guardians of the shroud to retest sample swatches from an area of the shroud both believers and skeptics agree is part of the original shroud and not a repair. Refusal to retest is based on the belief that retesting would require more samples to be removed from the valuable relic, thus damaging it further. Modern carbon dating technology, however, has become quite sophisticated, requiring ever smaller amounts of sample material, in the size range of an average fingernail. This seems quite small when taken from a piece of material approximately fourteen feet by four feet, or fifty-six square feet, and it need not come from an image area. The failure to take this additional definitive step to settle the question of the shroud's age ensures that the controversy will continue unresolved.

In 1996, Leoncio Garza-Valdes, a pediatrician with an interest in archaeology, examined a microscopic subset of fibers from the shroud and claimed they were covered with a "microbial coating" or "bioplastic" from bacteria and fungi. Such a coating, Garza-Valdes claimed, would skew the radiocarbon data to give a date younger than the shroud really is. Here was the answer that shroud believers were searching for. Referred to as a "bioplastic coating" by most people, the resulting material was "discovered" on "a few threads from the lower right corner of the shroud."[38] Garza-Valdes and a colleague, Stephen J. Mattingly, a microbiologist, examined the threads microscopically, noting a coating on the fibers that they concluded contributed significantly to the carbon-14 test resulting in a younger age for the shroud than it really is. The finding is not necessarily unreasonable on first consideration. What Garza-Valdes and Mattingly concluded was that the presence of contamination of living organisms on the test sample contributed to the test results giving a higher carbon-14 to carbon-12 and carbon-13 ratio, thus leading all three laboratories to the false conclusion that the linen shroud dated from 1260–1390 when in fact they were measuring a contaminated sample. They concluded the shroud must be much older, dating from the first century.

There are several problems with the findings of Garza-Valdes and Mattingly. Of course contamination might skew the results. This is why the samples were thoroughly cleaned prior to analysis. Just how clean is arguable, but they were cleaned to remove contaminants. Second, assuming contaminant material was present, Thomas J. Pickett, a physicist, calculated that for contaminants to skew the date from 30 A.D. to 1300 A.D. would require *twice as much contamination by weight* than the entire weight of the shroud itself.[39] Third, there is no evidence to prove the threads Garza-Valdes and Mattingly examined came from the Shroud of Turin. In fact, Turin's Cardinal Giovanni Saldarini questioned the source of the threads in Garza-Valdes's possession. The cardinal said during a telecast interview, "There is no certainty that the material belongs to the Shroud so that the Holy See and the custodian declare that they cannot recognize the results of the claimed experiments."[40] A remarkable statement coming from one of the "guardians" of the shroud. Fourth, if the claim that a "bioplastic coating" resulting from bacterial and fungal contamination can significantly skew radiocarbon dating is correct, then the field of archaeology will have to reevaluate a considerable number of its already tested artifacts. This can be done. Garza-Valdes and Mattingly claim to have a procedure to remove the "bioplastic coating" such that radiocarbon testing can be done on samples with and without cleaning to measure whether there is any difference in the dating, and if so, how great a difference. Fifth, Steven D. Schafersman, a geologist and microanalyst, in examining shroud fibers, states there is no "bioplastic coating" on any of the fibers. What Garza-Valdes and Mattingly observed as "bioplastic coating," Schafersman claims, is simply the "natural luster of linen fibers" that occurs with aging.[41] It would seem that Garza-Valdes and Mattingly need to devise experiments that prove their conclusion as to potential skewing of the date is correct. Even if there is a microbial coating of some sort on some of the shroud fibers, there is no scientific proof that such a coating would skew the date anywhere close to the thirteen hundred years the three laboratories determined. This is one of the major problems with the shroud. Claims continue to be made that are subject to scientific testing, but the definitive experiments are never carried out. If Garza-Valdes and Mattingly are right in their claims, let them carry out the experiments with appropriate controls (such as previously dated fabrics) to prove their theory.

The effort to discredit the original radiocarbon dating carried out by the three laboratories continues unabated. It is clear it will not come to any satisfactory resolution in which the two sides can agree without another round of supervised testing. It seems certain this will not be allowed. At the moment, controversy in the test results favors the advocates of authenticity. It should be remembered, however, that even if the cloth were dated to the period of Christ's death (circa 30 A.D.), that would not prove the cloth was the shroud that covered his body. It is the image on the shroud, not the cloth, that believers turn to in bolstering their claim that the shroud is authentic. The image is what really drives the advocates' claim of the shroud's authenticity. The image, the advocates point out, clearly is that of a man that bears all of the characteristics of someone who was crucified. Of course, it should if it were the creation of a medieval artist who wanted to convince people the shroud was the burial cloth of Jesus.

No amount of evidence is sufficient to overcome faith. The very definition of faith is a firm belief in something for which there is no proof.[42] There is no proof that the Shroud of Turin is the burial shroud of Jesus Christ. In the case of the Shroud of Turin, a firm belief in its authenticity continues in spite of no direct or indirect proof to support claims of its authenticity. Rather than attempt to overcome or challenge faith, a task with little hope of success, let us simply review the evidence and leave faith to the faithful.

The physical nature of the cloth itself speaks against its authenticity. The size and weave are contrary to the biblical description of the shroud, and the practice of the Jews in preparing the dead for burial in the time of Christ does not support the shroud advocates' claim of authenticity. Consider the size of the shroud, a single piece of fabric fourteen feet long. No cloth of that size is known to have survived or is even described in the scant literature for the first century A.D. The Bible states that a separate "napkin" (sudarium) was placed over the face of Christ, and yet the shroud, if authentic, shows no evidence of this being the case, thus refuting the Bible. The image on the shroud is of the entire body, including the head area, precluding the placement of a separate cloth or napkin.

Second, the weave of the shroud is inconsistent with the few surviving samples of the period. The twill pattern is more intricate a weave than the standard simple or basket weave of the period. A recent discovery of an authentic shroud fragment from the tomb of a wealthy individual from the same time period as Christ is in a simple basket weave pattern.[43]

Third, the image contains numerous areas of "blood" stains resulting from scourging, the crown of thorns, nail wounds, and the injury in Christ's side resulting from a spear. And yet, Jewish custom was to thoroughly clean the body before wrapping it in "linen clothes" (plural). The hair around the crown placed on Jesus's head bears "blood" rivulets or trickles, presumably from the thorns cutting into the scalp. This is completely inconsistent with what one expects from scalp wounds. The blood would not appear on the outer surface of the hair in rivulets, but would be matted in the hair, coming from the scalp beneath. Another point bears consideration. Blood does not dry as a red pigment. As blood oxidizes and dries it turns black, not bright red. Bright red is the depiction of blood by artists.

It is necessary that all of the alleged stains be examined in an effort to determine if they consist of blood or some other substance. In November 1973, the Italian commission appointed to examine the shroud in conjunction with its televised exhibition undertook an investigation of the "blood" stains. Among the studies carried out by this commission were certain tests specific for blood: tests for ultraviolet fluorescence, attempts to dissolve pigment granules with reagents typically used to dissolve blood, and the use of benzidene HCl. All of the tests were negative for blood, leading the commission to publicly state: "the generic tests for blood made in the laboratory of Forensic Medicine [Modena, Italy] would tend to exclude the presence of blood, *even of the slightest traces* in the Shroud fibers" (emphasis added).[44] This definitive statement has been ignored in the majority of articles and books discussing the nature of the image and the red stains associated with it. The advocates of the shroud's authenticity seem to accept the absence of positive results in testing for blood as inconclusive for the presence of blood. Any well-trained hematologist or forensic chemist would accept these results as evidence for the absence of blood.

The image itself has other anomalies. The length of the arms is significantly out of proportion to the rest of the body, giving it a rather grotesque appearance. The facial image on the shroud, however, is proportional, which is also problematic. If made while the cloth is draped over a face, which is three-dimensional, when the shroud is laid on a flat surface the face should appear distorted in width. It is not. And while believers in the shroud's authenticity do not accept the image as the work of a medieval artist, they have not been able to explain how it was made other than by a "burst of radiation" or another miraculous event.[45]

Of all the great variety of tests and analyses that have been carried out on the shroud, only one is definitive, and that is the one that deals with the linen cloth itself. All other tests, which involve samples extraneous to the linen fabric of the shroud, are by definition qualified. By that, I mean that tests on substances found on or bound to the linen fibers or surface of the shroud are secondary to the shroud. Pigment, images, dirt, dust, extraneous fibers, pollen, DNA, iron oxide, body fluid whether blood, saliva, tears, sweat, or any other substance may or may not be original to the fabric. There is no conclusive proof that the image or any other substance found associated with the shroud is original to the shroud. Most people believe the image along with the alleged blood stains, whether true blood or pig-

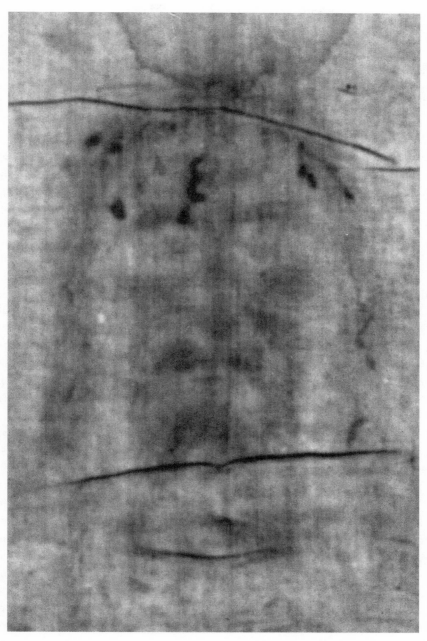

Close-up of the face image on the shroud. The dark areas allegedly represent blood and appear on the surface of the hair rather than on the surface of the skull. (Joe Nickell)

ment, were generated in close time proximity to the manufacture of the shroud, but that belief is supposition. The one truly definitive test of the shroud's origin is the radiocarbon dating tests carried out to establish the fabric's age. The carbon dating is definitive. This is why the advocates of the shroud's authenticity have devoted so much effort to discredit the radiocarbon results. No one disputes the methodology or the competence of the testing laboratories or scientists. Therefore, if one believes the shroud is the burial cloth of Christ it becomes essential to explain how a fourteenth-century date was obtained by carbon dating. As of this writing, no satisfactory answer has been forthcoming to invalidate the radiocarbon dating, although efforts continue.

Attempts to explain the medieval date for the shroud by suggesting contamination or skewing due to exposure to fire have been rejected by most, including serious believers in the shroud's authenticity. The claim that the testing sample did not come from the original shroud but from a fourteenth-century repair would be a valid criticism if true. The only question that remains is whether this claim is indeed correct. The basis for this claim has already been discussed and simply does not hold up under scrutiny. The question could be answered once and for all by simply taking another sample that all parties agree comes from the basic shroud and testing it by radiocarbon dating. That is not likely to happen because the guardians of the shroud will not permit it. Once was enough. If a second radiocarbon dating were to result in a fourteenth-century date, all claims to the shroud's authenticity would collapse.

Walter McCrone's analyses of the sticky-tape samples taken from the surface of both the nonimage and image areas of the shroud show the presence of substantial quantities of pigment and binding medium common to artists of the medieval period, supporting the findings of the Bishop of Troyes, whose investigation turned up the artist who confessed to painting the image.[46] The only way to dismiss McCrone's extensive studies is to believe he fabricated the results, or that someone altered the tapes by adding pigment and other substances to them before McCrone's tests were carried out. It must be pointed out that no one with reputable credentials has accused McCrone of fabricating his results. Instead, his work, like that of the 1973 Italian commission, has been simply ignored and treated by many believers as if it did not exist. By ignoring the data, it does not require explanation.

One study that will not be dealt with in any detail in this discussion is that of Max Frei-Sulzer, former director of the Zurich police science laboratory in Switzerland. At the time of the 1973 study Frei-Sulzer claimed to take several sticky-tape samples from the shroud that he later reported contained forty-four pollen samples, thirty-four of which were indigenous to Palestine or Turkey. Frei-Sulzer and others claimed the data provided proof the shroud came from the Holy Land. Frei-Sulzer's data have come under suspicion by individuals on both sides of the question of the shroud's authenticity, and have too many questionable aspects to be considered reliable.[47] The presence of pollen on the surface of the shroud, if true, only proves the shroud came into contact with the suspect plants or their airborne pollen. It contributes nothing to the age or origin of the cloth. However, Steven D. Schafersman claims Frei-Sulzer "fraudulently prepared" the tapes, adding pollen to his samples in an effort to prove the shroud had been in Jerusalem at the time of Christ.[48] Frei-Sulzer was later discredited as a forensic expert when he claimed the Hitler diaries were authentic (see chapter 3).

There is one other problem that is troubling concerning the image on the shroud. Kenneth L. Feder best summarized it in his book *Frauds, Myths, and Mysteries: Science and Pseudoscience in Archaeology.* Feder wrote: "Certainly the Gospels were not averse to proclaiming the miracles performed by Christ. A miraculous image of Jesus would have been noticed, recorded, and, in fact, shouted from the rooftops. But though the burial linens are seen and mentioned in the Gospel of John [19:40 and 20:7] there is no mention of an image on the cloth. In fact, there is no mention of an image on Jesus' burial garments anywhere in the New Testament. This is almost certainly because there was no image."[49] Feder makes a good point. With all the claims of a miraculous resurrection and ascension into heaven found in the New Testament, it is beyond belief that if there were a shroud with Christ's image boldly visible on it that his followers would not have spread the word of yet another miracle attesting to Christ's divinity. The cloth would have been shown again and again as a sacred relic proving Christ's divinity. And yet, there is no mention of the shroud in the New Testament or in any document for thirteen hundred years following Christ's death.

While science can explain the Shroud of Turin as the work of a fourteenth-century artist, it is insufficient to convince those who believe it to be the authentic burial shroud of Jesus Christ. It isn't clear that any amount of evidence can break through the faith of those who hold the object as the holiest of all religious relics. If authentic, the shroud would truly be a miracle, having survived two thousand years bearing an image that only a miracle can explain. The most unfortunate aspect of the shroud controversy is that access by scientists to the shroud is now barred, meaning anyone can make any statement about the shroud (scientifically or otherwise) and be assured their claims cannot be tested. If such a condition persists, the controversy will never be resolved and people will believe whatever they choose to believe. Simply stated, tell me what you want to believe and I will tell you what you will believe.

Suggested Reading

Adler, Alan D., Isabel Piczek, and Michael Minor, eds. *The Shroud of Turin: Unraveling the Mystery.* Alexander, N.C.: Alexander Books, 2002.

Gove, Harry E. *Relic, Icon, or Hoax? Carbon Dating the Turin Shroud.* Philadelphia, Pa.: Institute of Physics Publishing, 1996.

Guerrera, Vittorio. *The Shroud of Turin: A Case for Authenticity.* Rockford, Ill.: Tan Books and Publishing, 2007.

McCrone, Walter. *Judgment Day for the Shroud of Turin.* Chicago, Ill.: Microscope Publications, 1996.

Nickell, Joe. *Inquest on the Shroud of Turin: Latest Scientific Findings.* Amherst, N.Y.: Prometheus Books, 1998.

———. *Relics of the Christ.* Lexington: Univ. Press of Kentucky, 2007.

5

Skullduggery

The Man Who Never Was

On a December day in 2006, Dr. Jorn Hurum, associate professor of pale-ontology at the Natural History Museum at the University of Oslo, walked into a fossil fair in Hamburg, Germany. The fair was among the largest events of its type held annually in Europe. Thousands of people from around Western Europe attended the fair in search of commercially available fossils and to see the many interesting paleontological specimens on display. It was not Hurum's first visit to the fair, and he was not expecting to find anything out of the ordinary, but that is exactly what happened. Stopping by the table of dealer Thomas Perner, Perner told Hurum he had something "unbelievable" to show him, but needed to do so in private. The two met later that afternoon at a bar inside the exhibit hall. Perner showed Hurum a high-resolution color photograph of a fossil skeleton that literally shocked Hurum. He had never seen anything quite like it. If authentic, Hurum realized that the intact skeleton was that of an early primate, the special group or order that humans belonged to. But this fossil came from a special pit that dated the fossil creature as having died 47 million years ago. Hurum was dazzled by what he saw. The fossil represented what could well prove to be the most significant link in human evolution discovered to date. Hurum told Perner, "It's like finding the lost ark."[1]

Perner told Hurum the fossil was owned by a private collector who had decided it was time to sell the extraordinary specimen. Was Hurum interested? Yes, he was. The price? One million dollars. Hurum didn't flinch at this seemingly large sum of money for a fossil. If the specimen was authentic, and collected prior to 1995 (when the pit where it was discovered was designated a protected UNESCO World Heritage Site), Hurum would raise

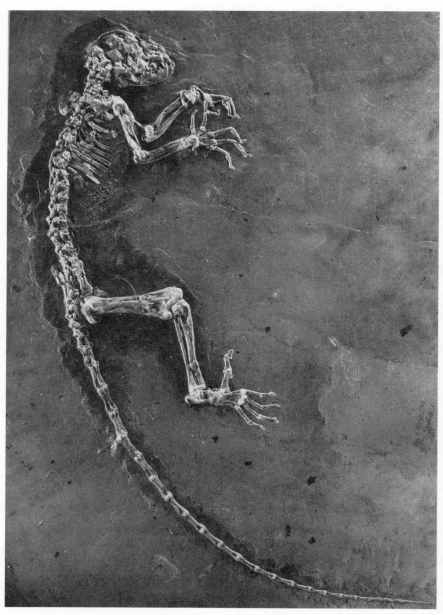

A complete 47-million-year-old fossil claimed to be the "missing link" between early primates and man. (Atlantic Productions)

the money from the Oslo Natural History Museum, where he worked. The rare *Darwinius masillae* fossil passed both tests, and the deal was consummated. Named "Ida" by Hurum, after his young daughter, Hurum believes Ida "will be the one pictured in the text books for the next one hundred years."[2]

Ida's significance comes from the fact that she (Ida is a female) is clearly a primate, and the most complete primate of that early period ever discovered.[3] The size of a modern house cat, not only does Ida possess a complete skeleton, but the fossil also includes a soft body (tissue) outline of the animal along with the contents of its digestive tract.[4] It was truly a unique specimen. In Ida's stomach were the remains of her last meal, an early prehistoric fruit. Shortly after ingesting the fruit, Ida is believed to have been overcome by a poisonous gas coming from the lake where she was drinking. Overcome, she fell into the lake and settled on the bottom, where she slowly fossilized.

The discovery of Ida and her introduction to the general public through the media is the latest in a long chain of discoveries in the general field of human evolution spanning over 150 years. That man should be interested in man and how the human species came to be is self-evident. Each new discovery is heralded as a breakthrough in advancing our knowledge of our own evolution. Man's quest for the "missing link" that bridged the gap between early primates and humans has spurred archeological exploration for over a century.[5]

As important as Ida is to the science of paleontology and human evolution, several other specimens have gathered similar attention at the time of their discovery, but none were heralded as being so important as the few fragments of bone discovered beginning in 1908 by Charles Dawson in an ancient gravel pit near the Sussex village of Piltdown in southern England. Like Ida's discovery a century later, Charles Dawson's find was received throughout the academic world as the most important find in the history of paleontology to that date. Here was the true "missing link" so many had been looking for that finally bridged the gap between humans and their ape relatives.[6] Dawson's man was part ape, part human.

At the time of Dawson's revelation to the archeological community few specimens had been discovered, resulting in an incomplete view of early man. His find consisted of several fragments of a cranium with human characteristics along with a fragment of a jawbone that bore strong characteristics of an ape, but with human-like teeth. This unique combination of a human skull with an ape-like jaw bearing human-like teeth fit many of the early scientists' ideas of what a "missing link" should look like. A missing link that had yet to be discovered. Dawson's find dazzled the world.

That man evolved over millions of years from earlier, more primitive specimens was still a young theory searching for evidence. To the world in general Dawson's discovery was the link that bridged the gap between ape and man, having characteristics from both. The discovery was clear proof of Charles Darwin's theory propounded in his revolutionary book *On the Origin of Species,* published fifty years earlier. Newspapers heralded the discovery with headlines like the one that appeared in the *Manchester Guardian,* "The Earliest Man. A Skull Six Million Years Old."[7]

One of the interesting aspects of Ida's discovery is that it was made by an amateur paleontologist and fossil collector. Charles Dawson, it turns out, was also an amateur paleontologist and collector. But unlike the discoverer of Ida, professional paleontologists recognized Dawson as an expert whose discoveries, knowledge, and scientific publications ranked him along with the better academicians in the field.

Dawson acquired an interest in antiquities at an early age, collecting fossils and educating himself such that by the end of his teens he had acquired both a substantial collection of artifacts and an unusual degree of knowledge. Born in 1864 into a prosperous family, he led an accomplished life, as did his two younger brothers, Hugh and Arthur. Hugh became vicar of Clandown in Somerset, near the town of Bath, while Arthur served in the Royal Navy before becoming the managing director of a major shipbuilding and arms manufacturing company. Arthur was knighted in 1909, around the time of the alleged Piltdown discovery.

Charles followed a different path than his two brothers, never attending a university but acquiring an education in archeology on his own. At the age of twenty he donated his impressive collection to the British Museum of Natural History, for which he acquired the title of "Honorary Collector." A year later he was elected a fellow of the prestigious Geological Society, and ten years after that he achieved his greatest honor when elected a fellow of the Society of Antiquaries of London. He could now proudly list his name in publications as "Charles Dawson, FGS, FSA," a considerable achievement in a nation filled with university-educated scientists.

Dawson's archeological pursuits remained an avocation throughout his life. His professional career was in the field of law, where he worked as a solicitor, eventually heading the firm of Dawson, Hart and Company, located in the village of Uckfield in Sussex, England.[8] Successful as a solicitor, Dawson devoted more and more time to his antiquarian interests, making

Charles Dawson wearing a ceremonial costume. (Miles Russell, *Piltdown Man*)

several prominent friends in the field, including Sir Arthur Smith Woodward, head of geology at the British Museum of Natural History located in London. The two men became fast friends, sharing their knowledge and love of geology and paleontology with each other.

Arthur Smith Woodward was a man of great accomplishment, highly respected, whose career prior to the Piltdown story was exemplary. Woodward's rise to prominence is a story akin to that of Horatio Alger. Born into modest means, he showed an early intense interest in archeology and collecting, much like his later friend Charles Dawson. Lacking a university degree, he accepted a low-level position with the Natural History Museum in London, and through self-education and hard work he rose to become head of its prestigious geology department. His achievements were many and his awards numerous. By the age of thirty-nine Woodward was elected a fellow of the Royal Society. During his years at the Natural History Mu-

Building where Charles Dawson had his law offices in the town of Uckfield. The firm still exists today as Dawson and Hart. (Photograph by the author)

seum he became close friends with Dawson. The two men, through their shared enthusiasm for archeology, corresponded regularly, sharing ideas. The stage was now set for what would become the greatest hoax in the fields of paleontology and anthropology.

On February 15, 1912, Dawson wrote a letter to Woodward. In the letter, Dawson revealed for the first time his find of fragments from a human skull in the ancient gravel pit on the estate known as Barkham Manor, not far from the village of Piltdown in Sussex. Dawson wrote: "I have come across a very old Pleistocene[9] (?) bed overlying the Hastings bed between Uckfield and Crowborough, which I think is going to be interesting. It has a lot of iron-stained flints in it, so I suppose it is the oldest known flint gravel in the Weald [forest]. I [found a] portion of a human skull which will rival *H. heidelbergensis* in solidity."[10]

Despite Dawson's astonishing revelation, the two men did not get together for another three months, although Dawson did send Woodward skull fragments and other mammalian animal fragments that supported his estimated age of the skull fragments as early Pleistocene. The discovery was made public in December 1912, ten months after Dawson informed

Arthur Smith Woodward (left) and Charles Dawson (center) pose for the camera in the summer of 1912. (Miles Russell, *Piltdown Man*)

Woodward, and as long as four years after Dawson claimed to have found the remarkable bones. Woodward enthusiastically accepted Dawson's finds. His reputation throughout the scientific community helped give Dawson's discovery considerable credibility.

The leading authorities of the period were thrilled. They had found exactly what they were looking for—a kind of hybrid creature, part human, part ape—and best of all, it was found in England. The cranium was human-like, while the jaw was ape-like, except for the two molars firmly imbedded in the jaw, which were definitely humanoid, not ape-like. The only problem with this creature was that it proved to be the opposite of what was eventually shown to be the case in man's evolution—human-like jaw and teeth with a smaller, underdeveloped cranium (brain). But that was to come later in the century. The pattern of man's emergence from his primate past showed his teeth evolving in advance of his brain capacity. This pattern, however, was not widely known at the time of Piltdown's discovery.

To better appreciate the significance of Piltdown Man, a little background is necessary. At the time of Dawson's discovery there were not many examples of hominid or human fossils, and basically none in England—or in all of the British Isles for that matter. The scientific community throughout Britain was feeling somewhat left out. Why was early man absent from British history? After all, Great Britain was certainly one of the greatest nations in every category, or every category except one, early man.

One of the characteristics that make an animal a "hominid" is the ability to walk upright on two legs. This is a somewhat simplistic statement, but necessary for our understanding of a complicated subject. The evolution of modern man took a major step forward (no pun intended) when his ancestor stood on two feet and left the habitat of the trees to walk onto the great savannah of Africa. Walking erect gave this ancestor a major adaptive advantage over his own ancestors and the other animals that roamed his habitat. Upright man could see farther across the savannah than most creatures on all fours. Walking upright is believed to have happened between 4 and 5 million years ago.

In 2005, scientists discovered the remains of a hominid in Ethiopia that walked around on two legs, fitting their prediction quite nicely. The fossil remains were dated to around 4 million years ago and were found not far from where the fossil remains of Lucy, a 3-million-year-old girl belonging to the genus *Australopithecus,* were discovered. The genus *Australopithecus* was a major breakthrough in the study of man's evolution. It was in this diminutive ancestor of modern man that paleontologists believe walking upright on two feet first occurred. As Darwin audaciously declared in his *Descent of Man,* published in 1871, "Man alone has become a biped."[11]

The earliest prehistoric ancestor of modern man (*Homo sapiens*) that is considered in the same group as modern-day man is named *Homo habilis. Habilis* emerged roughly 2 million years ago. This particular species is named *habilis* because it was accompanied by several stone tools and is believed to be the first or earliest of our ancestors to use tools. This feature, together with a brain shaped much like the later human brain, marks a significant point in human evolution. But we are still over a million years away from modern man.

All of the earliest fossil antecedents of modern man were found within Africa, suggesting that early man was restricted to that continent. Throughout the 4 million or so years that hominids were evolving, they slowly spread from Africa into the Middle East, Asia, and Europe. The discovery of fossils from regions outside of Africa is generally dated to around 1 million years and less. Java Man and Peking Man (members of *Homo erectus*), discovered in Asia, date to sometime between 700,000 years and 300,000 years ago, while Heidelberg Man (*Homo heidelbergensis*), a European discovery, dates to a period between 600,000 and 100,000 years ago. The well-known Neanderthal Man (*Homo neanderthalensis*) emerges on the scene 250,000 to 30,000 years ago, living throughout Europe. It is toward the end of the Neanderthals' reign that modern man (*Homo sapiens*) appeared. The discoveries of these early species of *Homo* occurred during the nineteenth century. Neanderthal skulls were first discovered in Belgium in 1829 and in Gibraltar in 1848, both before the more famous discovery in the Neander Valley near Düsseldorf, Germany, in 1856, three years before Charles Darwin's *Origin of Species* was published.

While Asia and Europe produced several specimens of early man, Britain found itself without a single representation. British paleontologists were derisively referred to by European paleontologists as "pebble hunters," a term that obviously did not sit well with Britain's scientific community. Enter Charles Dawson and Piltdown Man. Dawson's discovery vindicated British paleontology. It clearly demonstrated that the earliest ancestor to bridge the gap between man and ape was an "Englishman." Based on the fragment, the skull was large (estimated to be 1,100–1,400 cubic centimeters) and human, while the jawbone was "apish" in structure. The teeth, however, were clearly human. It was exactly what the early experts were looking for, a transition from ape-like to human dating from well before the current specimens known to paleontologists, 500,000 to 1.2 million years ago. And most important, it was found in England, right in the heart of the British Empire, where any thinking human being knew early man must have evolved. Dawson's find put England right at the top of the evolutionary tree of early man. The new species of human was given the name *Eoanthropus dawsoni,* meaning "Dawson's man of the dawn," or "Dawn Man" for short.[12]

Dawson officially announced his discovery at a special meeting of the Geological Society in London on Wednesday, December 18, 1912, to a crowded room of society members and press. Dawson was followed at the podium by Sir Arthur Smith Woodward, whose enthusiasm for Dawson's discovery was essential for Piltdown Man's credibility. By the end of the meeting, Woodward had dismissed the earlier specimens of Heidelberg Man and Neanderthal as dead ends in man's evolution, mere failures. But not Dawson's man. He was a link, not a dead end. Modern man descended from Piltdown Man, who would now take his rightful place as the true missing link.[13] And best of all, he was English.

Although Piltdown Man became widely accepted as a part of the evolutionary tree of humans, not all scholars were convinced of his authen-

An artist's rendition of Piltdown Man. (*Illustrated London News*, December 28, 1912)

ticity. In 1915, at the height of Piltdown Man's celebrity, Gerrit S. Miller, a curator of mammals at the Smithsonian Institution in Washington, D.C., published his analysis of Woodward's reconstructed skull of Piltdown. Miller concluded that the skull and jaw could not have come from the same animal. While the skull was human, Miller astonishingly concluded that

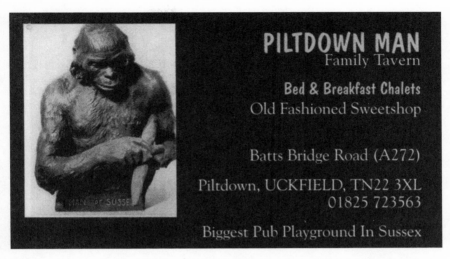

PILTDOWN MAN
Family Tavern

Bed & Breakfast Chalets
Old Fashioned Sweetshop

Batts Bridge Road (A272)

Piltdown, UCKFIELD, TN22 3XL
01825 723563

Biggest Pub Playground In Sussex

The business card of the Piltdown Man Family Tavern in Uckfield, England, bearing an artist's depiction of Piltdown Man using a tool. (Author's collection)

the jawbone came from a fossil ape. Forty years before the discovery was ruled a fraud Miller hit the nail squarely on the head. Unfortunately, he was rudely dismissed as having a "lack of perspective" and accused of setting out to "confirm a preconceived theory, a course of action which has unfortunately warped his judgment and sense of proportion."[14] Interestingly, this same sort of attack was leveled at Walter McCrone when he concluded the Shroud of Turin was a fake.

Dawson bolstered his claims by discovering fragments from a second Piltdown Man. Where this second fragment came from is still not known, but it did not come from the gravel pit at Barkham Manor, home of the first Piltdown Man. In a letter to Woodward dated July 3, 1913, Dawson wrote that he picked up "the frontal part of a human skull this evening on a ploughed field covered with flint gravel. It's a new place, a long way from Piltdown, and the gravel lies 50 feet below the level of Piltdown."[15] The new find was named "Barcombe Mills Man." Could one Piltdown Man be a mistake? Perhaps. But certainly not two. To make matters even more secure, Dawson found yet another fragment from a third location. This fragment was from the left side of the frontal bone, containing a portion of the eye orbit and root of the nose. This third specimen was named "Sheffield Park Man." Three specimens, all from different locales, sealed the claim. There could be no doubt Piltdown was real.

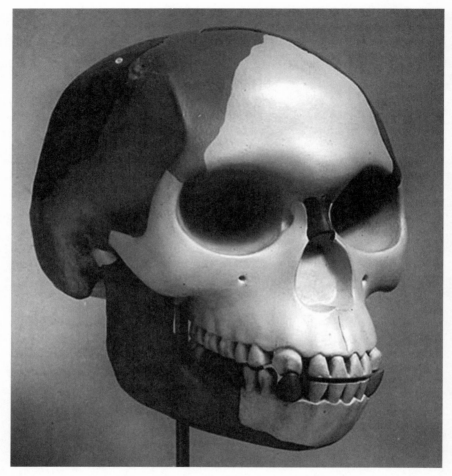

A reconstruction of Piltdown Man's skull by Arthur Smith Woodward. (Miles Russell, *Piltdown Man*)

Between 1915 and 1950, Piltdown Man remained a viable specimen of early man. His place as the missing link representing an intermediary transition from ape-like ancestors to early man was shaken somewhat over the years, and Piltdown Man slipped from his original place as the once heralded "missing link." He still remained, however, as one of the examples of early man. It was now a question of where to place the awkward, unconventional creature in the overall tree of early man, but most agreed that he belonged somewhere. The important thing to remember is that the signifi-

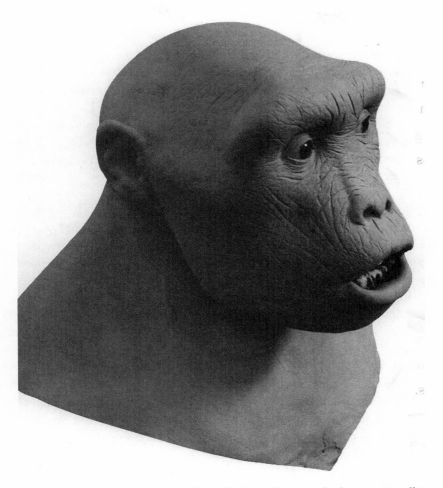

A reconstruction of the head and face of *Sahelanthropus tchadensis*, a 7-million-year-old hominid that contains features of both ape and later human hominids, making it the oldest known link between the apes and man. Piltdown Man was believed to fill this role when discovered. (Carl Zimmer, *Smithsonian Intimate Guide to Human Origins*)

cant features that made Piltdown so important initially, a human cranium and an ape-like jaw with human-like teeth, were the opposite of every other discovery since Piltdown Man. In later finds, it was always the jawbone and teeth that were human while the cranium was primitive and tended toward being ape-like.

A brief question of ownership arose when George Maryon-Wilson, the owner of Barkham Manor, and therefore owner of the gravel pit located on his estate, learned of the fossil finds through the national press reports. Maryon-Wilson wrote to the British Museum staking his claim and admonishing them "to kindly take care that they are not removed by Mr. Dawson or any other person, without my permission."[16] The question of ownership was soon resolved amicably when Maryon-Wilson authorized Woodward to offer the fossils to the museum. As such, they fell under the tight control of Woodward, who carefully guarded over them, making sure they were viewed only with his permission and under his watchful eye, thus limiting any further examination.

For the next forty years Piltdown Man held a special place on the tree of man's evolution. Revered by many of Britain's leading scientists, Dawson's "Earliest Englishman" was never seriously examined by forensic experts until 1949, five years after Woodward's death, when the science of chemistry caught up with anatomy.

Realizing the controversy associated with Piltdown Man, the British Museum agreed to allow certain tests on the various fragments recovered from the gravel pit, tests that were not available at the time of Piltdown's discovery. The earliest of these tests was one that measured the fluorine content of a specimen. Fluorine is a chemical element often found in low or trace amounts in groundwater. Bone will absorb fluorine and bind it chemically into its lattice-like matrix. The longer a bone is exposed to fluorine in the soil, the more fluorine will be bound by the bone, and this occurs whether the bone is living or dead. All parts of a skeleton in a grave, for example, should contain relatively similar amounts of fluorine when tested. Because the amount of fluorine in groundwater will vary from site to site, it is not possible to tell the age or date of a bone sample by its fluorine content. But, and this is important, all of the parts or fragments of bone from the same site should contain the same amount of fluorine. If bone specimens were added to a site at a later date than other bone fragments, they will differ in their fluorine content. Remember, the gravel pit contained fragments of animals that were removed along with the fragments from Piltdown Man's cranium and jaw.

In 1949, English anthropologist and paleontologist Kenneth Oakley developed a sensitive test for fluorine. He was granted permission by the British Museum to test the various animal and human fragments Dawson removed from the Barkham Manor gravel pit. When the fragments were tested, the animal fragments from the Lower Pleistocene period (1 to 2

Sir Arthur Smith Woodward standing alongside the memorial stone marking the gravel pit on Barkham Manor where Charles Dawson allegedly discovered the first relics of Piltdown Man. (Miles Russell, *Piltdown Man*)

million years old) and later Pleistocene period (800,000 to 100,000 years old) showed high fluorine content, as expected, while the Piltdown fragments (skull and jawbone) showed very low fluorine content. Oakley concluded, "None of the bones and teeth attributed to *Eoanthropus* [Piltdown

Man] belong to the Lower Pleistocene group" as claimed by *Eoanthropus*'s supporters.[17] In other words, Piltdown Man did not originally belong in the Barkham Manor gravel pit; he was added at a later date, a much later date.

While Oakley's results are consistent with Piltdown Man being something less than originally claimed, not everyone was convinced. One positive result Piltdown's proponents drew from Oakley's study was that the skull fragments and jawbone (and teeth) had the same low fluorine content, thus supporting the claim they belonged together, which only means they probably were of the same age and came from the same source. The controversy concerning the incompatibility of the human skull and ape-like jawbone continued to stir debate. Further evidence was necessary before Piltdown Man could be classified as a fraud.

In 1953, Joseph Weiner, a physical anthropology professor at Oxford University, undertook a study of the incompatibility between the ape-like jaw and humanoid teeth and skull. Even more puzzling to Weiner was the observation that the ape-like jaw had flat, worn-down molars never seen in any specimen to date. Either the teeth were added to the jawbone or the teeth were altered from their original ape-like structure to make them look human. Weiner set about to retest the fluorine content of the fragments and examine the teeth microscopically. The results were conclusive. The teeth had been altered. They were carefully filed down by a mechanical device, removing dentine and leaving fine file marks that were visible under microscopic examination. Weiner also conducted a second chemical test measuring the nitrogen content in the fragments. Nitrogen is a common element found in all amino acids, the chemical building blocks of proteins. Over long periods of time, the nitrogen is slowly and uniformly lost from the proteins. The results showed that the fragments from all of the specimens were modern. Weiner declared Piltdown a modern hoax.

In 1953, Weiner, along with Kenneth Oakley and Wilfred Le Gros Clark (a British surgeon and leading authority in human evolution), published the results of their study in the *Bulletin of the British Museum*.[18] In their conclusion they wrote: "From the evidence which we have obtained, it is now clear that the distinguished paleontologists and archeologists who took part in the excavation at Piltdown were the victims of a most elaborate and carefully prepared hoax." They went on to state: "The faking of the mandible and canine is so extraordinarily skillful, and the perpetuation of the hoax appears to have been so entirely unscrupulous and inexplicable, *as to find no parallel in the history of paleontology discovery*" (emphasis added).[19]

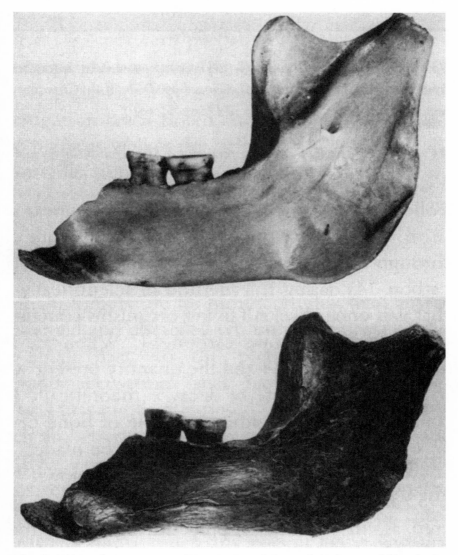

The mandible of an orangutan (above) altered to simulate the mandible of Pilt-down Man (below). (Miles Russell, *Piltdown Man*)

"Victims?" Perhaps the authors were so naive as to believe none of the original players who discovered and promoted Piltdown Man had a role in creating him. Or were they simply covering themselves from possible libel lawsuits? In fairness, the three men were scientists and could only base their conclusions on the scientific data. Who created Piltdown and seeded his fragments in the gravel pit was beyond their research. In the end, Piltdown Man was shown to be entirely modern. The skull fragments were later dated to come from the medieval period, around 1400 A.D., while the jawbone came from an orangutan and was judged to be around five hundred years old. All of the fragments showed clear evidence of deliberate staining designed to give the appearance of antiquity to the bones.

The question that soon followed revelations that *Eoanthropus dawsoni,* commonly known as Piltdown Man, was a fake was who was responsible? Who had opportunity, and knowledge, and most importantly, motive? Was it a hoax gone awry? A prank that simply meant "gottcha" that quickly escalated and got out of hand? Or was it a deliberate and malicious hoax intended to further reputations, or perhaps to destroy reputations? All of these conjectures are possible and all have been considered. The men involved in the early evaluation and promotion of Piltdown Man had impeccable credentials and their reputations were above reproach. So who was responsible for the hoax?

Perhaps the best indication of the success of the perpetrator is seen in the number of suspects that have been proposed in the years since the hoax's exposure. Upward of a dozen persons have been accused of initiating the fraud or conspiring in its creation. Among the suspects are men of great esteem and reputation, including the likes of Sir Arthur Conan Doyle, the creator of Sherlock Holmes.

The unexpected early death of Dawson in 1916, only four years after he introduced his "Dawn Man" to the world, removed the principal witness who knew all of the facts associated with the discovery. Adding to this void is the unfortunate fact that all of Dawson's private papers were accidentally destroyed in 1917 in a fire. Of course, Dawson and his colleagues who were involved early on were dead when the hoax became known. The intervening years between Dawson's death and the exposure of the hoax were crucial years when controversy over the fossil find was still being debated in some scientific quarters. Having Dawson available to defend his discovery and answer questions and criticism during the intervening years would have probably brought the matter to an earlier conclusion. With the principals dead, speculation about the culprit or culprits flourished. It is interesting that Dawson's reputation was such that he was not immediately recognized as the possible perpetrator, but rather the victim.

Who are the principal suspects and why are they suspected? Everyone who visited or had access to the gravel pit in the first twelve years

The gravel pit at Barkham Manor, 1913. Charles Dawson holds a sieve while Arthur Woodward examines its contents. Digger Venus Hargreaves stands to one side holding a pick. (Miles Russell, *Piltdown Man*)

of the twentieth century, including anyone closely associated with Charles Dawson, becomes a suspect. First and foremost is Arthur Smith Woodward, Dawson's closest friend and companion, and an esteemed scientist who promoted Piltdown Man's authenticity up until his own death in 1944. Next is a young Jesuit priest and ardent amateur geologist, Marie-Joseph Pierre Teilhard de Chardin, a companion of both Dawson and Woodward who spent time digging with them in the gravel pit at Barkham Manor. These two men, along with Dawson, were closely associated with the physical aspects of the case, having opportunity, knowledge, respect, and perhaps motive.

After Dawson, Woodward, and de Chardin, the list of bona fide suspects begins to weaken, ranging from interesting to ridiculous. Ridiculous in the sense that some of the names proposed are considered solely because they possessed a dislike for one or another of the principal players. The most interesting and most seriously considered among the "weak" list is Sir Arthur Keith, a conservator with the Hunterian Museum of the Royal College of Surgeons. Further down the list are William Johnson Sollas, Oxford University professor of geology; William Ruskin Butterfield, museum curator at the Hastings Museum; Grafton Elliot Smith, professor of anatomy at the University of Manchester; John Hewitt, professor of chemistry at Queen Mary College, London University; Martin Hinton of the British Museum; Frank Barlow, a model maker at the Natural History Museum; Samuel Woodhead, public analyst for east Sussex; and the famous writer of mystery, Sir Arthur Conan Doyle. Conan Doyle, the creator of Sherlock Holmes, adds a certain notoriety to the story. A surprising suspect to most people, Conan Doyle had motive, access, and the capability of pulling off the great hoax.

This is a large number of people, many with impressive credentials and plenty of character references. But that is what often makes hoaxes so intriguing. Not one of the suspects is readily identifiable by some flaw in their character. To the contrary, they all appear to be professional men whose conduct in matters other than Piltdown is above reproach.

The conclusion of modern-day authors who have investigated the numerous accusations made against Sollas, Butterfield, Smith, Hewitt, Hinton, Barlow, and Woodhead is that the accusations were baseless, more often reflecting personal animosities against them than substantive fact. There is no need in this review to go through each of their cases, dismissing them as unrealistic. Instead, let us look at those suspects for which there is some evidence to support their possible involvement.

Let's begin with one of the least likely of those on the short list, Arthur Keith. Keith, initially on unfriendly terms with Woodward, eventually became one of Piltdown's stronger advocates, although he always had some lingering doubts. Keith was probably the scientist Dawson should have contacted first, rather than Woodward. At the time of the discovery Keith was perhaps the leading scientist in the study of human fossils. He became president of the Royal Anthropological Institute, London. Dawson later explained to Keith that he felt bound to take the fragments to Woodward because they were such close friends. Keith said he understood. Following his death in 1944, Woodward's wife asked Keith to write a foreword for Woodward's book *The Earliest Englishman,* and Keith agreed. Even here, Keith hedged his wholehearted endorsement of Piltdown Man.

Keith became a target of one of the later Piltdown fraud-busters, Ian Langham, an Australian science historian who mentored Keith. Langham was in the process of gathering research for a book on the Piltdown hoax when his sudden death in 1984 interrupted his work. Frank Spencer, a Long Island University professor, took the project over at the request of Langham's family. The resulting book was titled *Piltdown: A Scientific Forgery.*[20] In the book, Spencer devoted the concluding chapter, titled "Be-

Sir Arthur Keith, 1912. Keith at the time of the Piltdown discovery was England's leading anatomist and a member of the Royal College of Surgeons of England. He was considered a leading authority on the study of fossils. (Frank Spencer, *Piltdown: A Scientific Forgery*)

yond a Reasonable Doubt," to Keith, accusing him of being Dawson's collaborator. Spencer concluded that Langham was convinced that Keith and Dawson conspired together to create Piltdown Man from a modern human skull and the jawbone of a modern orangutan. (The fact that Piltdown was concocted from modern specimens had been demonstrated before Spencer's book was published.)

The smoking gun in Langham and Spencer's study comes from a diary Keith kept that Langham discovered one afternoon while conducting research at the Royal College of Surgeons in 1979. Reading Keith's diary entries from the time of the announced discovery of Piltdown in December 1912, Spencer found one entry dated December 22, 1912, that caught his attention. Simply put, Keith describes his week, mentioning that he wrote an article for the *British Medical Journal* on December 16, which appeared on December 21. Keith also mentions attending the meeting of the Geological Society on December 18, where Dawson and Woodward revealed their stunning find at the gravel pit near Barkham Manor. Spencer noted, however, that the article published on December 21 covering the meeting and giving many details concerning the gravel pit and bone fragments was written on December 16, according to the entry in Keith's diary, two days *before* the meeting on December 18, when the details were revealed for the very first time. How, Spencer asked, could Keith know about such details two days before they were released? Without going into detail about what specific things Keith wrote in his article, Spencer concludes it was Keith who planted the bone and jaw fragments. He knew all along about the details of the fragments that Dawson presented in his lecture.

To further support his case against Keith, Spencer found another entry in the diary dated January 4, 1913, two weeks after the earlier entry, where Keith tells of his visit along with his wife to Uckfield (Piltdown) to see the site where the exciting discovery was made. The trip, according to Spencer's reading of the entry, was unsuccessful—"Didn't see the gravel bed anywhere."[21] Keith also notes in his diary that he had never been to the site before. So, as late as January 4, Keith had yet to visit the gravel pit. And yet he described the pit in detail in his article. How could Keith describe the gravel pit in detail in his December 16 article if he had never been to it?

Spencer was not finished in his investigation of Keith. Two weeks after Keith's apparently aborted visit to Uckfield (Piltdown) to see the pit, he wrote another article that appeared in the journal *Sphere* on January 18 in which he again described the gravel pit in detail. Spencer notes that according to Keith's diary he was busy at work during the entire period January 5 through 18. This means he must have visited the pit prior to January 4, the date of his aborted first trip to the pit area. Here is the smoking gun. Keith is obviously fabricating his knowledge and involvement with Piltdown. He knew about the details of the bone fragments before the December 18 meeting, as evidenced by his diary entry stating he wrote the article on December 16, and must have visited the gravel pit at some point prior to writing his second article of January 18. Spencer concludes this could only have taken place through collusion between Keith and Dawson. At this point in our story a "mysterious stranger" appears to help support Spencer's claim against Keith.

Mabel Kenward, the daughter of the tenant that lived at Barkham Manor, was twenty-seven years old at the time of the Piltdown discovery. She told of an incident that seemed innocuous at the time but which was seized upon by Spencer as supporting his claim. One evening while observing the area around the gravel pit from Barkham Manor, Kenward "saw a tall man come up, not even up the drive, but across the fields—must have gotten over the hedges and ditches even to get there . . . and he walked to the pit and started scratching about . . . so I said excuse me are you an authorized searcher? . . . he didn't say one word . . . off he went the same way across the fields . . . he was dressed in an ordinary grey suit but he had gum boots [Wellington boots] on and he was very tall . . . a man in his forties."

Gate covering the entrance to Barkham Manor. The gravel pit where Dawson made his first discoveries is located at the end of the road shown here. (Photograph by the author)

Part of Barkham Manor. Woodward's monument marking the site of the gravel pit can be seen in the far distance in the center of the photograph. (Photograph by the author)

Keith fit Kenward's description, in that he was tall and in his forties. According to Spencer, Langham believed this mysterious visitor was Arthur Keith, and so did he.[22]

There is more to Spencer's argument accusing Keith of conspiring with Dawson, but it falls far short of the evidence discussed so far. What of Spencer's conclusions based on Keith's diary entries? John Evangelist Walsh, in his definitive study, *Unraveling Piltdown*, explains Keith's visit to Uckfield. Keith and his wife did see the pit where the discovery was made during their January 4 visit. Walsh points out that a careful reading of the diary entry does not lead one to conclude that Keith never made it to the pit. The crucial entry reads, "boys told us where Sussex skull found: fir avenue leading to farm—white gate: on Delta plateau above the Ooze. Didn't see the gravel bed anywhere."[23] Walsh points out, correctly in my opinion, that Keith used the precise term "gravel bed," and not "gravel pit." The bed is in the bottom of the pit. Remember, Keith was a world-class geologist and as such would have selected his terminology carefully. Walsh goes on to point out that the pit was completely filled with water, thus obscuring the gravel bed. In his January 18 article published in *Sphere*, Keith described the gravel pit as being "now full of water, owing to the heavy rains."[24]

As to the all-important observation by Spencer that Keith wrote his December 16 article describing details of the Piltdown discovery two days before the information was publicly released at the meeting of the Geology Society on December 18, Walsh points out, again correctly, that the article was not published until December 21, five days after it was written, and three days after the meeting. Routinely, submitted drafts were held for correction or additional editing up to the day before a journal went to press. This would have allowed Keith to make additions as late as December 20. Walsh also points out that the editorial offices of the *British Medical Journal* were located less than two blocks from Keith's office in the Royal College of Surgeons building. It is only reasonable that Keith edited his article after listening to Dawson's presentation on December 18, before its publication on December 21.

Leaving aside arguments involving character and reputation, the evidence against Arthur Keith falls quite short of that needed to even suspect him of complicity with Dawson, or anyone else, in the hoax. Unfortunately, Keith was not around to explain his diary entries, leaving Spencer a free hand to interpret them the way he wanted them to read. It is another example of following the facts where you want them to take you rather than following them wherever they may lead.

If the fraudulent construction of a new specimen of early man was not enough of an interesting story on its own, add to it the literary world's greatest mystery writer, Sir Arthur Conan Doyle. Conan Doyle is as legitimate a suspect in the fabrication of Piltdown Man as many of the names on our lesser list. To Conan Doyle, nothing was as it seemed. He reveled in misleading his readers, thereby enhancing Holmes's ability to solve crimes. His Sherlock Holmes was unparalleled in his uncanny analytical ability to examine the most innocuous bit of evidence and extract detailed information. A trained medical doctor himself, Conan Doyle's Holmes was a scientist par excellence. Conan Doyle loved hoaxes and fabrications, but only of the most sophisticated type.

Conan Doyle lived eight miles from Barkham Manor and the famed gravel pit. Like Dawson, he had a keen interest in fossils and paleontology, using them in his writing, and he is known to have visited the site on at least three occasions in 1912 shortly after the announcement of the discovery.[25] And interestingly, Conan Doyle and Dawson were friends. Both were members of the Sussex Archaeological Society, and Dawson and his wife were even houseguests of Conan Doyle around the time Dawson announced his discovery.[26]

Conan Doyle certainly had opportunity, but did he have motive? It seems he did. By the time of Dawson and Woodward's announcement of the discovery of Piltdown Man in the gravel pit at Barkham Manor and Piltdown II at Sheffield Park, Conan Doyle had apparently lost interest in fossils and human evolution, and much of everything else, including Sherlock Holmes. For the last ten or twelve years before his death in 1930, Conan Doyle devoted most of his energy to spiritualism. During this period he lectured, wrote articles and books, and attended séances promoting the spirit world. The great scientist of mystery and cryptic evidence seemed to have lost all of his rigorous skepticism he imparted to Holmes in dealing with hoaxes and fraud.

As a promoter of the spirit world, Conan Doyle came under increasing ridicule by the scientific community. The master of evidence had become something of a joke who no longer had the ability to examine evidence when it came to spiritualism. One can easily imagine Conan Doyle setting out to teach the arrogant scientists who ridiculed him a lesson. With his knowledge of paleontology, and access to fossil material from his own collection, and his wounded pride, it was plausible to some that Conan Doyle planted the Piltdown specimens in the gravel pit one afternoon while playing a round of golf on the course nearby. Motive and opportunity. Conan

Doyle had both, but that is a long way from committing fraud, even for a brilliant mind like his.

In addition to motive and opportunity, Conan Doyle would need access to fossil specimens—in particular, an early orangutan jaw and fossil hippopotamus teeth and other Pleistocene animal specimens that were found along with the cranium and jawbone fragments. It appears Conan Doyle did have such access. In his carefully researched treatise, *Unraveling Piltdown,* John Evangelist Walsh reviews the evidence for Conan Doyle's access to everything needed to salt the gravel pit at Barkham Manor. Drawing from an article by John Winslow in *Science 83,* Walsh points out that the legitimate animal fossils found in the gravel pit, which gave credibility to the discovery and supported Dawson's dating to the Pleistocene period, came from the Mediterranean area, particularly Malta and Tunisia.[27] In 1907 Conan Doyle and his new (second) wife traveled extensively to these places. In 1909 they visited Tunisia and the western Mediterranean. Conan Doyle had access to fossils of the type recovered in the gravel pit as a result of his own serious collecting.

Of course, circumstantial evidence is a mixed bag when it comes to determining guilt or innocence. It can have no bearing on the subject, or it can have direct bearing. Conan Doyle had opportunity, motive, and the skill or ability to perpetrate the Piltdown hoax. None of the evidence proves that he was the hoaxer. It is only because of his fame as a master of mystery and a skillful interpreter of evidence that he appears as a suspect at all. Enticing as it is for us to think Conan Doyle was behind the hoax, he was not.

The best evidence in support of Conan Doyle's innocence comes from the masterful studies of Miles Russell, an archeologist at Bournemouth University. Russell has eliminated all of the suspects on the short and long lists by showing beyond a reasonable doubt that the real culprit is Charles Dawson. Russell's conclusions are not based on any of the finds at Barkham Manor (Piltdown I) or Sheffield Park (Piltdown II) or Barcombe Mills (Piltdown III). Rather, they are based on what amounts to the entire corpus of Dawson's work as an archeologist over a period of several decades. This corpus includes a long list of spectacular finds—more than any one archeologist might reasonably expect in a lifetime.

Dawson's recognition as one of the leading British archeologists of the time came from his numerous discoveries of important artifacts, ranging from fossil remains to iron statuettes to Roman tiles. At least thirty-eight of his several dozen dramatic finds are shown by Russell to be fake.

Among Dawson's many discoveries is a small iron statuette purportedly recovered from an old Roman slagheap by workmen obtaining material for road repair.[28] Dawson represented the artifact as having been made of cast iron. Ironworking during the Roman occupation of Britain was believed to be carried out by working the material by hand, yielding only wrought iron. To convert iron ore into the molten iron used in casting requires temperatures of 1,200 degrees and above, while it is believed the Roman smelting process did not achieve temperatures over 900 degrees, rendering the iron soft or "spongy," allowing it to be shaped by hammering. Dawson's claim would make his statuette the oldest cast-iron artifact in all of Europe. When his statuette was presented to the Royal Academy it was met by some of the experts with skepticism, while others concluded it was made from wrought iron, not cast as Dawson claimed. Dawson spent some effort in attempting to convince the scientific community as a whole that the statuette was cast and dated from the Roman occupation. According to Miles Russell, "if Dawson's statuette had indeed been cast, then the whole world of iron making in Europe would be turned on its head."[29] Just as the study of man's evolution would be turned on its head had Piltdown Man been genuine. Dawson, it seems, had a knack for turning the scientific world on its head with stunning discoveries, much the way Mark Hofmann continued to turn up astounding documents that changed Mormon Church history.

In order to determine whether the statuette was made of cast or wrought iron, a sample taken from the statuette was analyzed by W. C. Roberts-Austen, a professor of metallurgy at the Royal School of Mines and an assayer to the Royal Mint. By examining the crystalline structure of the metal, Roberts-Austen concluded the statuette was not cast, but had been wrought, thereby saving the history of iron making from major revision. Nonetheless, if the statuette was from the Romano-British period, it was still a major find. While the conclusion that the statuette was not made of cast iron answers one important question, it does not answer the question of fraud. Was the statuette fabricated, and if so, by whom?

There are several aspects of Dawson's statuette that cast doubt on its authenticity. Dawson claimed it was found in 1877 and that he purchased it in 1883 from the workman who found it. For some unexplained reason Dawson withheld the discovery until 1893, when he showed it to A. W. Franks, head of Roman antiquities at the British Museum in London. Franks presented the statuette to the membership of the Society of Antiquaries that same year, where its authenticity came under question by sev-

The Beauport
Park Statuette,
photographed by
Charles Dawson.
(Miles Russell,
Piltdown Man)

eral prominent members of the society. Dawson seems to have pulled back
in his effort to have the statuette accepted as the oldest example of cast iron
in European history. Between 1893 and 1903, Dawson had another analysis of the statuette made, this time by the analyst of the Royal Arsenal, who
surprisingly declared the piece to be made of cast iron. Dawson was obviously elated.

That same year, the Sussex Archaeological Society opened an exhibit
in which the statuette was placed on display with the bold claim that it was
made of cast iron. Dawson wrote an article describing the exhibit, using
it as a vehicle to release details about the statuette that he had kept secret
for the previous twenty years. The finder of the statuette was a man named

William Merritt, a nineteen-year-old laborer digging in the Roman iron-working site for road building material. According to Dawson, Merritt also found two coins, one of Trajan (emperor from 98 to 117 A.D.) and one of Hadrian (emperor from 117 to 138 A.D.), conveniently confirming the dating of the statuette to the Romano-British occupation of Britain. When Dawson purchased the statuette from Merritt in 1883, Merritt claimed the coins were sold many years earlier (presumably in 1877) to another archeologist-collector, James Rock. The question arises, why didn't Rock buy both items? Selling them together would have increased the value for the seller and enhanced the purchase of the buyer by having dated coins from the same strata of the slagheap. Secondly, why did Merritt, who discovered the piece in 1877, wait six years before selling the statuette to Dawson (in 1883), and why did Dawson wait ten more years before having it presented before the Society of Antiquaries in 1893? And why did Dawson not reveal Merritt as the discoverer of the statuette until 1903? One obvious explanation for the twenty-year delay is that the principal parties were now all dead, and no longer available to tell their stories, if indeed they had stories to tell. Twenty-six years after its alleged discovery in 1877, the history of the statuette was hazy, and only Dawson knew any of the details. The original slagheap was completely used up by 1890, leaving no trace for further examination.

Taken by itself, the Beauport Park Statuette is little more than a mistaken modern copy of an early Roman figurine. At its worst, it is a modern replica of a Roman bronze statuette known to be authentic. The evidence, however, falls short of proving beyond a reasonable doubt deliberate fraud on the part of its creator. (Merritt? Or Dawson?) Dawson clearly seemed determined to prove the statuette genuine, even manipulating subsequent analyses until he got the answer he wanted. This is not the behavior of an objective scientist, but rather that of an advocate.

When considered along with the totality of Dawson's amazing finds, culminating with Piltdown Man in 1912, however, it adds to the indictment of Dawson as a fraud whose fabrications perverted science and seriously damaged the early study of man's evolution. The story of the Beauport Park Statuette is only one in a long succession of archeological firsts by Charles Dawson, many of which are now considered bogus.

During the years covering the discovery of dozens of artifacts, Dawson acquired his reputation as an outstanding amateur archeologist, garnering several honors. But the one big honor eluded him, election as a fellow into the Royal Society of London for Improving Natural Knowledge, known as the Royal Society. Had he not died within four years of his Piltdown discoveries he probably would have achieved his goal, and perhaps, as some have speculated, knighthood. On the other hand, had Dawson lived another twenty to thirty years he may well have been exposed as the creator of one of science's greatest hoaxes. As it is, he probably escaped both knighthood and ignominy by his early death.

The sad impact of Piltdown Man on the study of man's evolution has best been stated by Joseph S. Weiner in his dramatic exposé of the hoax, titled *The Piltdown Forgery*, published in 1955:

> The end of Piltdown Man is the end of the most troubled chapter in human paleontology. From the first moment of the introduction of *Eoanthropus dawsoni* to the scientific world, the complexities and contradictions of the "enigma," as [Sir Arthur] Keith continued to call him, took up quite unduly and unnecessarily the energies of students of Man's evolution. This ill-begotten form of primitive man in the several hundred papers devoted to him received as nearly as much attention as all the legitimate specimens in the fossil record put together.

Suggested Reading

Russell, Miles. *Piltdown Man: The Secret Life of Charles Dawson and the World's Greatest Archaeological Hoax.* Stroud, Gloucestershire, England: Tempus Publishing, 2003.

Spencer, Frank. *Piltdown: A Scientific Forgery.* London, England: Natural History Museum Publications, Oxford Univ. Press, 1990.

Tudge, Colin. *The Link.* New York: Little, Brown, 2009.

Walsh, John Evangelist. *Unraveling Piltdown: The Science Fraud of the Century and Its Solution.* New York: Random House, 1996.

Weiner, Joseph S. *The Piltdown Forgery.* 1955. Reprint, New York: Dover Publications, 1980.

Zimmer, Carl. *Smithsonian Intimate Guide to Human Origins.* New York: HarperCollins, 2005.

6

The Missing Pages from
John Wilkes Booth's Diary

I have a greater desire and almost a mind to return to Washington and in a measure clear my name. Which I feel I can do.

—John Wilkes Booth

We have Booth's diary, and he has recorded a lot in it. . . . It concerns you for we either stick together in this thing or we will all go down the river together.

—Edwin M. Stanton, allegedly quoted
in George W. Julian's diary

The epigraph by John Wilkes Booth that appears above can be found in Booth's little diary or memorandum book, currently on display in the museum in Ford's Theatre. Booth made the entry during his attempted escape while hiding in a pine thicket, waiting until it was safe to cross the Potomac River into Virginia following his murder of Abraham Lincoln. The entry has spurred conspiracy-minded individuals for more than 140 years in their quest to prove that Lincoln's assassination was part of a grand conspiracy between members of his own administration and the Confederate government. Beginning in 1865, when Union prosecutors tried to prove that Jefferson Davis was behind Lincoln's murder, to more modern times, when self-professed historians claim Edwin Stanton engineered the president's death, reams of mysterious documents have surfaced which, if true, would force a rewriting of American history in shocking terms.[1] It all began when the assassin's diary was found on his body after he was killed

During his escape following his shooting of Lincoln, John Wilkes Booth kept a small diary recording his thoughts. (Author's collection)

at the farm of Richard Garrett near Bowling Green, Virginia, on Wednesday, April 26, 1865. What happened to that diary shortly after its discovery forms the basis of one of history's more successful hoaxes, which included the forging of documents and the salting of archives in an effort to shock the public into believing a sensational crime had occurred involving treason at the highest levels of government.

Our story begins on April 25, eleven days after Booth fatally shot Lincoln and after he had safely crossed the Potomac River with his cohort Davy Herold, when three former Confederate soldiers took them to the farm of Richard Garrett, a Virginia tobacco farmer. Garrett, believing the two men were also Confederate soldiers on their way home, offered them food and rest. Booth and Herold bedded down in the Garretts' tobacco barn, content that they were safe for the time being. Around three o'clock in the morning,

Abraham Lincoln.
Photograph by
Alexander Gardner,
February 5, 1865.
(Author's collection)

however, they were suddenly awakened by the sound of horses and men shouting. Stirring from their sleep, the two men peered between the open slats of the tobacco barn. In the moonlight they could make out a troop of Union cavalry gathered in front of the Garrett farmhouse.

After twelve days of hard searching, Union soldiers finally had caught up with Booth and Herold a hundred miles south of Washington, deep in Confederate Virginia. Based on a telegram received in the War Department telegraph office on Monday, April 24, Lafayette C. Baker, head of the National Detective Police, had sent two of his detectives and a troop from the 16th New York Cavalry to King George County, Virginia, in pursuit of the two fugitives. The detectives accompanying the squad of cavalry received a tip that one of the Confederate soldiers who aided the two men could be found in Bowling Green. Rousting the soldier from a dead sleep

The Richard Garrett farmhouse where Booth died early on the morning of April 26, 1865, twelve days after he began his escape. (Author's collection)

shortly after midnight, the detectives convinced him he should give up the two fugitives for his own safety. Realizing he had no choice, the soldier led the troopers to the Garrett farmhouse, where they learned that Booth and Herold were sleeping in the nearby tobacco barn.[2]

Surrounding the barn, the detectives began negotiating with Booth to surrender. After a bravado performance in which Booth tried to convince the soldiers to give him a fair chance to shoot it out with them, the barn was set on fire in an attempt to force Booth into surrendering. Herold had surrendered earlier without a struggle. As the fire raged through the barn, a shot rang out and Booth fell to the barn floor mortally wounded. The shot came from the pistol of Sergeant Boston Corbett, one of the troopers of the 16th New York. When questioned later, Corbett said he saw Booth raise his carbine as if he were going to shoot at the officers standing outside.[3] Corbett's act would eventually be used by conspiracy theorists, who claimed he violated orders not to shoot Booth, but to take him alive. Corbett, the theorists explain, was under secret orders from Secretary of War Stanton to

An engraving depicting Booth's final moments before dying on the porch of the Garrett farmhouse. (*Frank Leslie's Illustrated Newspaper,* May 13, 1865)

make sure Booth was not taken alive, so as to prevent him from revealing that Stanton and others were behind Lincoln's murder.[4]

The mortally wounded Booth was dragged from the burning barn and carried to the porch of the Garrett house, where he was laid out on a small mattress. The bullet had passed through his neck, severed part of his spinal cord, and left him paralyzed from the neck down. As Booth lay dying, Lieutenant Colonel Everton Conger, head of the search party, noticed his lips moving as if he were trying to speak. Leaning over and placing his ear close to the dying man's mouth, he heard Booth say in a halting whisper, "Tell . . . my . . . Mother . . . I . . . die . . . for . . . my country."[5]

It was a few minutes past seven o'clock on the morning of April 26, 1865, when Booth died. Before his body was shipped back to Washington, Conger carefully went through the contents of Booth's pockets, making a written inventory of each item. He found a small stickpin inscribed, "Dan Bryant to J.W.B.," a small boxed compass, a file with a cork stuck on the sharp end (for protection), a small pipe, a large handful of shavings (to use as a fire starter), a spur, a bank draft made on the Ontario Bank of

The triumvirate that resulted in Booth's capture and the recovery of his diary. From left: Lieutenant Luther B. Baker, Colonel Lafayette C. Baker (head of the National Detective Police), and Lieutenant Colonel Everton Conger. (Author's collection)

Canada for 61 pounds, 12 shillings, and 10 pence (the equivalent of $300 in gold or $660 in U.S. currency—greenbacks), and the small memorandum book, which Booth used as a diary during his flight.[6] Inside the diary were five photographs of women he had known—four actresses and his fiancée, Lucy Hale.

The items were carried back to Washington and turned over to Stanton in his office in the War Department. The bank draft, compass, carbine, Bowie knife, and brace of pistols taken from Booth and Herold were introduced at the conspirators' trial by the prosecution as exhibits.[7] The small memorandum book, or diary, however, was never produced and remained in Stanton's safe, seemingly forgotten at the time of the trial. The diary surfaced two years later when it was introduced as evidence during the impeachment trial of President Andrew Johnson in the House of Representatives. Although the diary was known to have existed at the time of the Lincoln conspiracy trial, neither the prosecution nor the defense nor

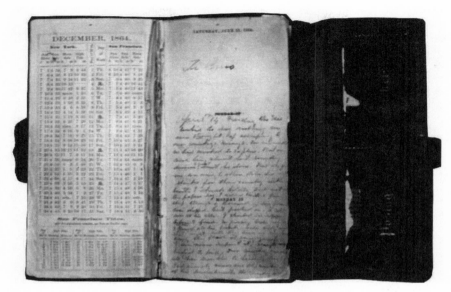

John Wilkes Booth's little memorandum book, often referred to as his diary. It was found on his body after his death by Lieutenant Colonel Everton Conger and Lieutenant Luther B. Baker and turned over to Secretary of War Edwin M. Stanton. (National Park Service)

the nine military officers serving as judge and jury questioned its absence. Not even the press raised questions about the diary or why it was not introduced at the trial.

When the diary was finally examined, it was found to have several dozen pages missing. Lafayette C. Baker was called as a witness at Johnson's impeachment trial in 1867 and engaged in the following exchange:

> Q. You are still of the opinion that the book [Booth's diary] is not now in the condition it was when you first saw it?
> A. That is my opinion.
> Q. Did you see the Secretary of War count the leaves at the time you and [Lieutenant Colonel Everton] Conger were together at his house?
> A. No, I think not.
> Q. Did you count the absent leaves or stubs?
> A. No sir; I never saw any stubs until I saw them here.

Q. Do you mean to say that at the time you gave the book to the Secretary of War there were no leaves gone?

A. I do.

Q. That is still your opinion?

A. That is still my opinion.[8]

Conger also appeared as a witness. His testimony went somewhat differently:

Q. To whom did you deliver them [articles taken from Booth's body at the Garrett farm]?

A. To Mr. Stanton.

Q. Did he retain possession of the diary?

A. Yes, sir.

Q. Do you know who has it now?

A. Judge Holt [Judge Advocate General Joseph Holt].

Q. Do you know when he received it?

A. I do not.

Q. Who was present when you delivered the diary to Mr. Stanton?

A. Colonel L. C. Baker.

Q. Have you seen that diary since?

A. Yes, sir; I saw it today.

Q. State whether it is in the same condition as when you delivered it to Mr. Stanton.

A. I think it is.

Q. Have you examined it closely?

A. I have.

Q. Are there any leaves cut or torn out?

A. Yes, sir.

Q. Were they torn out when you first had possession of it?

A. There were some out and I think the same.[9]

The conflict between Baker's and Conger's testimony was never resolved. It should be noted that Baker was not present at Booth's capture, and that it was Conger who removed the diary from Booth's body and examined it. What we do know for a fact is that dozens of pages were missing from Booth's diary at the time of his capture, and that at least two of the pages were removed by Booth to use for writing notes intended for Dr. Richard Stuart when Booth and Herold stopped at the Stuarts' house. This occurred on Monday, April 24, while Booth and Herold were at a cabin preparing to leave for Port Conway on the Rappahannock River. Booth was miffed at Stuart's failure to allow him to spend the night in his house and wrote him a note expressing his disapproval of Stuart's behavior. The "missing" pages became one of the first of many controversial questions to come out of the Lincoln assassination. Conspiracy theorists became convinced they contained the key to who really was behind Lincoln's assassination. The very notion that pages were missing suggested a cover-up.

Jumping forward to the year 1937, Otto Eisenschiml, a chemist turned historian, published his infamous book, *Why Was Lincoln Murdered?* The book caused a seismic upheaval among history buffs and the public in general.[10] Eisenschiml, through clever innuendo and manipulation of facts, framed a series of questions that pointed an incriminating finger at Lincoln's secretary of war, Edwin Stanton, accusing him of masterminding Lincoln's assassination. Up to this point, there was never any suggestion that Stanton or anyone else in Lincoln's administration had anything to do with his death.

One of the entries Booth made in his diary was a statement that caught Eisenschiml's attention: "To night I will once more try the river [Potomac]

Some conspiracists believe Secretary of War Edwin McMasters Stanton deliberately withheld Booth's diary because its content implicated him and other prominent people in Lincoln's murder. (Author's collection)

with the intent to cross; *I have a greater desire and almost a mind to return to Washington and in a measure clear my name. Which I feel I can do*" (emphasis added). How could Booth possibly clear his name? What did he mean when he wrote those words? Eisenschiml seized on Booth's remark as a launching pad for his bizarre theory that Stanton, along with other powerful figures in the North, wanted Lincoln out of the way so they could deal with a defeated South without his interference. To accomplish this, Stanton turned to Booth as the instrument to remove Lincoln by capture or assassination. Never once did Eisenschiml consider that Booth was acting on behalf of the Confederate government, and therefore serving a different cause. Underlying Eisenschiml's theory of Stanton's involvement was his belief that Stanton had been informed that a plot was afloat and did nothing to stop it from taking place.[11]

Eisenschiml also claimed that Lincoln was refused protection at the same time he wrote that the president's bodyguard was derelict in his duty, thereby allowing Booth easy access to Lincoln. Both claims are false. Lincoln never requested protection, and his bodyguard that night, John F. Parker, accompanied him to the theater. Once inside, Parker's job was done until it was time for the president to leave. Lincoln's valet and personal messenger, Charles Forbes, sat outside the box and screened visitors who wished to see the president. He allowed at least three people to enter at different times during the evening. Unfortunately, Booth was one of the three.

Eisenschiml further claimed that if General Grant had accompanied Lincoln to the theater as originally planned, Booth would never have been able to pass Grant's military guards, thus protecting Lincoln as well as preventing his own assassination. Eisenschiml claimed that Stanton ordered Grant not to go to the theater with Lincoln, and Grant dutifully complied. Apparently Eisenschiml believed Stanton was senior in command to the commander in chief. Another false claim. Grant was free to attend the theater with the Lincolns that night but chose to travel with his wife to New Jersey to see their children. Like Lincoln, Grant often moved about Washington unaccompanied by military guards or aides, including those occasions when he attended the theater. Just two months earlier, on February 10, Grant accompanied Lincoln to Ford's Theatre to see Booth's brother-in-law, John Sleeper Clarke, in a comedy entitled *Love in Livery.* No military guards were posted at the president's box, and several people freely entered the box with messages for Lincoln. The event was described in the *Washington Evening Star* the next day.[12]

While Eisenschiml went to ridiculous extremes in attempting to implicate Stanton in Booth's plot, he did not claim that Stanton withheld the diary to cover up his role in Lincoln's murder. Rather, he believed that Stanton withheld the diary because its contents would have benefited some of the defendants on trial for Lincoln's murder. "Booth's notebook," Eisenschiml wrote, "showed plainly that, up to the last day, kidnapping and not murder had been the goal of the conspirators."[13] While Booth initially plotted to kidnap Lincoln, he changed his plan to murder days before April 14. Here again, Eisenschiml overreached. Did Eisenschiml really believe Booth and his cohorts could kidnap the president of the United States and transport him 120 miles through enemy-occupied territory without someone getting killed? If Booth and his cohorts had no intention of killing anyone, why were they carrying guns during their aborted kidnap plot on March 17, 1865?

While Eisenschiml raised several questions about the assassination, he never questioned the missing pages. That was left to later conspiracy advocates, who, although lacking Eisenschiml's reputation as a historian, equaled his audacity in attempting to rewrite history.

In November 1975, thirty-eight years after Eisenschiml first accused Stanton of involvement in Lincoln's murder, a rumor spread that the long-sought missing pages had at last been discovered in the possession of a Stanton descendant, and that they were filled with incriminating evidence not only resurrecting Otto Eisenschiml's theory of Stanton's role in Lincoln's murder, but naming dozens of other high-ranking politicians and prominent people as accomplices. Two students of the case, James O. Hall and Richard Sloan, were particularly interested in pursuing the claims. Hall was the acknowledged scholar on the subject and spent countless hours investigating the various conspiracy theories associated with Lincoln's murder. Sloan was the editor and publisher of a popular Lincoln newsletter, *The Lincoln Log,* which devoted much of its space to the assassination. If the rumor about the missing pages was true, their exposure could result in the rewriting of American history. Sloan doggedly pursued the rumors and was able to make contact with a man who claimed to have access to the missing pages.

At first, Sloan's informant insisted on anonymity, referring to himself only as "Mr. X."[14] Eventually Sloan gained Mr. X's confidence, and he revealed himself to be Joseph Lynch, a dealer in rare books and Americana living in Worthington, Massachusetts. Lynch told Sloan that he discovered the missing pages in 1974 in the possession of one of Stanton's great-granddaughters. She had contacted him for an appraisal of some artifacts. (She

The dean of Lincoln assassination scholars, James O. Hall spent several years demolishing the numerous unfounded myths associated with Lincoln's murder, including the missing pages from Booth's diary. (Kieran McAuliffe)

also insisted on anonymity, Lynch claimed). Hall had many questions for Lynch, but he was sure that if he pressed for an interview Lynch might be scared away. So Hall fed some of his questions through Sloan, who reported back to him. The whole affair had an air of mystery and intrigue. Lynch never gave Sloan his personal telephone number, always using a pay phone when contacting Sloan.[15] It was reminiscent of Bob Woodward and Carl Bernstein's adventures with "Deep Throat" in their investigation of the Watergate cover-up. Sloan kept his newsletter readers informed of the latest news as it became available to him.[16] Readers of the *Lincoln Log* could not wait for the next issue with its tale of the missing pages.

As word of the discovery of the missing pages spread, a motion picture studio in Salt Lake City, Sunn Classic Pictures, expressed an interest in obtaining the rights to them for use in a major motion picture about the Lincoln assassination. The pages were the stuff great movies were made of. Lynch, claiming to act as the Stanton heir's intermediary, negotiated with David Balsiger and his partner, Charles Sellier, of Sunn Classic Pictures for the use of the missing pages along with other related documents that

Lynch claimed were in her possession. Balsiger allegedly paid $39,000 for the right to read the material and take notes.[17] They soon acquired a full transcript of the missing pages, again through Lynch's efforts. Balsiger and Sellier wanted to see the original pages, but Lynch claimed the Stanton heir would not permit anyone but him to see them, claiming they were kept in a bank safe-deposit box. In October 1977, Sunn Classics, without ever having seen the original pages, released the movie and a paperback book under the title *The Lincoln Conspiracy.*[18]

Lacking the necessary expertise to evaluate the transcripts, Balsiger and Sellier had hired Ray A. Neff as a consultant. Neff, a professor of health sciences at Indiana State University, was well known in assassination circles for his bizarre theory that Booth escaped capture from the Garrett farm, eventually making his way to Guwahati, India, where he died in 1883. Similar to the plot outlined in the missing pages, Neff claimed that Stanton and his cronies were behind Lincoln's murder. Neff had amassed a vast collection of documents that supported his theory. The documents, all typescript copies, spelled out in detail the who and why of Lincoln's murder. None of the original documents existed; only typed copies were in Neff's possession. Neff's collection neatly dovetailed with the missing pages.

In 1961, sixteen years before the release of the movie, Neff had convinced Robert Fowler, the editor of *Civil War Times Illustrated,* that his unorthodox claims fingering Stanton for Lincoln's murder were true. In 1961, the centennial year of the start of the Civil War, Fowler ran a sensational article in his magazine titled "Was Stanton behind Lincoln's Murder?"[19] The article was based on the "new discoveries" by Neff that he made available to Fowler. Neff's most sensational claim involved the man behind Booth's capture, Lafayette C. Baker, head of the National Detective Police. Neff claimed to have discovered cipher messages written in the margins of a book originally owned by Baker. Neff also claimed to have found the book in a used bookstore in Philadelphia. According to Neff, Baker, privy to Stanton's treasonous plans, came to fear for his life because of what he knew. After several scrapes with near death, Baker allegedly succumbed to arsenic poisoning in 1868, murdered to keep him from exposing the other plotters. According to the ciphers Neff discovered in Baker's book, Stanton headed a group of over fifty prominent people in the North who sought to remove Lincoln once the war was won. It was an astonishing claim.

Neff's treasure trove included: secret service files pilfered from Baker's agency by one of his top agents, Andrew Potter; an unpublished diary of a congressman, George Julian; old letters, book manuscripts, deathbed confessions, secret cipher-coded messages, dozens of rare photographs, and secret correspondence intercepted by Secretary of War Edwin Stanton.[20] The documents literally ran into the thousands of pages. The discovery of such a wealth of previously unknown material was unprecedented in the annals of historical research. It was this "gold mine" of incriminating documents that consultant Neff brought to Balsiger and Sellier and which, together with the missing pages from Booth's diary, were used as the basis for their movie and book.

There was a problem, however. In the years following the 1961 article in *Civil War Times,* several historians presented evidence that Neff's claims were based on faulty research and fabricated documents (one historian referred to them as "ingenuine").[21] They were found to contain wrong names, wrong dates, wrong places, and wrong relationships, which seriously challenged their authenticity. Most disturbing of all, every one of Neff's documents was a typescript copy of an original that no longer existed.[22] Not a single original document survived.

Between 1977 and 1981, the revamped *Civil War Times,* under its new editor, William C. "Jack" Davis, ran a series of editorials retracting the 1961 article.[23] Davis wrote, "Rarely does a magazine print a retraction or refutation of one of its own articles, but this is precisely what we do now. It is a debt we owe to the cause of history."[24] Davis wrote that if they are not "outright forgeries, [they] are so highly suspect as to make them inadmissible as evidence in any serious investigation."[25]

Davis, however, was referring only to the documents in Neff's collection, not the missing pages of Booth's diary. What about these pages? Unlike the Neff material, the originals of the missing pages allegedly still existed, although they were unavailable for historians to examine. When pressed to produce the original pages, Lynch claimed the owner was reluctant to release them because of her concern the documents might legally belong to the federal government, and she did not want to become embroiled in a messy legal battle.[26] This argument fails, however. A person's private diary or journal, even if used as evidence in a murder trial, remains the property of the individual. Whatever the real reason, the alleged original pages remained hidden away from scholarly examination.

One of the caveats that raised doubts over the authenticity of the missing pages was Lynch's claim that they had faint blue lines printed on them while the diary displayed in Ford's Theatre was believed to contain pages without blue lines. Hence, the missing pages were not from the Booth diary. Lynch received permission from Michael Harman, custodian of the relics in the Ford's Theatre collection, to examine the diary firsthand. To his delight, he found that the diary had the same faint blue lines as the missing pages. They had not been noticed before. Lynch further reported that he found "suspicious erasures . . . and evidence of invisible ink that was beginning to show up" on several of the pages. But his most shocking conclusion was that the writing in the diary was forged![27] It wasn't, Lynch said, Booth's handwriting.

The forgery claim made no sense at all. When Balsiger learned of Lynch's "findings," he sent Ray Neff, now working for Balsiger, to Washington in hopes of having him examine the diary and photograph the pages using ultraviolet and infrared illumination in an effort to confirm Lynch's claims. As incredible as it sounds, Harman granted Neff permission to examine the diary!

James O. Hall, on learning that Neff had photographed the diary on behalf of a commercial movie studio, became concerned that the pictures would become the property of Neff and Balsiger and that other researchers would not have access to them. Any claims made about secret writing or evidence of tampering or forgery could not be independently verified. Hall was concerned because of Neff's involvement in the earlier controversy about Lafayette Baker's alleged secret cipher markings that William Davis had termed "ingenuine."[28] Hall's concern was that Neff was working as a consultant for a private, profit-making company whose financial interests would be seriously jeopardized if the documents in question proved fraudulent. The National Park Service had no way of protecting itself should a controversy later arise. Hall suggested that the FBI be requested to carry out a thorough analysis of the diary, including Booth's handwriting. He had recently uncovered two important letters written by Booth shortly before the assassination that had been misfiled in the National Archives. Their provenance was solid. They could be considered authentic samples of Booth's handwriting in determining the legitimacy of the handwriting in the diary.

To everyone's surprise, the Park Service rejected Hall's suggestion. The principal reason they gave was that the diary was fragile, and any further handling might damage it. But the damage had already been done when the Park Service granted a private citizen exclusive access to the diary. Faced with the Park Service's decision to deny further access to the diary, Hall sought the help of influential friends, who contacted several political leaders, including Vice President Walter Mondale and Senator Hubert Humphrey. The Park Service, under political pressure, suddenly had a change of heart and announced they would turn the diary over to the FBI's forensic laboratory for analysis. Hall, in writing to FBI Director Clarence Kelly, said, "It is our hope that you will use the most sophisticated means to photograph each and every page of this diary, to bring up whatever is there or to demonstrate that nothing is there."[29] Hall went on to point out that a claim had been made that the writing in the diary was not that of John Wilkes Booth and that the forgery was committed to aid in a massive government cover-up. The analysis of the handwriting by FBI experts would settle the question once and for all.

The FBI's report stated that "no invisible writing, unusual obliterations or alterations or any characteristics of a questionable nature were found" and that "the handwriting in the diary was prepared by the writer of the specimens furnished by the National Archives[30] known to be in the handwriting of John Wilkes Booth."[31] No invisible writing, no secret (encoded) writing, no altered writing, and no erasures were found. Several of the stubs left behind when pages were removed showed signs of handwriting. There were faint blue lines printed on each of the dated pages, just as Lynch claimed. Hall's fears were put to rest. In all, the FBI report noted that a total of forty-three sheets (eighty-six pages) were missing from the diary.[32]

Now that the FBI had answered any questions concerning the diary's condition, attention turned to what was written on those alleged missing pages that Joseph Lynch claimed he had uncovered. Richard Sloan suggested Lynch meet with Hall. He pointed out that sooner or later Lynch or Sunn Classic Pictures would have to produce proof that the pages existed and were real. Hall, after all, was the leading authority on the assassination, and if anyone could authenticate the missing pages it was him. Lynch appeared nervous at Sloan's suggestion. He told Sloan he didn't trust historians. Lynch felt they would take advantage of him or misquote him.[33] After considerable cajoling and prodding by Sloan, Lynch agreed to meet with both men, in a hotel room in White Plains, New York. Once the two men met, Lynch overcame his distrust of Hall and gave him a copy of the full typescript of the pages. In return, he asked Hall for his evaluation of their authenticity. Hall agreed. From Lynch's perspective, Hall's approval would blunt any criticism.

Following are excerpts taken from the typescript provided to Hall:

I [Booth] have finally decided to take the step which I hoped would not be necessary. Sent a message by a friend to Jefferson Davis and await summons from him.

I received instructions to proceed to Montreal and wait upon Clement Clay and Jacob Thompson. I am to proceed at once.[34]

Clement C. Clay and Jacob Thompson, two Confederate emissaries of Jefferson Davis, were sent to Montreal in April 1864 to establish a secret service operation working out of neutral Canada. Davis authorized $1 million in gold to finance a series of attacks against the North in an effort to demoralize its citizens, resulting in Lincoln's defeat in the fall elections.

Clay and Thompson finally arrive and inform me if I were willing to undertake a mission for the Confederacy, they could use my services.

I ran into John Surratt the other day and by a conversation, he told me that he was now serving the Confederacy as a courier between Washington, Richmond, and Canada.

John Surratt, Mary Surratt's son and a cohort of Booth, worked as an agent for the Confederate State Department, reporting directly to Judah P. Benjamin, the Confederate secretary of state.

He comes tonight bringing with him four trusted friends he swears by. We are to meet at Ella Washington's boarding house in Washington.

Surratt brought to me this morning Thomas Jones, Dr. Mudd, and Col. Cox.
Jones said that he had a brother-in-law who could also be enlisted [Thomas Harbin] but that the brother-in-law had to support his family and would require $100 a month. When I go South, he will introduce me to him.

Thomas Jones served during the war as the Confederate Signal Service's chief agent in Charles County, Maryland. Early in the war Jones lived in a house on a high bluff overlooking the Potomac River with a clear view of the Confederate signal camp on the Virginia side. Following Lincoln's assassination, Jones hid Booth and Herold in a pine thicket for five days, caring for them before putting them safely across the Potomac River. Jones's brother-in-law was Thomas Harbin, also a Confederate agent. Harbin had served as postmaster in Charles County before the war. Several years after the war Harbin was interviewed by George Alfred Townsend, a highly respected newspaper reporter and author. Harbin told Townsend that Dr. Mudd introduced him to Booth at a prearranged meeting at the Bryantown Tavern on December 18, 1864. As a result of the meeting Harbin agreed to join Booth's kidnap plot. Once Booth and Herold crossed the Potomac River following Lincoln's murder, Harbin arranged for them to be taken to the summer home of Dr. Richard Stuart, where they hoped to receive food and rest. Stuart refused Booth lodging and sent him to the cabin of William Lucas, a free black, where the two fugitives spent the night.

> In Richmond, I saw Judah Benjamin first. He brought me to Vice-President Stevens and the two of them and I went to see Jefferson Davis.

> I received instructions in all detail and an order for $70,000 drawn on a friendly bank.

> In Philadelphia today I met with Jay Cooke. After waiting for an hour and a half, he entered the room with great apology citing as his reason for the delay—press of business.

Cooke was a prominent banker and financier who used his own bank and influence with other bankers to raise large sums of money for the government by selling government bonds. By January 1864, Cooke had raised over $600 million to help Lincoln finance the war and keep it going.

> The discussions that we had concerning the project he was very concerned with being compromised, but said that he would arrange for me to meet a number of people who have interests in the plans, in New York on Friday next at the Astor House.

> Cooke brought his brother Henry—greeted me warmly and said he thought most highly of Judah Benjamin and anyone who that wily fox, Benjamin, would send would be the best man available.

Henry Cooke was a journalist who in 1856 used his paper, the *Ohio State Journal,* to get Salmon P. Chase elected governor of Ohio. In 1861 he became head of his brother's bank in Washington, and in 1862 he became president of his brother's street railway system that ran between Washington and Georgetown.

> We had lunch, then went to a room where the people present were a number of speculators in cotton and gold.

> Present were Thurlow Weed, a person by the name of Noble, a man by the name of Chandler, a Mr. Bell—who said he was a friend of John Conness.

Weed was the political "boss" of the Whig and, later, Republican parties in New York. He supported William Seward for the Republican nomination for president in 1860. Isaac Bell was a cotton merchant. Zachariah Chandler was a Radical Republican senator from Michigan (1857–1875) and a constant thorn in Lincoln's side. He was also a business associate of John Conness, senator from California.

> Answering a knock on my door this morning, I found Lafayette Baker on my doorstep. I thought the end had come.

Baker was head of the War Department's National Detective Police (NDP), which after the war became the Secret Service. Baker had a shady reputation for bending the law in carrying out his investigations, but he was very effective at dealing with corrupt government and military individuals.

> But instead, he handed me letters from Jefferson Davis, and Judah Benjamin, and from Clement Clay. I gave him the money and sent a message to Richmond. I don't trust him. I wait for answer. I receive reply, my orders—trust him! I do not!

Davis was president of the Confederate States. Benjamin was the Confederate secretary of state at the time of Lincoln's assassination, and Clay was a Confederate diplomat who became one of two commissioners Davis sent to Canada to carry out undercover actions against the North.

> He [Senator John Conness] also said Montgomery Blair was with us, but that Blair had to be careful. He was watched constantly.

Montgomery Blair served as Lincoln's postmaster general. He resigned in 1864, forced out of Lincoln's cabinet by the Radical Republicans.

Baker comes and brings with him Col. Conger. I told Baker to have him leave because I did not know him and talking to too many people can be dangerous.

Lieutenant Colonel Everton J. Conger was a detective in Lafayette Baker's NDP. He was the ranking officer in charge of the troop of cavalry that captured Booth and Herold at the Garrett farm. Conger removed the diary from Booth's body and turned it over to Stanton. One conspiracy theory has Conger shooting Booth under orders from Stanton to prevent Booth from implicating Stanton and others should he be taken alive.

[Judah] Benjamin says that the Jacobeans [word missing] received their promises and their money.

Jacobean was a social club of the Republican Party.

I purchased a carbine entirely covered in leather. I darken it with lamp black.

Booth purchased a Jenks carbine on March 20.

I took Paine and Surratt with me and we waited on the road near the garden. In the late hours of the morning we heard a horse approaching. It was him. It was dark and I waited until he was 25 or 30 yards from me. I fired! I saw his hat fall.
　　Paine fired twice. He stayed in the saddle and galloped away. Within minutes they pursued us. Within two miles, we eluded them. Another failure!

Paine was an alias used by Lewis Powell. This excerpt apparently refers to the incident in which Lincoln had his hat shot off of his head while approaching the main gate to the Soldiers' Home, where Lincoln and his family stayed during the summer months. Lincoln later made light of the incident, saying it was an accidental stray shot. Ward Hill Lamon, Washington marshal and a close friend of Lincoln, believed it was an assassination attempt. Lincoln's hat was later recovered by a sentry, who said it had a bullet hole through it.

I met Conger at the Herndon House. He was in mufti and warned no new attempts until we have a new plan.

The Herndon House was a boarding house located one block from Ford's Theatre. Booth paid for a room for Lewis Powell. Booth, Powell, George Atzerodt, and David Herold met in Powell's room around seven o'clock on the evening of April 14 to go over Booth's assassination plans.

If I try again without orders they will find me in the Potomac along with my friends.

Paine said he would kill the tin soldier if I wished. I told him not to.

The "tin soldier" presumably refers to Lafayette Baker.

A new plan—other arrangements to be made. I am to have charge.

The "new plan" was presumably an assassination plan.

I believe that Baker and Eckert and the Secretary are controlling our activities and this frightens me.

Thomas T. Eckert was the U.S. assistant secretary of war and head of the war department's telegraph office.

I have found the additional men needed. The routes are arranged. It is too late to withdraw.

By the almighty God, I swear that I shall lay the body of this tyrant upon the altar of Mars. And if by this act I am slain, they too shall be cast into Hell for I have given information to a friend who will have the nation know who the traitors are.
     Pax Vale[35]

Mars is a reference to Secretary of War Stanton. *Pax Vale* means "Peace and Farewell."

So here are a series of diary entries that clearly indict Stanton and several of those around him in Booth's plot to assassinate Lincoln. In analyzing the transcript, there are several things to consider. First is the alleged "Stanton heir," who Lynch claimed owned the missing pages. When Hall contacted the known descendants of Edwin Stanton, none of them were aware of the missing pages or of any other documents relating to Lincoln's assassination. When confronted with this finding, Lynch claimed the great-granddaughter was descended from an illegitimate child of one of Stanton's sons. This claim, however, is difficult to believe without some sort of documentary proof. Lynch was unable to produce any evidence to support his claim other than his own word. Why such an important document as pages from Booth's diary would descend through an illegitimate child is equally puzzling.

The second consideration is the internal evidence of the transcript. Even the best of fabricators make mistakes. One need only read the first two sentences to see that the transcript is problematic. The entry reads: "They say that Jubal Early has attack[ed] Rockville and even though one can see the flames and hear the gunfire, no one knows how the battle goes. At lunch someone said that Lincoln and Stanton had almost been killed when a shell burst within five feet of them on the parapet of Fort Stevens."

This entry clearly places Booth in Washington at the time of Confederate Jubal Early's attack. In early July 1864, Early marched out of the Shenandoah Valley with orders to attack Washington and sack parts of the city. The objective was to force Grant to send part of his army facing Lee around Richmond and Petersburg to Washington, thus relieving pressure on Lee. On July 9, Early pushed aside a delaying force under Union major general Lew Wallace near Frederick, Maryland, and marched south toward the capital. Early's forces reached the outlying environs of Washington near Silver Spring on July 11, where his troops were stopped at Fort Stevens. A Federal force from the 6th Army Corps arrived just in time to repel the Confederate attack.

Fort Stevens was located a short distance from Soldiers' Home, where Lincoln was staying with his family at the time of Early's attack. On July 12, Lincoln visited the fort and climbed atop the parapet to watch the action. His recognizable form drew Confederate fire, and an army surgeon standing next to Lincoln was shot in the hip, knocking him from the parapet.

While the entry in the alleged diary indicates Booth was in Washington at the time of Early's raid, he was, in fact, several hundred miles away in Franklin, Pennsylvania, tending to his oil investments. On June 7, 1864, Booth wrote to Isabel Sumner, a sixteen-year-old girl he was courting at the time, "I start tomorrow for the mountains of Penn. Where I remain about three weeks."[36] The correspondence continued through the end of August. On July 14, Booth wrote to Isabel from New York City, "I have just returned from the mountains of Penn—God bless you."[37] Booth's trip to Pennsylvania is corroborated by his brother Junius, who wrote in his diary for June 9, "John & Joe Simonds left for Oil City [Pennsylvania]."[38] Clearly, whoever fabricated the missing pages was unaware of these letters in the possession of a descendant of Isabel Sumner.

The next questionable entry reads, "At a party given by Eva's parents, I met Senator John Conness. Conness says Eddie and he are friends from the days in California in '55 and '56."

Conness was a senator from California (from March 3, 1863, to March 3, 1869) who switched from the Democratic Party to the Republican Party in 1864. The transcript supplied with the Sunn Classic Pictures promotional material identifies "Eddie" as John Wilkes Booth's older brother, Edwin Booth. Of the known letters written by Booth, three mention his brother Edwin by name. The first is a letter to Edwin with the salutation "Dear Ted."[39] The remaining two letters are to friends, in which Booth calls his brother "Ned" ("I am glad Ned is doing well,"[40] and "When did you see Ned?").[41] The name "Eddie" is absent from any known writing of Booth or, for that matter, any of the other members of the Booth family.

The fifth entry in the diary reads: "John Morgan is dead. Another brave spirit has paid the ultimate price for his patriotism. I met him years ago at a soiree in New Orleans. He was a gentleman and we will miss him."

John Hunt Morgan was a brigadier general in the Confederate army who mostly operated behind enemy lines as a guerilla raider. Morgan was engaged in several small operations that gained him fame as a dashing cavalier. He was killed on September 4, 1864, in Greeneville, Tennessee, while attempting to escape from Union cavalry that had surrounded his headquarters. The only time that Booth was in New Orleans was the period from March 6 through April 3, 1864, five months prior to Morgan's death. Booth was fulfilling an acting engagement at the time while Morgan was carrying out raids in Kentucky, including Mt. Sterling (March 22) and Danville (March 24). At the time of Booth's engagement, New Orleans was occupied by Union troops, making it doubtful if not impossible for Morgan to attend a soiree where he allegedly met Booth.

The next entry notes that Grant has advanced to within seven miles of Richmond. This occurred on September 28, 1864. It reads: "I have finally decided to take the step which I hoped would not be necessary. Sent a message to Jefferson Davis and await summons from him." The timing is off in this entry. We know that Booth made his decision to kidnap Lincoln in late July, not October. During the first week of August, Booth summoned two old friends from his Baltimore boyhood days, Samuel Arnold and Michael O'Laughlen, to meet with him in his room at Barnum's City Hotel in Baltimore. It was during this meeting that Booth told Arnold and O'Laughlen of his plan to capture Lincoln and turn him over to authorities in Richmond.

The next troublesome entry claims that Booth, along with Lewis Paine (Powell) and John Surratt, lay in wait for Lincoln near his summer residence at Soldiers' Home. As he approached Booth fired once and Paine fired twice. Booth writes, "I saw his hat fall." In the companion book version of *The Lincoln Conspiracy* movie, the date taken from the missing pages for this failed attempt on Lincoln's life is March 22. Apparently the person who wrote the diary was unaware that Booth was in New York City on March 22 and Lincoln was not staying at the Soldiers' Home. The records of the National Hotel, where Booth stayed when in Washington, show he checked out on March 21 and took the 7:30 P.M. train to New York. There is a record of Booth sending a telegram from the St. Nicholas Hotel in New York to Louis Weichmann at the Surratt boarding house on March 23. Booth did not return to the National Hotel until the evening of March 25. The "hat incident" occurred in August 1864—not in March, according to those people close to Lincoln who were aware of it.

These errors, Booth's presence in Washington at the time of Early's attack, the use of the name "Eddie" when referring to Edwin Booth, the alleged meeting between Booth and Morgan in New Orleans, the timing of Booth's decision to kidnap Lincoln, and his attempt to shoot Lincoln on March 22, 1864, when he was actually in New York City are careless mistakes that point to the missing pages as being fabrications. The disposition of the real missing pages is unclear. We know Booth used two of the sheets (four pages) to write notes to Dr. Stuart. The other forty-one sheets (eighty-two pages) were more than likely also used by Booth as note paper. One thing seems clear, however: they were not used by Booth to record the bogus writings that appear in the typescript Lynch claimed came from Booth's diary and which David Balsiger and Charles E. Sellier Jr. relied on.

There are other documents that Sunn Classic Pictures and David Balsiger relied on that also appear to be fabricated. The principal one is a supposedly unpublished entry from the journal of George Washington Julian, a Radical Republican congressman from Indiana. Sunn Pictures accepted the passage as proof the pages were authentic. The alleged entry in Julian's journal shows that Booth's diary was intact when it was turned over to Stanton, just as Lafayette Baker and those who believed in Stanton's complicity in Lincoln's murder had claimed. The entry describes how the diary turned up in Stanton's office on April 24, two days before Booth was cornered and killed at the Garrett farm. Just how the diary turned up in Stanton's office before Booth's capture is an amazing story that *The Lincoln Conspiracy* writers try to explain.

According to Balsiger's scenario, Booth's diary was not found on his body on April 26 as most history books claim. It was found by one of Lafayette Baker's alleged Indian scouts, Whippet Nalgai, lying in the tall grass along the banks of a creek where Booth left it by mistake during his attempted escape.[42] Working separately from the Union search party that eventually cornered Booth, Nalgai found the diary with several other items belonging to Booth at the spot where Booth and Herold landed early Monday morning after crossing the Potomac River on the night of April 23–24. Booth had rested along the bank of the creek while Herold sought the help of Mrs. Elizabeth Quesenberry, a Confederate agent who lived nearby. Thomas Jones had told Booth to seek out Mrs. Quesenberry, who he was certain would help the two men. After listening to Herold's story, Quesenberry sent for Thomas Harbin, the agent Booth had enlisted in December 1864 with the aid of Dr. Samuel Mudd. Harbin arranged for horses and a guide to take Booth and Herold to the summer home of Richard Stuart in King George County, Virginia. According to *The Lincoln Conspiracy*, Booth mistakenly left the diary and several other items in the tall grass while waiting for Herold to return from Quesenberry's house. Later that same day, while searching for Booth, Whippet Nalgai discovered the diary. Nalgai rushed the diary back to Washington and delivered it personally to Lafayette Baker, who gave it to Stanton on Monday, April 24.[43] After examining the diary, Stanton summoned to his office the three Radical Republicans involved in his plot to kill Lincoln: George Julian, Senator Zachariah Chandler of Michigan, and Senator John Conness of California.

Julian describes the scene in Stanton's office in the April 24 entry of his journal. Julian wrote that on entering Stanton's office he "sensed something was amiss." Stanton told him, "We have Booth's diary, and he has recorded a lot in it." Senator Conness, who was scanning the pages when Julian arrived, was "moaning repeatedly, 'Oh, my God. I am ruined if this ever gets out.'"[44] Stanton took the diary from Conness and asked Julian to look at it. Julian demurred. "I was better off not reading it," he later wrote in his journal. Stanton pressed him in threatening language: "It concerns you for we either stick together in this thing or we will all go down the river together." Stanton gave the diary to Thomas Eckert, his assistant, and told him to secure it in his iron safe, warning those in the room, "We cannot let it out."[45] The excerpt is sensational to say the least, and it confirms the claims made in the missing pages.[46]

Following his death in 1899, Julian's journals containing the alleged passage passed to his daughter, Grace Julian Clarke. In 1926 she loaned them to Indiana historian Claude Bowers, who was working on his anti-Radical book, *The Tragic Era*.[47] According to an explanatory statement in the Neff-Guttridge Collection at Indiana State University written by Neff,[48] Bowers "photographed the journal pages without Grace Clarke's knowledge."[49] Neff claimed that Bowers transcribed the photographic copies in the presence of an Indianapolis businessman by the name of Hugh Smith. Smith then took the transcribed copies and had them notarized. According to Neff, Bowers for some strange reason then destroyed the photographs, leaving only the transcribed copies. Smith, thinking ahead, "took one [of Bowers's transcribed copies] back to Indianapolis to have proof of the journal entries should Bowers ever need support in the future."[50] Why do you suppose Bowers destroyed the photographs? Why would he need to substantiate his writings? And why did he rely on Hugh Smith to provide that support? Why didn't he simply keep the photographic copies in his own files? Bowers never made any claims or statements in his writings that referred to the alleged Julian excerpts that implicated Stanton and the three Republicans in Lincoln's murder. None of Bowers's writings refer to Booth's diary or to missing pages. None of Neff's claims makes any sense.

In 1974, Neff claims, he met with Smith in Muncie, Indiana. Using the third person, Neff wrote in a memo for the record: "During our interview with Hugh Smith he showed us the Photostats and said he had decided to destroy them. He did, however, permit us to have them transcribed in the presence of a notary public."[51] Smith, emulating Bowers before him, then destroyed his copies, leaving Neff with the only surviving copy of Julian's "unpublished" excerpt. Neff's "copy" of the "excerpt," now part of the Neff-Guttridge Collection at ISU, is the sole evidence for the strange meeting that Neff and Balsiger claim took place in Stanton's office.

But once again, the devil is in the details. Unbeknownst to Neff and the authors of *The Lincoln Conspiracy* at the time of publication, authentic excerpts from Julian's diary had appeared in a 1915 issue of the *Indiana Magazine of History*. Even more fortuitous, the key entry for April 24, the very date on which Neff claims Stanton allegedly revealed the contents of the missing pages to Conness and Julian, is among the published entries. It reads:

> Monday, [April] 24th
> On Saturday last we had General Rosecrans before our committee, and his account of the campaign of Western Virginia makes Mc-Clellan look meaner than ever. On last Friday went with Indianans to call on President [Andrew] Johnson. Governor Morton transgressed the proprieties by reading a carefully prepared essay on the subject of reconstruction. Johnson entered upon the same theme, indulging in bad grammar, bad pronunciation and much incoherency of thought. In common with many I was mortified.[52]

This represents the entire entry for April 24, 1865. There is no mention of a meeting in Stanton's office, of Booth's diary, or of Stanton's warning that everybody will go down the river together if they don't stick together. Did the editor of the *Indiana Magazine of History* decide to delete such an important part of the entry, leaving out the incredible story of what took place in Stanton's office? It seems unreasonable. If the editor had such sensational material proving treason within Lincoln's own cabinet, why would he withhold it from the public? Even more puzzling, why would Claude Bowers, a historian so strongly anti-Radical Republican, withhold such anti-Radical information from his book? The whole thesis of Bowers's book was to condemn the Radical Republicans. He could have driven a stake through the very heart of the Radical Republicans by exposing this treasonous plot involving Stanton.[53]

In an attempt to locate the alleged "unpublished" portion of Julian's journal, historian Hall sought the help of curators at the Indiana State Library, where Julian's papers reside, and at the Lilly Library at the University of Indiana, where the Claude Bowers papers are housed. Their efforts came up empty. There were no "unpublished" portions of the journal, no correspondence pertaining to the "unpublished" version, no notes by Bowers or anyone else, no photographs, photostats, or photocopies, and no typescripts. There was nothing in the Claude Bowers papers to indicate that he made copies before returning Julian's journals to Grace Clarke.[54]

Once again, fortune smiled on the seekers of truth. It turns out that Bowers was not the only historian Grace Clarke allowed to use the journals for research. Mabel Engstrom, a graduate student at the University of Chicago, was allowed to use them in researching her master's thesis on George Julian (which she submitted in 1929). In 1977, Mabel Engstrom, now Mabel Herbert, wrote to the managing editor of *Civil War Times Illustrated*, who was investigating the question of Booth's diary and the alleged missing pages. Engstrom wrote: "I just cannot remember reading anything in the journal which stated that Julian was aware of any plot relating to the assassination of Lincoln. Of course, it has been fifty years or so since I read the journal. However, I think I would have remembered such an important statement if it had been in the journal."[55] It is highly unreasonable to believe that Mrs. Herbert, a graduate student preparing her thesis, would not remember such a dramatic entry. Her recollections only cast further doubt on the authenticity of the "unpublished excerpt" from the journal.

It appears no one in Stanton's office that day bothered to ask how Booth's diary turned up in Stanton's office while he was still at-large. It is an important point because all of the evidence places the diary on his body at the time of his death. Indeed, at least four eyewitnesses reported seeing Booth and his diary south of the Potomac River *after the date* that the diary was allegedly found in the tall grass where Booth rested.

The first of these witnesses was Dr. Richard Stuart. On the night of April 23, Booth and Herold arrived at his summer home in King George County, Virginia, ten miles south of the Potomac River. After crossing the river, Thomas Harbin had arranged to have the men taken to Stuart's house. The doctor allowed the two men into his home long enough to eat, but he refused them shelter. Instead, he sent them a short distance away to the cabin of William Lucas, where they spent the night. The next morning Lucas's son, Charlie, took Booth and Herold to the Rappahannock River crossing at Port Conway, where they ran into three Confederate soldiers.

While at the Lucas cabin, Booth, angered by Stuart's lack of hospitality in refusing shelter to him, decided to insult Stuart by offering to pay for the small amount of food they received. Booth tore a leaf from his diary and used it to write a note offering Stuart $5.00. Deciding that was too much, Booth slipped the note back in his diary, tore a second page from it, and wrote a second note offering $2.50. In his sworn statement to authorities, Stuart described the note as "a leaf from a memorandum book rolled around and the money rolled up in it."[56] Booth sent the note to Stuart via Lucas on the very day Julian's purported journal entry said the diary was in Stanton's possession. The first note, offering $5.00, was found by detectives tucked in Booth's diary when it was recovered.[57]

The second witness to Booth's having the diary in his possession after April 24 was William Garrett, the oldest son of Richard Garrett. Booth and Herold arrived at the Garrett farm on the evening of Monday, April 24.

William Garrett later told detectives that on April 25 he saw Booth seated on the porch, where "he had *a small memorandum book* in his hand and was writing in it" (emphasis added).[58]

The third and fourth witnesses are the two detectives that cornered Booth at the Garrett farm, Everton Conger and Luther B. Baker. Both testified to removing Booth's diary from his body on April 26. During the conspirators' trial in 1865, Luther Baker gave the following testimony: "We took all the papers from his pocket—as soon as we removed him from the barn, and delivered them to Colonel Conger. . . . They were *a diary,* three drafts or checks, and forty-five dollars in greenbacks" (emphasis added).[59]

At the 1868 impeachment trial of Andrew Johnson, Baker testified a second time and was asked: "Who took the memorandum book from his [Booth's] pocket?" Baker replied, "Colonel Conger. He looked at it and handed it to me. I looked at it, and then we put it in a handkerchief with other things."[60]

There can be no doubt that Booth had the diary on him when he was killed. The missing pages and the excerpt from Julian's journal are pure fabrications in support of the myth that Stanton engineered Lincoln's assassination. Clearly, the fabricator of the pages was not a Stanton descendant. Hall and Sloan were never absolutely sure that it was Lynch. If it was not Lynch and not a "Stanton descendant," then there must have been another party working through Lynch. The producers at Sunn Classic Pictures were careful to refer to them as the "purported missing pages," leaving doubt as to their authenticity, thereby having their cake and eating it too. Like the numerous other myths associated with Abraham Lincoln, the myth of the missing pages and Stanton's complicity in Lincoln's death will continue to live on, finding new believers in future generations. As Lincoln once said, "You can fool some of the people all of the time and all of the people some of the time, but you can't fool all of the people all of the time"—or did he?[61]

Suggested Reading

Steers, Edward, Jr., ed. "Missing Pages, John Wilkes Booth's Diary." *The Lincoln Assassination Encyclopedia.* New York: HarperCollins, 2010. 375–376.
———. "The Missing Pages From Booth's Diary." *Lincoln Legends.* Lexington: Univ. Press of Kentucky, 2007. 177–202.
Verge, Laurie. "Those Missing Pages From the 'Diary' of John Wilkes Booth." *The Lincoln Assassination,* vol. 1. Clinton, Md.: Surratt Society Publication, 2000. Section IV, pages 13–22.

Acknowledgments

This book is drawn from several authors whose works are listed at the end of each chapter. My writing is the synthesis of the research they carried out in producing their fine studies. In particular, I am indebted to John Lukacs, Robert Harris, Miles Russell, Linda Sillitoe, Allen Roberts, Robert Lindsey, Walter McCrone, and Joe Nickell. I am indebted to each of them, and heartily recommend their works to the reader. I am especially indebted to Joe Nickell, Senior Research Fellow at the Committee for Skeptical Inquiry, for his invaluable suggestions for improving the manuscript, and for his generous foreword. Joe has been an indefatigable soldier in the front line battling paranormal hoaxes and myths for decades. His endorsement of this book is an honor. I also want to acknowledge with thanks the help of Terry Alford, professor of history at Northern Virginia Community College. Terry has been a longtime friend whose work on the Lincoln assassination and the life of John Wilkes Booth I have long admired. His thoughtful suggestions have overcome several deficiencies in the early drafts of this work. I also want to thank Miles Russell, senior lecturer in prehistoric and Roman archaeology at the School of Applied Sciences, Bournemouth University, England. Miles generously provided his collection of images that accompany the chapter on Piltdown Man. His book, titled *Piltdown Man,* contains the most reliable research on this fascinating subject. I also thank my longtime friend Joe Nichols, who has devoted many hours to reading and offering suggestions on virtually all of my writing for the past thirty years. I have come to rely on his many thoughtful suggestions and am indebted to him. I also thank Richard Sloan for providing me with his research into the missing pages of Booth's diary. I thank Cornelia Schnall of Landov Media for her help in providing several of the images relating to the Hitler diaries. I am indebted to two longtime colleagues and friends, Kieran McAuliffe and Jim Hoyt. I can state without reservation that without their help this, and my other works, would never have come into print. I especially want to thank Derik Shelor, my copyeditor, whose pointy pencil and eagle eye saved many mistakes and grammatical errors on my part. He has my gratitude and thanks for conscientious effort as he should have yours as well. Any mistakes are solely due to me. And last but not least, I want to thank the staff of the University Press of Kentucky: Anne Dean Watkins, Bailey Johnson, Mack McCormick, Cameron M. Ludwick, and Stephen Wrinn. I have always received wonderful support from this group and appreciate being one of their many authors.

Notes

1. Oath of a Freeman

1. Linda Sillitoe and Allen Roberts, *Salamander* (Salt Lake City, Utah: Signature Books, 1988), 87.

2. Robert Lindsey, *A Gathering of Saints: A True Story of Money, Murder, and Deceit* (New York: Simon and Schuster, 1988), 66.

3. Ibid., 65–68.

4. Hugh Nibley, quoted in ibid., 69.

5. Sillitoe and Roberts, *Salamander,* 251.

6. Ibid., 289–291.

7. Ibid., 292.

8. Simon Worrall, *The Poet and the Murderer* (New York: Plume Group, 2002), 4.

9. Ibid., 249.

10. Edward Steers Jr., "A Puttin' on (H)airs," *Lincoln Herald* 91, no. 3 (fall 1989): 86–90.

11. Worrall, *The Poet and the Murderer,* 45–46.

12. Todd Axelrod, *The Handbook of Historical Documents* (Neptune, N.J.: TFH Publications, 1992).

13. Worrall, *The Poet and the Murderer,* 48.

14. Justin G. Schiller, "In the Beginning . . . A Chronology of the 'Oath of a Freeman' Document as Offered by Schiller-Wapner," in *The Judgement of Experts,* ed. James Gilreath, 9 (Worcester, Mass.: American Antiquarian Society, 1991).

15. Ibid, 11.

16. "Preliminary Report on the Examination and Analysis of the 'Oath of a Freeman,'" in Gilreath, ed., *The Judgment of Experts,* 22.

17. James Gilreath, "Schiller-Wapner Galleries Offers the 'Oath' to the Library of Congress," in Gilreath, ed., *The Judgment of Experts,* 58.

18. Marcus A. McCorison, "Found at Last? The 'Oath of a Freeman,' the End of Innocence, and the American Antiquarian Society," in Gilreath, ed., *The Judgment of Experts,* 69.

19. Excerpts from the interviews appear in Gilreath, ed., *The Judgment of Experts.*

20. Roderick McNeil, "Scanning Auger Microscopy for Dating Two Copies of the 'Oath of a Freeman,'" in Gilreath, ed., *The Judgment of Experts,* 119.

21. Ibid.

22. Ibid., 116.

23. www.mormoninformation.com/hofmann.htm (accessed 2011).

2. Pearl Harbor

1. Gordon W. Prange, *At Dawn We Slept: The Untold Story of Pearl Harbor* (New York: McGraw-Hill, 1981), 539–540.

2. Walter Davenport, "Impregnable Pearl Harbor," *Collier's,* June 14, 1941, 11.

3. Quoted in George Victor, *The Pearl Harbor Myth: Rethinking the Unthinkable* (Washington, D.C.: Potomac Books, 2007), 171.

4. When war did break out, the navy estimated it needed seventy thousand new officers to fight a Pacific war. It was able to accomplish this incredible increase in its officer corps through an ingenious program dubbed V-12.

5. Victor, *The Pearl Harbor Myth,* 189.

6. "United States House of Representatives elections," en.wikipedia.org/wiki/United_States_House_of_Representatives_elections, 1942 (accessed 2011).

7. Quoted in Prange, *At Dawn We Slept,* 584.

8. Prange, *At Dawn We Slept,* 587.

9. Ibid., 587.

10. Ibid., 588.

11. Ibid., 589.

12. Ibid., 594.

13. Roberts Commission, "Attack upon Pearl Harbor by Japanese Armed Forces: Report of the Commission Appointed by the President of the United States to Investigate and Report the Facts Relating to the Attack Made by the Japanese Armed Forces upon Pearl Harbor in the Territory of Hawaii on December 7, 1941," 77th Congress, 2nd sess., U.S. Senate, Document No. 159 (Washington, D.C.: GPO, 1942), 1 (cited hereafter as Roberts Commission report). Prange, *At Dawn We Slept,* 595–599.

14. Roberts Commission, "Attack upon Pearl Harbor," 1.

15. Ibid., 20.

16. On May 25, 1999, the U.S. Senate attempted to set the record straight, passing a resolution exonerating Kimmel and Short by a 52 to 47 vote. The resolution stated that the success of the Japanese attacks was "not a result of dereliction of duty" by Short or Kimmel.

17. Former secretary of the navy Frank Knox died of a heart attack on April 28, 1944. Roosevelt appointed James V. Forrestal as his replacement on May 19, 1944.

18. Prange, *At Dawn We Slept,* 81.

19. Ibid., 681.

20. Quoted in ibid., 675–676.

21. Ibid., 682.

22. Quoted in Victor, *The Pearl Harbor Myth,* vii.

23. Victor, *The Pearl Harbor Myth,* 302.

24. Lieutenant Commander Kenneth Landis, USNR (ret.), and Staff Sergeant Rex Gunn USAR (ret.), *Deceit at Pearl Harbor* (N.p.: 1st Books Library, 2001).

25. Francis L. Loewenheim, Harold D. Langley, and Manfred Jonas, eds., *Roosevelt and Churchill: Their Secret Wartime Correspondence* (New York: Dutton, 1975).

26. The Gestapo is mistakenly believed by most people to have been headed by the infamous Heinrich Himmler. Himmler was head of the entire Reich security agency, of which the Gestapo was only one section.

27. Robert S. Wistrich, *Who's Who in Nazi Germany* (London: Routledge, 1995), 49–50.

28. John Lukas, "The Churchill-Roosevelt Forgeries," *American Heritage,* November–December 2002, 66.

29. Ibid., 65–67.

30. Ibid., 66.

31. Gregory Douglas, *Gestapo Chief: The 1948 Interrogation of Heinrich Müller,* 3 vols. (San Jose, Calif.: Bender, 1998).

32. Douglas, *Gestapo Chief,* 3:50.

33. Ibid.

34. The original transcript used the letter "A" for FDR, and the letter "B" for WSC. The initials are used here so as to avoid any confusion.

35. The base was located in Tankan Bay at Etorofu in the Kurile Islands, the northernmost chain of the Japanese archipelago.

36. This force presumably was to attack the Philippine Islands shortly after the attack on Pearl Harbor.

37. The complete transcript of this alleged telephone conversation appears in Douglas, *Gestapo Chief,* 3:78–82.

38. Landis and Gunn, *Deceit at Pearl Harbor,* 235.

39. Ibid., 225.

40. Lukacs, "The Churchill-Roosevelt Forgeries."

41. "John Lukacs," en.wikipedia.org/wiki/John_Lukacs (accessed 2011).

42. Lukacs, "The Churchill-Roosevelt Forgeries," 66–67.

43. In a search of the wartime correspondence between Roosevelt and Churchill, I found that Roosevelt began his communications with the salutation "Dear Winston" on at least three occasions, while Churchill began his correspondence with the salutation, "Dear Mr. President" on one occasion. The remaining 1,700-plus communiqués lack any salutation. None of the correspondence contains the salutation "Franklin." See Francis L. Lowenheim, Harold D. Langley, and Manfred Jonas, eds., *Roosevelt and Churchill: Their Secret Wartime Correspondence* (New York: Saturday Review Press/Dutton, 1975).

44. Lukacs, "The Churchill-Roosevelt Forgeries," 67.

45. Loewenheim et al., eds., *Roosevelt and Churchill,* 164–166.

46. Ibid., 166–167.

47. Douglas, *Gestapo Chief,* 3:98.

48. Lukacs, "The Churchill-Roosevelt Forgeries," 65–67.

3. Hah Hitler!

1. Hans Bauer, *Hitler at My Side* (Houston, Tex.: Eichler), 184.

2. Ibid., 184.

3. en.wikipedia.org/wiki/Hugh_Trevor-Roper (accessed 2011).

4. Kristen Robinson, "Trevor-Roper, Hugh," in *The Encyclopedia of Historians and Historical Writing,* vol. 2, ed. Kelly Boyd, 1024–1025 (London: Fitzroy Dearborn, 1999).

5. H. R. Trevor-Roper, *The Last Days of Hitler* (New York: Macmillan, 1947), 243–246.

6. James P. O'Donnell, *The Bunker* (Boston: Houghton Mifflin, 1978), 232.

7. Linge's and Guensche's interrogations by Stalin's NKVD agents may be found in Henrik Eberle and Matthias Uhl, eds., *The Hitler Book: The Secret Dossier Prepared for Stalin from the Interrogations of Hitler's Personal Aides* (New York: Public Affairs, 2005).

8. Trevor-Roper, *The Last Days of Hitler.*

9. Recent DNA testing on the skull fragment believed to be Hitler's determined the sex of the fragment to be female, leading to the conclusion it came from Eva Braun Hitler's skull.

10. Norman Cameron and R. H. Stevens, eds., *Hitler's Table Talk, 1941–1944: His Private Conversations* (1953; reprint, New York: Enigma Books, 2008).

11. Robert Harris, *Selling Hitler: The Story of the Hitler Diaries* (London: Faber and Faber, 1986), 19.

12. The letters turned out to be "FH," but Heidemann and others confused the gothic letter "F" with "A" at first. It was not until much later that experts pointed out that the forger made a mistake and purchased the letter "F" thinking it was an "A."

13. Charles Hamilton, *The Hitler Diaries: Fakes That Fooled the World* (Lexington: Univ. Press of Kentucky, 1991), 19.

14. Harris, *Selling Hitler,* 101–102.

15. Ibid., 93.

16. Ibid., 114.

17. Ibid., 116.

18. Ibid., 118.

19. Priesack was disappointed at the diary's mundane content. See ibid., 118.

20. Ibid., 135.

21. Cameron and Stevens, eds., *Hitler's Table Talk.*

22. Harris, *Selling Hitler,* 158–159.

23. Adolf Hitler, *Hitler's Second Book*, ed. Gerhard Weinberg (New York: Enigma Books, 2006).

24. Harris, *Selling Hitler*, 158–159.

25. Ibid., 241–248.

26. Ordway Hilton quoted in ibid., 193.

27. Quoted in ibid., 196.

28. Harris, *Selling Hitler*, 195.

29. Quoted in ibid., 24.

30. Ibid., 258.

31. Trevor-Roper quoted in ibid., 261.

32. Hamilton, *The Hitler Diaries*, 108.

33. Gerhard Weinberg, *A World at Arms* (Cambridge, England: Cambridge Univ. Press, 1994); Hitler, *Hitler's Second Book*, ed. Gerhard Weinberg.

34. Harris, *Selling Hitler*, 266.

35. Schulte-Hillen quoted in ibid., 281.

36. Harris, *Selling Hitler*, 307.

37. Deborah E. Lipstadt, *History on Trial: My Day in Court with David Irving* (New York: HarperCollins, 2005), xvii–xviii. See also Richard J. Evans, *Lying about Hitler: History, Holocaust, and the David Irving Trial* (New York: Perseus Books, 2001).

38. Harris, *Selling Hitler*, 320.

39. Russell Watson with Theodore Stanger, Ron Moreau, Maks Westerman, and Tessa Namuth, "Uncovering the Hitler Hoax," *Newsweek*, May 16, 1983, 56–57.

40. Hamilton, *The Hitler Diaries*, 75.

41. Ibid.

42. Ibid., 76.

43. Ibid.

44. Harris, *Selling Hitler*, 321.

45. Ibid., 322–323.

46. The telegram from Hitler to Mussolini is one example.

47. Harris, *Selling Hitler*, 368.

48. Ibid., 324–325.

49. Ibid., 345.

50. Max Domarus, *Hitler: Speeches and Proclamations, 1932–1945*, 4 vols. (1962; Mundelein, Ill.: Bolchazy-Carducci, 1997).

51. Harris, *Selling Hitler*, 355.

52. This is the same Kenneth Rendell that authenticated the famous "Salamander Letter" for Steve Christensen and the poem by Emily Dickinson for Daniel Lombardo, the curator of Special Collections at the Jones Library in Amherst, Massachusetts. In his defense, Rendell was not alone. The forger of those two documents, Mark Hofmann, had fooled all the experts.

53. Kenneth Rendell, "Cracking the Case," *Newsweek*, May 16, 1983, 58–59.

54. Friedrich Zimmermann quoted in Harris, *Selling Hitler*, 357.

55. Harris, *Selling Hitler,* 377.

56. Ibid., 378.

57. Hamilton, *The Hitler Diaries,* 159.

58. Ibid., 171.

59. Ibid., 136–137.

60. http://en.wikipedia.org/wiki/Gerd_Heidemann (accessed 2011).

61. Rupert Murdoch quoted in Harris, *Selling Hitler,* 368.

4. The Shroud of Turin

1. Joe Nickell, *Relics of the Christ* (Lexington: Univ. Press of Kentucky, 2007).

2. The report is reproduced in part in Joe Nickell, *Inquest on the Shroud of Turin: Latest Scientific Findings* (Amherst, N.Y.: Prometheus Books, 1998), 12–13.

3. Margaret de Charney was later excommunicated for her refusal to return the shroud and for her sale of it to the House of Savoy (Nickell, *Inquest on the Shroud of Turin,* 19; Nickell, *Relics of the Christ,* 130).

4. Quoted in Nickell, *Relics of the Christ,* 131.

5. Nickell, *Relics of the Christ,* 116.

6. Barnabas Lindars, *John* (Sheffield, England: Sheffield Academic Press, 1990), 63.

7. Stephen L. Harris, *Understanding the Bible* (Palo Alto, Calif.: Mayfield Publishing, 1985), 355.

8. *The Illuminated Bible,* King James Version (Chicago: Columbia Educational Books, 1941), St. John 19:38–42, 20:1–7.

9. M. Balter, "Clothes Make the (Hu) Man," *Science* 325, no. 5946 (September 11, 2009): 1329.

10. David Sox quoted in Nickell, *Inquest on the Shroud of Turin,* 35.

11. David Sox quoted in Nickell, *Relics of the Christ,* 134. Sox resigned from the British Society for the Turin Shroud when he concluded the shroud was a forgery.

12. Such preparation, however, would presumably entail cleaning the body prior to applying the oils and spices. This is in keeping with Jewish custom and the biblical description given in John 19:40.

13. Nickell, *Relics of the Christ,* 132.

14. The report is quoted in Walter McCrone, *Judgement Day for the Shroud of Turin* (Chicago, Ill.: Microscope Publications, 1996), 5–12.

15. Ibid., 134.

16. McCrone was the founder and director of the McCrone Research Institute, located in Chicago, Illinois. Among the many artifacts McCrone evaluated was the Vineland Map, owned by Yale University, which he concluded was a forgery based on his chemical analysis of certain pigments and inks. McCrone died in 2002.

17. Nickell, *Relics of the Christ,* 151.

18. McCrone, *Judgement Day,* 78–79.

19. Ibid., 156.

20. Ibid., 156–157.

21. Ibid., 166.

22. The refractive index is a measure of the speed at which light passes through a substance. It is expressed as a ratio of the speed of light through a vacuum over the speed of light through the test subject. The refractive index of water is 1.33. The light may also change the angle of its direction as a result of the medium through which it passes. This is another test of the subject medium. It should be noted that McCrone was the only researcher/examiner who tested the refractive index of the material on the shroud.

23. McCrone, *Judgement Day*, 151.

24. Agreement reproduced in ibid., 74.

25. Ibid, 152.

26. W. C. McCrone and S. A. Skirius, "Light Microscopical Study of the Turin 'Shroud,'" Part I, *Microscope* 28, nos. 3 and 4 (1980): 105; W. C. McCrone, "Light Microscopical Study of Turin 'Shroud,'" Part II, *Microscope* 28, nos. 3 and 4 (1980): 115; W. C. McCrone, "Light Microscopical Study of the Turin 'Shroud,'" Part III, *Microscope* 29, no. 19 (1981): 19.

27. "STURP—Shroud of Turin Research Project," http://www.shroudstory.com/topic-STURP.htm (accessed 2011).

28. "A Summary of STURP's Conclusions," Final Report (1981), available at "STURP—Shroud of Turin Research Project," http://www.shroudstory.com/topic-STURP.htm (accessed 2011).

29. Kenneth L. Feder, *Frauds, Myths, and Mysteries: Science and Pseudoscience in Archaeology* (New York: McGraw-Hill, 2008), 296–297.

30. Nickell, *Inquest on the Shroud of Turin*, 150.

31. Radiocarbon 14 dating of the Shroud of Turin, Wikipedia: http://en.wikipedia.org/wik/radiocarbon_14_dating_of_the_Shroud_of_Turin_note-Damon_Nature-48.

32. Feder, *Frauds, Myths, and Mysteries*, 303.

33. Nickell, *Relics of the Christ*, 136.

34. P. E. Damon et al., "Radiocarbon Dating of the Shroud of Turin," http://www.shroud.com/nature.htm (accessed 2011).

35. McCrone, *Judgement Day*, 245–246.

36. Raymond N. Rogers, "Studies on the Radiocarbon Sample from the Shroud of Turin," *Thermochimica Acta* 425 (2005): 189–194.

37. Joe Nickell, "Claims of Invalid 'Shroud' Radiocarbon Date Cut from Whole Cloth," *Skeptical Inquirer* 29, no. 3 (May–June 2005), 14–15 (also available online at http://www.csicop.org/specialarticles [accessed 2011]).

38. Jim Barrett, "Science and the Shroud: Microbiology Meets Archaeology in a Renewed Quest for Answers," *Mission*, http://www.uthscsa.edu/mission/spring96/shroud.htm (accessed 2011).

39. Thomas J. Pickett, "Can Contamination Save the Shroud of Turin," *Skeptical Briefs* (June 1996), 3.

40. Barrett, "Science and the Shroud," 5.

41. Steven D. Schafersman, "A Skeptic's View of the Shroud of Turin: History, Iconography, Photography, Blood, Pigment, and Pollen" (2005), available at http://cybercomputing.com/freeinquiry/skeptic/shroud/schafersman_skeptics_view_of_shroud.pdf (accessed 2011). This is an excellent discussion of the evidence for and against the shroud's authenticity.

42. *Merriam-Webster's Collegiate Dictionary*, 10th ed. (Springfield, Mass.: Merriam-Webster, 1996), 418.

43. Mati Milstein, "Shroud of Turin Not Jesus', Tomb Discovery Suggests," National Geographic News (December 17, 2009), http://news.nationalgeographic.com/news/2009/12/091216-shroud-of-turin-jesus-jerusalem-leprosy.html (accessed 2011).

44. Quoted in McCrone, *Judgement Day*, 11.

45. Nickell, *Inquest on the Shroud of Turin*, 85–94.

46. Ibid., 13.

47. A discussion of Frei-Sulzer's results may be found in McCrone, *Judgement Day*, 27–30, along with a listing of the plant sources of the pollen in Appendix One, 291–308. Joe Nickell, "Scandals and Follies of the 'Holy Shroud,'" *Skeptical Inquirer* 25, no. 5 (September–October 2001), 19–20.

48. Schafersman, "A Skeptic's View of the Shroud of Turin."

49. Feder, *Frauds, Myths, and Mysteries*, 301.

5. Skullduggery

1. Colin Tudge, *The Link* (New York: Little, Brown, 2009), 202.

2. Ibid., 3–15.

3. Jens L. Franzen et al., "Complete Primate Skeleton from the Middle Eocene of Messel in Germany: Morphology and Paleobiology," *PLoS ONE* 4, no. 5 (2009), available at http://www.plosone.org (accessed 2011).

4. Ibid., 1.

5. Within months of her introduction to the general public and scientific community, Ida came under challenge. A number of experts in the field expressed doubts about Ida's significance, pointing out that Ida is too old "to reveal anything about the evolution of humans. The earliest putative human ancestors are a mere seven million years old." See Kate Wong, "Weak Link," *Scientific American* (August 2009), 24.

6. "Missing link" is a misnomer. That a single creature spanned the change from ape to human never occurred, and paleontologists and anthropologists do not believe there is such a link. The link, if such is the case, is a series of evolutionary changes that occurred throughout several early creatures, the features of which came together in the earliest recognizable hominid.

7. Quoted in Miles Russell, *Piltdown Man: The Secret Life of Charles Dawson and the World's Greatest Archaeological Hoax* (Stroud, Gloustershire, England:

Tempus Publishing, 2003), 8. The fragments were estimated by Dawson and Woodward to be approximately 1 million years old, not 6 million.

8. The firm exists today as Dawson and Hart and still resides in Uckfield.

9. The Pleistocene period began a million years ago, at the end of which modern man first appears.

10. Quoted in Russell, *Piltdown Man,* 149. Heidelberg man is believed to have lived from the mid- to late Pleistocene, the period from 600,000 to 100,000 years ago.

11. Charles Darwin, *The Descent of Man, and Selection in Relation to Sex* (London: J. Murray, 1871), 4.

12. Russell, *Piltdown Man,* 19.

13. John Evangelist Walsh, *Unraveling Piltdown: The Science Fraud of the Century and Its Solution* (New York: Random House, 1996), 30.

14. Quoted in Michael Farquhar, *A Treasury of Deception* (New York: Penguin Books, 2005), 123–124.

15. Quoted in Russell, *Piltdown Man,* 231.

16. Quoted in ibid., 171.

17. Quoted in ibid., 190.

18. J. Weiner, K. Oakley, and W. Clark, "The Solution of the Piltdown Problem," *Bulletin of the British Museum (Natural History) Geology* 2, no. 3 (November 1953): 139–146.

19. Weiner et al., "The Solution of the Piltdown Problem," 146. Quoted in Russell, *Piltdown Man,* 196.

20. Frank Spencer, *Piltdown: A Scientific Forgery* (London: Natural History Museum Publications, Oxford Univ. Press, 1990).

21. Walsh, *Unraveling Piltdown,* 153.

22. Spencer, *Piltdown,* 238 n 10.

23. Quoted in Walsh, *Unraveling Piltdown,* 160.

24. Walsh, *Unraveling Piltdown,* 161.

25. Joseph S. Weiner, *The Piltdown Forgery* (1955; reprint, New York: Dover Publications, 1980), 105.

26. Walsh, *Unraveling Piltdown,* 13.

27. J. Winslow and A. Meyer, "The Perpetrator at Piltdown," *Science 83* (September 1983): 33–43.

28. The considerable mound of slag remaining from Roman smelting operations was used for repairing roads in the area for decades, until the material was exhausted.

29. Russell, *Piltdown Man,* 63.

6. The Missing Pages from John Wilkes Booth's Diary

An earlier version of this chapter appeared in Edward Steers Jr., *Lincoln Legends* (Lexington: Univ. Press of Kentucky, 2007), 177–202.

1. In recent years, three books have appeared claiming that Lincoln's murder was the result of conspiracies involving members of Lincoln's own cabinet and prominent northern politicians and businessmen in league with their Confederate counterparts: Leonard F. Guttridge and Ray A. Neff, *Dark Union: The Secret Web of Profiteers, Politicians, and Booth Conspirators That Led to Lincoln's Death* (Hoboken, N.J.: John Wiley and Sons, 2003); Charles Higham, *Murdering Mr. Lincoln: A New Detection of the 19th Century's Most Famous Crime* (Beverly Hills, Calif.: New Millennium, 2004); John Chandler Griffin, *Abraham Lincoln's Execution* (Gretna, La.: Pelican, 2006).

2. Edward Steers Jr., *Blood on the Moon: The Assassination of Abraham Lincoln* (Lexington: Univ. Press of Kentucky, 2001).

3. Statement of Boston Corbett, NARA, RG94, M-619, reel 456, frames 0248–0257.

4. No such orders were given according to Lieutenant Colonel Everton Conger, the detective in charge of the search party. See Conger's statement, NARA, RG 94, M-619, reel 455, frames 0691–0703.

5. Statement of Everton Conger.

6. For a full description of the search of Booth's body, see the testimony of Everton J. Conger in Edward Steers Jr., ed., *The Trial: The Assassination of President Lincoln and the Trial of the Conspirators* (Lexington: Univ. Press of Kentucky, 2003), 93.

7. For a list of exhibits, see Steers, ed., *The Trial*, ci–ciii.

8. Testimony of Lafayette C. Baker, *Impeachment Investigation: Testimony Taken Before the Judiciary Committee of the House of Representatives in the Investigation of the Charges Against Andrew Johnson*, 39th Congress, 2nd sess., and 40th Congress, 1st sess., 1867 (Washington, D.C.: Government Printing Office, 1867), 458.

9. Testimony of E. J. Conger, *Impeachment Investigation: Testimony Taken Before the Judiciary Committee of the House of Representatives in the Investigation of the Charges Against Andrew Johnson*, 39th Congress, 2nd sess., and 40th Congress, 1st sess., 1867 (Washington, D.C.: Government Printing Office, 1867), 323–324.

10. Otto Eisenschiml, *Why Was Lincoln Murdered?* (Boston: Little, Brown, 1937).

11. This idea is reminiscent of the controversy surrounding President Roosevelt, who critics claim knew the attack on Pearl Harbor was coming and did nothing to prevent it.

12. *Washington Evening Star,* February 11, 1865, page 2, col. 4.

13. Eisenschiml, *Why Was Lincoln Murdered?,* 139.

14. Richard E. Sloan, telephone interview with the author, April 4, 2006.

15. Ibid.; Richard Sloan, "The Case of the Missing Pages," *Journal of the Lincoln Assassination* 9, no. 3 (December 1995): 38–44. The *Journal of the Lincoln Assassination* is a privately printed newsletter edited by Frederick Hatch and published by Autograph Press, P.O. Box 2616, Waldorf, MD, 20604.

16. Sloan reported the story in *The Lincoln Log*, beginning with the November–December 1976 issue (vol. 1, no. 11) and continuing through the October–November 1977 issue (vol. 2, no. 6).

17. Richard D. Mudd, telephone interview with the author, January 3, 1998. In the same telephone conversation Richard Mudd told the author he received $1,500 to serve as a consultant to Sunn Classic Pictures.

18. David Balsiger and Charles E. Sellier Jr., *The Lincoln Conspiracy* (Los Angeles: Schick Sunn Classic Books, 1977).

19. Robert Fowler, "Was Stanton behind Lincoln's Murder?" *Civil War Times Illustrated* 3, no. 5 (August 1961): 6–23.

20. Balsiger and Sellier, *The Lincoln Conspiracy*, 8.

21. William C. Davis, "Behind the Lines," *Civil War Times Illustrated* 21, no. 7 (November 1981): 26.

22. Among the many items obtained by Neff is a collection of documents known as the "Chaffey Papers." Included is an original (holograph) letterbook of James and John Chaffey whose contents date from 1831 to 1838 and have nothing to do with the Civil War or Lincoln's assassination. The remaining papers are typescript copies made by Neff.

23. William C. Davis, "Behind the Lines: Caveat Emptor," *Civil War Times Illustrated* (August 1977): 33–37; William C. Davis, "Behind the Lines: 'The Lincoln Conspiracy'—Hoax?," *Civil War Times Illustrated* (November 1977): 47–49; William C. Davis, "Behind the Lines," *Civil War Times Illustrated* 21, no. 7 (November 1981): 26–28.

24. Davis, "Behind the Lines," 26.

25. Davis, "Behind the Lines: Caveat Emptor," 37.

26. Sloan, "The Case of the Missing Pages," 39.

27. Ibid., 40.

28. Davis, "Behind the Lines," 26.

29. Sloan, "The Case of the Missing Pages," 43.

30. The two specimens of Booth's writing supplied by the National Archives are the "To whom it may concern" letter dated 1864 and the "Dearest Beloved Mother" letter to Mary Ann Holmes Booth dated 1864. The two letters were discovered by James O. Hall in 1977 in the files of the Justice Department in the National Archives. For the complete text of these letters, see John Rhodehamel and Louise Taper, eds., *"Right or Wrong, God Judge Me": The Writings of John Wilkes Booth* (Chicago: Univ. of Illinois Press, 1997), 124–127, 130–131.

31. J. Dunning, "Examination of John Wilkes Booth's Diary," Report of the FBI Laboratory, Federal Bureau of Investigation, Washington, D.C., No. 95-216208, October 3, 1977.

32. Ibid.

33. Sloan, "The Case of the Missing Pages," 40.

34. The entire transcript of the missing pages was first published in the *Surratt Courier* 19, no. 10 (October 1994): 3–9, edited by Laurie Verge.

35. Laurie Verge, ed., "Those Missing Pages from the 'Diary' of John Wilkes Booth," *Surratt Courier* 19, no. 10 (October 1994): 3–9.

36. Rhodehamel and Taper, eds., *"Right or Wrong, God Judge Me,"* 111.

37. Ibid., 114.

38. Junius Brutus Booth Jr., diary, 1864, Folger Shakespeare Library, Washington, D.C. Joe Simonds was Booth's close friend and business partner in Booth's oil venture.

39. Rhodehamel and Taper, eds., *"Right or Wrong, God Judge Me,"* 45.

40. Ibid., 83.

41. Ibid., 86.

42. There is no record that Baker employed or used Indian scouts in any of his operations.

43. Guttridge and Neff, *Dark Union,* 175.

44. The version in *Dark Union* differs slightly from the version in the Neff-Guttridge Collection, in which Conness is quoted as saying, "Oh my God, Oh my God."

45. Guttridge and Neff, *Dark Union,* 175–176.

46. The excerpt from Julian's diary currently resides in the Neff-Guttridge Collection in the Special Collections Department of the Cunningham Memorial Library at Indiana State University. The collection consists of materials collected over the years by Ray Neff, the consultant to Sunn Classic Pictures who provided the documents used to make *The Lincoln Conspiracy.*

47. Grace Julian Clarke to Claude Bowers, July 22, 1926, Manuscript Department, Lilly Library, Indiana University, Bloomington, Indiana.

48. Neff donated his entire collection to Indiana State University, which unwisely accepted it and treated it as authentic.

49. Appendix 4, "George Julian's Diary," Neff-Guttridge Collection. See also *Dark Union,* "Sources on Notes," chapter 13, page 258: "Claude Bowers, preparing his book, *The Tragic Era,* borrowed the 1865 diary and photographed its pages without Grace Clark's [*sic*] knowledge."

50. Appendix 4, "George Julian's Diary," Neff-Guttridge Collection.

51. Ibid. Although the explanatory document refers to both Guttridge and Neff being present, Guttridge stated in a telephone conversation with the author on October 15, 2003, that he was not present during the Smith interview or during the transcription of the alleged Smith copy.

52. "George W. Julian's Journal—The Assassination of Lincoln," *Indiana Magazine of History* 11, no. 4 (December 1915): 324–337.

53. Appendix 4, "George Julian's Diary," Neff-Guttridge Collection.

54. In addition to the research librarian's search of the Julian and Bowers papers, the curator in charge of the Claude Bowers papers wrote the following: "we keep very complete-use files and we have no record of Mr. Neff making use of our materials, either in person or through correspondence" (Saundra Taylor to James

O. Hall, May 26, 1977, Manuscript Collection, Lilly Library, Indiana University, Bloomington, Indiana).

55. Mabel M. Herbert to Charles Cooney, September 12, 1977, original in possession of William C. Davis, photocopy in the author's files.

56. Statement of Richard Stuart, NARA, RG 153, M-599, reel 6, frame 0209.

57. The two notes were introduced as evidence at the time of Andrew Johnson's impeachment hearing. They subsequently disappeared and were never seen again.

58. Statement of William Garrett, NARA, RG 94, M-619, reel 457, frames 0499–0525.

59. Statement of Luther B. Baker, aboard the *Montauk,* April 26, 1865, NARA, RG 94, M-619, reel 455, frames 0665–0686.

60. Testimony of Luther B. Baker, *Impeachment Investigation: Testimony Taken Before the Judiciary Committee of the House of Representatives in the Investigation of the Charges Against Andrew Johnson,* 39th Cong., 2nd Sess., and 40th Cong., 1st Sess., 1867 (Washington, D.C.: Government Printing Office, 1867), 478–490.

61. For an in-depth discussion of this famous quote attributed to Lincoln, see Steers, *Lincoln Legends,* 89–101.

Index